The Last Bastion

The Last Bastion

The Suppression and Re-emergence of
Witchcraft, the Old Religion

Ralph Harvey

ZAMBEZI PUBLISHING LTD

First published in 2005
by Zambezi Publishing Ltd
P.O. Box 221 Plymouth,
Devon PL2 2YJ (UK)
Fax: +44 (0)1752 367 300
email: info@zampub.com
www.zampub.com

British Library Cataloguing in Publication Data:
A catalogue record for this book
is available from the British Library

ISBN 1-903065-40-2

Cover design: © 2005 Tom Paddle
Photos (pp. 172-177):
© 2005 John Hooper / Hoopix (labelled),
others: © 2005 Ralph Harvey
Editor: Sasha Fenton
Layout / typesetting: Jan Budkowski
Printed in the UK by Antony Rowe Ltd
135798642

Review extracts for The Last Bastion

The Last Bastion fills the gap left by Doreen Valiente's long out-of-print work. My own ongoing researches into the origins of the modern witchcraft revival are pointing increasingly to Sussex as a major source, which is why Ralph Harvey's book is so timely. It should be an essential addition to the library of anyone interested in the background to this spiritual path.
Philip Heselton

Ralph Harvey's book will ensure that his extensive knowledge of Traditional Sussex Witchcraft will be saved. This book contains an amazing amount of information and lore on the old ways of the Sussex Witch. Whether you are a beginner or an experienced practitioner, you will find this book captivating, enjoyable and informative. Highly recommended.
Merlyn, Editor of Witchcraft & Wicca Magazine, Children of Artemis

Ralph Harvey is regarded as one of the country's foremost and leading Wiccan High Priests, and is classed as an authority on the Old Religion of Witchcraft. His expert knowledge of the subject is clearly evident in this informative and fascinating book. Highly recommended and definitely one for your bookshelf, this is an exceptional book by an extremely exceptional man.
Lawrence Dean, Paranormal researcher and psychic healer.

When I read that Ralph had recently initiated his 100th High Priestess, I realised that he has been busy living and working craft, rather than seeking the glory of writing about it.
Ralph takes the reader on a historical narrative journey...from the earliest times until more modern incidents. He lifts the lid on some of the truth behind the Pickingill Covens, and dismisses rumours with indisputable facts.

Ralph is a true Gentleman and Priest of the Craft; Audrey, his wife of 50 years, is everything a Priestess should be. It's a shame there are not more people like these.
Five Pentacles, John Randall, Pentacle Magazine

Reviews in full – just for reference

On the subject of witchcraft in Sussex, "The Last Bastion" fills the gap left by Doreen Valiente's long out of print and now rare work, "Where Witchcraft Lives".

My own ongoing researches into the origins of the modern witchcraft revival are pointing increasingly to Sussex as a major source, which is why Ralph Harvey's book is so timely. It should be an essential addition to the library of anyone interested in the background to this spiritual path.
Philip Heselton

With the world changing so rapidly, there is always the risk of losing ancient wisdom forever. Thankfully, Ralph Harvey's book will ensure that his extensive knowledge of Traditional Sussex Witchcraft will be saved. This book contains an amazing amount of information and lore on the old ways of the Sussex Witch. Whether you are a beginner or an experienced practitioner, this is a book you will find captivating, enjoyable and informative, highly recommended.
Merlyn, Editor of Witchcraft & Wicca Magazine, Children of Artemis

Ralph Harvey is regarded as one of the country's foremost and leading Wiccan High Priests, and is classed as an authority on the Old Religion of Witchcraft. His expert knowledge of the subject is clearly evident in this informative and fascinating book, detailing the history of Wicca in Sussex.

The craft's legends, herbal and ancient cures are skillfully recounted as well as the numerous events and incidents that have occurred over the years as he promoted the Old Religion.

Highly recommended and definitely one for your bookshelf, this is an exceptional book by an extremely exceptional man.
Lawrence Dean, Paranormal researcher and psychic healer.

It's not often you get an exclusive extract and book review from such a distinguished source, but that's what happened with this one. We are the first or review this initial offering from the head of Sussex Witchcraft. I originally wondered why Ralph hadn't written anything publicly before, but when I read that he had recently initiated his 100th High Priestess, I realised that he has been busy living and working craft, rather than seeking the glory of writing about it. This is something that some of the authors on a few rosters should take note of – less books, more substance!

Ralph takes the reader on a historical narrative journey about the rites, trials and rituals of the Sussex Witch - from the earliest times until more modern incidents. He lifts the lid on some of the truth behind the Pickingill Covens, and dismisses rumours with indisputable facts.

Ralph is a true Gentleman and Priest of the Craft, and Audrey, his wife of 50 years, is everything a Priestess should be – between them they have revised, updated and reworked the more outmoded and unrepresentative craft workings, making a lean, dynamic and workable synthesis of Traditional and Gardnerian crafts. It's a shame that there are not more people like these.
Five Pentacles, John Randall, Pentacle Magazine

Dedication

This book is dedicated to my loving wife Audrey, who has stayed the course of more than fifty years of marriage through all its trials and tribulations. For her, for richer or for poorer meant just that, and we have known riches and experienced hard times. We have feasted on Ambrosia and we have drunk Nectar with the Gods, and we still appreciate the simplicity and comradeship of a cup of tea. Feast and famine have often followed one upon the other, but the overriding factor has been our undying love for each other and the fact that our marriage has been blessed with five lovely children brought up to high standards and who stand proud.

I therefore equally dedicate this book to:

Deirdre Susan, my first-born

Martin Anthony Graham, who swiftly followed

Karen Ingrid, who also quickly followed

Vanessa Melanie, who equally was not far behind

Finally, yet importantly, Wayne Ian Stuart, who came along unexpectedly several years later, making five!

Acknowledgments

To my ever-faithful personal assistant of many years standing, Petra Ginman. She has laboured long and hard for many years on film scripts and other books and her only complaint was, "My fingers are getting tired". Without her devotion and loyalty, many of our projects would never have borne fruit. She is both a valuable PA and friend.

To my High Priestess of the Order of Artemis, Lyn Baylis, whose position until recently made it impossible to name her. Also, to all the loyal members of Artemis who follow the original religion of this country unswervingly, and the order of Witchcraft that I founded.

To Tom Paddle, a most talented artist who painted the front cover for this book.

To John Hooper of Hoopix for his photography, which he supplied without charge in the furtherance of the Craft.

A big thank you to Horsham Museum and Library for allowing me the countless hours of research while discovering the roots of "Hang Town".

To Lewes Castle Museum and Library for all their help and untiring assistance in uncovering the roots of the Kemp family, and for being allowed unfettered access to all their records of Witch Trials.

To Rye Town Hall for all their help and assistance in researching old Witchcraft Archives and researching John Bread, who was gibbeted there.

To Graham King at the famous Witchcraft Museum in Boscastle, for his assistance and access to his records. I passed him one of the earliest Books of Shadows from the 1950s.

To the Honourable Olivia Robertson of the Fellowship of Isis for the wonderful month we spent with her and Lord and Lady Strathlock at Huntingdon Castle, when Audrey was ordained there. For what we learned from her... not forgetting the fairies, of course.

To John Belham-Payne for all his help in researching the yet unpublished works of Doreen Valiente and for permission to publish extracts from her works and for supplying photos for this book.

To Jonathan Tapsell and Justin Hankinson of Hexagon Archive for all their help over the years and for the enlightening programmes on the Craft that we did together.

To Carol Spencer, the original land owner of the sacred coven site near Warnham, and Jennifer de Sanchez, the current owner of the land upon which it is situated, the eternal blessings of the Witches for all your kindness and hospitality. I feel that I must record that when Jennifer was negotiating buying the house and land from Carol, she dropped the bombshell - "Oh, by the way, it comes complete with Witches on - is that alright?" Well, it was, and the new owner also became our benefactor. There is to be a great civic ceremony in 2005, with new blessing to be bestowed.

In addition, a very big thank you to Witches and covens worldwide for supplying me with so much material that would otherwise have been lost.

To all the loyal followers of The Order of Artemis – a huge big thank you.

To Dave Taylor - a police officer who dared to go public with his Wiccan faith, and to his wife Sally, the Witch Queen of Kent, whose circular underground temple could be flooded by the sea in an instant - all the ceremonies went swimmingly, might I say!

To Levanah Shell Bdolak of the Clearsight Organisation, who personally organised and sponsored my tour of the USA in 2003, and who has been such a close and most generous friend - a highly spiritual and motivated lady from whom I have learnt much. A very big thank you.

To all those whose positions in society as judges, lawyers, Members of Parliament, police officers, doctors and nurses do not allow them to be recognised even now. Athene, Tanith, Cernunnos, Herne, Aradia, Isis, Astarte, Faunus and Feronia, plus Circe and our Aphrodite and many, many others.

To Emrys and Sarah of the Cromlech Covenant for their most valued friendship and the wonderful introduction they so kindly wrote for this book – a big thank you. Emrys himself is a true master of magic and together we have invoked power within the sacred confines of Stonehenge, an awesome experience!

And, last but by no means least, to Eight Horses of the Navaho tribe, our guide in the desert and with whom we shared a magical experience in a sweat lodge, together with our host Levanah, and whom we saw performing the sacred rituals of Coyote, Bear, Elk and Buffalo in the swirling smoke of the lodge.

A Special Acknowledgment

It so happens that, just as this book is reaching its final editing stage, the dreadful floods of August 2004 have devastated part of the Witchcraft Museum in Boscastle.

For the moment, nobody knows how much damage has been caused. Neither does anyone know how many of the valuable books, papers and other artefacts that were stored in various parts of the museum have survived. I'm sure that Graham will be interested in receiving suitable items for the museum and he may put out a call for help. If so, please watch for news and developments on his website (www.museumofwitchcraft.com) and other suitable sites and publications.

There are financial appeals going out all around various parts of the West Country, as spotted by my eagle-eyed publishers. While money is always useful in such instances, it cannot replace the history that has been lost. Only you can help Graham to do that.

Disclaimer

This book will be available in many countries around the world, and we furnish the following information in order to comply with various regulations as far as possible. The intention of this book is to provide information and to entertain. It is sold on the understanding that the publisher and the author are not engaged in rendering legal, medical, advisory or any other professional services, and cannot be held responsible for the outcome in whatsoever manner the contents may be used. If expert assistance is required in connection with any subject matter linked to this book, the services of a competent professional should be sought.

No warranties, either express or implied, are made by the author or the publisher regarding the contents of this book. It is not intended to reprint all linked information that is otherwise available, but to complement, amplify and supplement other data on the subject matter herein. The reader is urged to read all other available pertinent material and to tailor the information herein to the reader's individual needs accordingly.

The material herein does not profess to disclose any form of get-rich scheme, or to be absolutely or categorically effective, and the spiritual aspect of the contents affirms that it should never be seen solely in terms of moneymaking or self-aggrandisement.

Every effort has been made to make this book as complete and accurate as possible, especially due to but not restricted to the necessary limitations of size and content, and the contents are not presented as categorical claims in any manner whatsoever by either the author or the publisher, nor are the viewpoints expressed herein to be considered as any more than data available for the reader to use in arriving at the reader's own personal conclusions. Therefore, the text should be used as a general guide and not the ultimate source of data on the subject matter concerned. Should any material inaccuracies come to light, future editions will incorporate these as and when practical.

The author and the publisher shall have no liability or responsibility to any person or entity with respect to any loss or damage caused or alleged to be caused, directly or indirectly, by the use or misuse of information contained in this book. Should the content matter in any way not comply with local regulations or restrictions pertinent to the reader, now or in the future, the reader is strongly urged to comply with any such regulations. It is impossible for the author or the publisher to control where or how this book is made available for public consumption and they cannot accept any responsibility for any possible contraventions accordingly.

If the reader does not wish to be bound by the above parameters, this book may be returned to the publisher in acceptable condition for a full refund.

Contents

Foreword

Ralph Harvey must rank as one of the most extraordinary men it is my privilege to know. On the anniversary of his seventy-fifth birthday, a time when most folk are thinking in terms of slippers and bus-passes, Ralph was to be found ten thousand feet up in the sky strapped to a young female parachute-instructor, swinging gently under a canopy in a free-fall parachute experience. For an encore, he flew his first fighter plane, a Harvard T6G, which is based on the wartime Mustang. I mention this because it illustrates his vivacious nature so well.

I belong to the Cromlech Covenant, where the emphasis is on producing what might be called "renaissance" men and women - multi-talented people with a wide range of skills and interests.

My dear friend Ralph is just such a person, with skills as an equestrian, actor, writer, stuntman, linguist, medievalist and historian - to name just a few. Truth is stranger than fiction - and Ralph's exploits throughout his life lend weight to that saying. However, this brief preface is not the place to explore this aspect of the man: I merely want to cast a glimmer of light on the Witch and his milieu.

He has always been different from those around him. Even as a young boy, while his school chums played football and cricket, he would be found in the woods studying insects and other animals and indulging his particular fascination for amphibians. Continuously castigated by his teachers for his "strangeness", he eventually earned the epithet "the wild boy of the woods".

It was while wandering the fields of Berkshire on such an expedition that he met a Romany Gypsy girl from the nearby encampment in Scours Lane or "Gypsy lane", as the locals knew it. She belonged to one of the few remaining tribes then still living in horse-drawn caravans. Every year the gypsies migrated to Tile Hurst alongside the river Thames, where they plied their pegs and palmistry to all. Perhaps the travellers saw something in the young "Chavvie": we shall never know; but for whatever reason, they made him welcome, and before long the young Ralph's face became a familiar sight in their midst.

However, this was in the gloaming of the Second World War. Rationing was introduced within months of the commencement of that dreadful conflict, and in a short space of time, the people of Great Britain found themselves struggling to survive. Root vegetables became the mainstay of the diet; cricket pitches, lawns and people's gardens were turned into vegetable plots. Any scraps would be fed to a scrawny hen in the hope that she would lay the occasional egg to introduce a little protein into the sparse diet. Nothing was wasted in those desperate times. Ralph noticed the small section of meat – two ounces once a week – that his family were allowed, but over in the gypsy encampment his friends fed sumptuously on rabbit, hare and pheasant. It was not long before they took him on their foraging expeditions and taught him the art of poaching. He learnt to study the striations in the grass that showed which way an animal regularly travelled, how to track spoor and how to set snares and nets. He was never keen on the use of the snare, so he was taught the art of the catapult - silent and deadly - which soon became his favourite hunting tool. His friends introduced him to fungi and edible berries, and so it was that he supplemented his family and that of his neighbours' with a bountiful supply from Nature's parlour.

The war years taught him many other things at the hand of the Romany. These people were living repositories of the knowledge of the "Old Ways". As medicines and other standard cures became difficult to obtain, the urbanites suffered, but the gypsy women simply went into the countryside and came back with a variety of herbs and plants, from which they concocted their own medicines.

Ralph's role as "auxiliary" provider for the family came to an abrupt end when, at the age of eighteen, he was conscripted into the RAF. He found himself rubbing shoulders with people from every occupation. The call-up knew no bounds of class distinction, so rich and poor all ended up "square bashing" in the services. Strange to say many were glad of it, for the alternative was to end up down the mines, hewing coal or mineral ores for the war-effort, under the auspices of Aneurin Bevan, Minister of Labour.

At Padgate RAF training camp, Ralph met many girls in the WAAF (Women's Auxiliary Air Force) and within a few weeks, he had formed a close friendship with Rachael, who was another Romany gypsy, in addition to a former nurse called Anne. Old cures, medicines and folklore were a frequent topic of conversation among them, but it was the spiritual side of Rachael that struck home the most, as Ralph learned of old Witchcraft practices that were retained secretly within the tribes.

In those days, the foreign religion (Christianity) held absolute power, and being forced into Church parades and compulsory Church attendance did little to endear a freethinking youth. This simply reinforced the deep fear of Churches that had been engendered in Ralph. This stemmed from an event that occurred when he was seven, when he found himself locked in a Church hall with many other children by a drunken (and subsequently unfrocked) clergyman. The trauma caused by the screaming and ranting of this "Man of God", has echoed all down the years, and I suppose we should be grateful to the great Goddess who, in the guise of this priest, set Ralph on the pagan path. However, I digress…

Ralph was eventually sent into the desert in Aden, in the Yemen, attached to the 4001st Armoured Car Flight, Aden Protectorate Levees. Here he would spend long periods on patrol. In the way of soldiers everywhere, the men grumbled and swore as the endless vistas of sand, rock and scrub filled their long days and nights. They read and re-read books and letters, cigarettes ran out and utter boredom became the order of the day. To Ralph, the desert night brought enchantment as centipedes, snakes, scorpions and spiders brought the apparently dead sands to life.

None of his comrades could understand how he could spend hours transfixed, watching ant columns as they crossed the desert surface. Here in the vast emptiness, he could feel his soul stir and hear "The Lords of the outer Spaces" whisper to him in the guise of desert winds, gently, oh so gently, touching his heart. Slowly but inexorably, the Pagan in him awoke.

After demobilisation, Ralph started to study esoteric religion, Paganism and folklore seriously. He went looking for his Gypsy friends, but they had moved on from Scours Lane because a large stadium complex had encroached onto the lands they once occupied. He was never to see them again. Even their lane has long since disappeared, though the giant horse trough carved out of solid granite for their horses to drink from remained up to a few years ago. In later years, it was planted with daffodils and tulips, bearing silent witness to a way of life long gone.

In 1954, Ralph married his beautiful wife, Audrey. This was a strange match, given his leanings, for she was a practicing Baptist and Sunday school teacher. She accepted his practices because of her deep love for him, but she would have no part of them, having been brought up to believe that everything occult was evil. This belief was not lessened when strange things started to happen around the house while Ralph experimented with the "tele-sciences". More than once, after an unsuccessful foray into the world of ritual magic, he would return from his temple despondent at having failed to move a single object telekinetically, only to find as they were about to go to bed, that wild poltergeist-like activity would become activated around the house. In time, as he became more proficient in these arts and Audrey became more accepting – unlike more than one Reading University student who stayed with them as a paying guest in those days, who packed their bags and left the "haunted house".

The couple had five children, so they moved to a larger house in Blenheim Road in Reading. They found themselves living in an actual haunted house, which had been the domain of a young woman who had died in the early 1900s. This woman had been the mother of two young children. She appeared so frequently to their own children that they gave her the affectionate nickname of Fred. This was because, at first, they took her for a male, but it was when the children started to speak of the "lady'" who sat and spoke to them at night, that it was realised that "Fred" was a woman and so was promptly renamed "Frederica". Frederica became so attached to the children that when they grew up and married, she followed them from house to house. Frederica still flits from one to the other as Ralph and Audrey's children bring up their own young families in their turn. Though she always returns to Ralph and Audrey where to this day, she makes her presence felt by behaving mischievously, delighting in taking and hiding things, then making them appear in full view, usually in an unlikely and prominent position. Her favourite is to remove a plant pot and hold it tantalisingly before them but just out of reach. This has left many a visitor to their home dumfounded.

These early visible manifestations of Frederica's earthly form fuelled Ralph's fascination with the unknown. In 1952, this fascination – or perhaps obsession – led via a circuitous route to his initiation into the Storrington Witches' coven. These ageing Witches were thought to be the remnants of one of the famous nine covens founded by the legendary Old George Pickingill. These Witches adhered strictly to the old ways, though in reality, they had merely (though no less importantly) been guided by Pickingill.

By now, the Harvey family had moved to Sussex. It was there that Ralph came to form his own order, which was to become the "Order of Artemis". He had realised that the Craft form known as "Traditional Witchcraft", as practiced by his initiators, was badly in need of a "bit of a cleanup", albeit with a feather duster. In modern parlance: a slight "makeover" to bring it into the Twentieth Century, just as Gardner was doing with his own branch of the Craft. "Artemis" gradually evolved into the form in which it is known today. It is traditional but it adopts the middle way, letting go outdated traditions, but retaining the innermost secrets, such as the passing of the secret names of the Goddess at the Third Degree. However, more of that later...

With the passing of the years, Audrey had become accustomed to coven meetings in the house, Ralph had abandoned High Ritual Magic and the accompanying disturbing phenomena had now ceased. He had successfully incorporated a lower grade of Ritual Magic into Witchcraft practices, with the emphasis on healing.

Thus, Audrey's interest grew. She turned her back on the "foreign religion" and sought initiation at the hands of Len and Anna, Wiccan Priest and Priestess. The two were descended from Rae Bone, who had been Gerald Gardner's High Priestess, who ran the local Gardnerian "Acorn" coven. Sadly, the group disintegrated when Len and Anna parted, before Audrey could take her second and Third Degrees. However, Tom and Mabs Penfold, who had both been initiated into Rae Bone's coven years before, and who now ran a flourishing coven in Hove, Sussex, invited Audrey to join them. It was from Tom that she received her second and Third Degrees. The transformation was now complete, as a one time Baptist became a Witch! Mabs and Tom were reciprocally initiated into Artemis, and likewise Ralph accepted Gardnerian initiation at the hands of Mabs Penfold. From then on, the two traditions worked closely side by side for many years.

Now fifty years on, Ralph has become known as the leading exorcist in this country. He runs the largest coven in Britain, having personally initiated over one hundred women into the group, many of whom have themselves in turn founded covens worldwide, as his book will show. A renowned lecturer on

Witchcraft and folklore, he is sought by groups as diverse as the Women's Institute, Rotary clubs, Round Table, The Young Farmers Institute and Pagan Moots. He lectures regularly at the acclaimed annual Occulture festival in Brighton. The Encyclopaedia of Witchcraft and Neo Paganism, published in 2003, devoted over three full pages to him and the Order of Artemis. He is also a regular contributor to television.

Ralph was recently invited to conduct a lecture tour of the USA by Levanah Shell Bdolak of the Clearsight Organisation, where he met a large variety of covens and groups, all avid for information on traditional British practices in the "Old Country". One group in California is run by Carol, a Sussex Witch and High Priestess originally initiated by Ralph in the 1980s. Upon reaching her Third Degree, Carol emigrated to the USA, where she took on a Cherokee shaman as her High Priest. She has been a major influence on local covens since her arrival there. Like Ralph, she was amazed to find just how far the Craft had evolved away from its simplistic and traditional roots. This was mainly due to the influx of Italian *Stregas* (Witches); the essentially British core had been "Latinised", but she was also gratified to find that some of that core had survived intact. In Arizona, Ralph and Audrey stayed on Native American reservations (the proud and unconquered Hopi and Navaho tribes resent the term 'Indian'"), where the pair added to their already vast knowledge of the spiritual practices of these people. Ralph has now been invited to lecture in Florida and Portugal. The Order of Artemis now has covens in the USA, Canada, Australia, New Zealand, Germany, France and other European countries, in addition to Scotland, Wales and Eire.

From the New Forest of Hampshire to the Downs of Sussex, a new age has been born as the original religion of this country has risen, phoenix-like, from its own ashes. This has been fanned and fuelled by Ralph and his compatriots (many of whom have passed on to the Summerland). Sussex is truly "The Last Bastion" of the Native religion of England, and

Sussex can take pride in its history, not only of being able to resist the foreign religion's yoke, but by virtue of Ralph's presence, being the forerunner in this renaissance of Witchcraft and its spread across the world.

This, then, is the story of the Craft. Ralph, one of the few remaining "Old Ones", shows the worship of the old ways of the God Cernunnos and his consort Ceridwen, the Goddess and Earth Mother. You will find the book fascinating, as 50 years of Witchcraft of the past and present unfold within its pages.

Pagan history will show the great debt that is owed to this intriguing man, whom I am proud to call my friend.

Sn. Emrys
Grand Master of the Cromlech Covenant
Sussex, 2004

Dark Clouds on the Ḫorizon

The hills of Sussex are emerald green havens of tranquillity, and the rich brown fertile earth that surrounds them has fed the county since time immemorial. One may ask why it should not? For its rich soil has been fertilised by blood since the beginning of time itself. Invasions and countless raids have devastated its people over the centuries. Villages and towns have been lost beneath its soil, only to be found by archaeologists aeons later.

The Romans came, followed by Saxon mercenaries and Danish pirates. Vikings roamed at will, as did Frankish marauders. French privateers regarded Sussex as a source of rich and easy booty: ultimately, it would fall to the Norman invaders in the battle of 1066, changing Sussex history forever. It was not the first time the county had suffered so completely, for she had previously endured 400 years of Roman occupation. Saxons came and Saxons went, as did all the other raiders, but the Romans and the Normans came to stay.

Before them, the South of England had been divided between the warring factions of the Atrebates, Regnenses and Cantiaci, but it was the Regnenses that were opposed on all sides. Over the years, they had become so integrated with one particular raider who had also settled on their land, that these indigenous peoples were now regarded as Saxons. Outsiders referred to them as the Suth Seaxe or South Saxons, and it was from this definition of the Suth Seaxe that the word Sussex was born.

This proud and independent territory eventually succumbed to the invaders, but out of this eternal and constant conflict and turmoil emerged a race of hardy, resolute people, who carried that unmistakable stamp that labelled them "Sussex Folk". Sussex men and women had defied the depredations over the centuries and survived them, until they emerged as a hardy breed of Celt and Roman, laced with the blood of a hundred raiders.

It was Sussex that refused to bow the knee to the doctrine of St Augustine. Why should they yield to a strange newcomer's religion when they had resisted hundreds of years of invasion? It was not in their nature to accept a new religion, with which they could not identify and which was contrary to their Pagan beliefs and heritage. As they stood by, county after county fell to the new religion, the old ways were swept aside and in their wake came the Xtian priests with a Bible in one hand and a sword in the other, determined to convert or slay.

NB: For those who are new to Witchcraft, the word Xtian is used here to signify the new religion that ousted and replaced the original.

It took many years of preaching and internal conflict from Land's End to John O'Groats, but in the end, the British counties all fell to the blandishments of fine words from the Xtian newcomers. Lancashire, Durham, Essex and Warwickshire had swiftly succumbed, with only the West Country and Sussex remaining. Devon and Cornwall eventually gave way, although their old traditions died hard and many in the remaining counties only paid lip service to the new religion. However, stubborn and obstinate Sussex held out to the bitter end. She could not go it alone, surrounded now as she was by Xtian counties, and so slowly and reluctantly, she too gave way and accepted the Xtian yoke.

Xtian priests moved in, destroying Pagan Temples, filling in the holy wells, diverting sacred streams, and felling the Sacred

Oaks and Groves. The populace looked on bewildered at the vandalism of these newcomers, who preached eternal life but seemed hell bent on destroying so much of the works of Nature. Thus, it was that the Old Ways went underground as Sussex joined the rest of the country and paid lip service to the new religion, while secretly adhering to the Old. How right they were to do so, for suppression of their ways was not long in coming. Firstly, it was simple chastisement followed by penances and fines. Then whippings and brandings, culminating in death by hanging or burning at the stake for loving the Old Gods or for the crime of rejecting the new Messiah. Free will and free choice were abolished – the Church would brook no opposition.

Sullenly, the Sussex people entered the new Churches that were appearing all over the county, desecrating the ancient sites of worship as the newcomers built their towering citadels upon them. Now, if they wanted to get onto the land they once loved so dearly and were accustomed to worship on, they had to enter the strange and gloomy buildings where the priests dolefully expounded misery on earth. The priests promised that the faithful who accepted everything the Church dictated, and who religiously obeyed their teachings (including donating a tithe of all they earned) would receive the rewards of their earthly labours in the Xtian paradise to come. This was a premise that had no evident hope of ever being fulfilled.

How different were the strange men in their simple gowns and shaven heads, who never smiled, compared to the joyousness of their own priests, who laughed and sang with the people. How they missed the tinkle of their priestess's laughter as they cavorted around the circle, daring any male who could to catch them. When they compared the droll sermons that were delivered each Sunday to the exuberance of a Pagan Sabbat, they failed to see how a strange religion that had entered from the East could have grown in ascendancy so fast. What was the attraction of a doctrine that gave misery today in theoretical exchange for glory up in the clouds tomorrow?

The people loved the depictions of their own God, the Lord Cernunnos, with his smiling eyes and perpetual grin. They adored the festivals of wine where he and Bacchus would become the same: and when they would drink, eat and carouse until dawn in honour of the forest spirits. Then, as dawn broke, they would all rise and dutifully pour a libation of wine onto the rich Sussex earth in gratitude to the Old Ones who had granted them such bountiful harvests. Equally, they adored the Goddess of Fertility and Love who unashamedly portrayed her inner sexuality, and who proclaimed herself as joy in the heart of man. "All rituals of Love and Laughter are mine," she declared; and each act of love was a dedication and tribute to her.

Oh how different to the newcomers who abjured sex and condemned woman as the source of all evil and original sin. This was especially so when they compared their continual filling of their drinking horns during their revelry with the niggardly sip of communion wine that the Xtian priests allowed them in the church. No, this new faith did not make sense to them. A village headsman commented after having been compelled to attend one of these Church services that the priest gave out no more than a single loaf of bread and a small flagon of wine to the entire congregation. This was in a ceremony that was a form of ritualised cannibalism when Xtians ate the flesh of their God and drank his blood in the ceremony that they called communion. "Why?" he exclaimed, "My wife would drink a quart of ale and an entire flagon of wine at a single sitting when we all meet. And our ceremony of cakes and wine compareth not to the morsel of bread this priest gives! And afterwards, they hold not the *agape*, the traditional love feast we all adore".

Neither did Sussex men and women understand the strange effigy these Xtians worshipped, for it was a horrendous depiction of a man in agony nailed to a cross. This in itself amazed them. How could anyone worship such an act of sheer cruelty? They worshiped and loved the gentleness of the

Goddess, whose Priestesses would stand sky-clad, with legs apart, in a sign of fecundity and with arms outstretched, depicting the sacred Pentacle. This was a form of beauty that they understood. There was no shame in nudity for either sex, for they were children of Nature. The invaders wished to destroy the Goddess and to substitute a stern and forbidding God in her place.

"This is not for us," they decided. Let them go their way and we will go ours. Then if our ways are forbidden, we will go underground and worship in secret - and thus it was. Sussex never received the vitriolic onslaught of Xtian persecution that other counties endured. Although over a few centuries, by the simple process of ensuring that all children received a Xtian education, the basics of the new religion took root. "Give us a child until it is seven" said the priests, "and we will give you a Xtian for life!"

Thus, Pagan ways and Pagan practices were suppressed in Sussex, but the Pagano/Wiccan inheritance remained. When the Witch-hunters entered Sussex, seeking those they termed "The Hidden Children of the Goddess", they found nothing. The village people hid their wise men and women and the persecutors went away empty handed. Sussex can proudly hold her head up and say, "We did not yield." In a 200-year span from 1500 to 1700, in what we now refer to as the burning days, only eighteen Witches were ever taken from Sussex, and of these, less than half suffered the death penalty. Compare this record with a single week in Essex, when over 250 Witches were on trial at one time, and when there were mass hangings with over 3,000 who were awaiting "examination".

Did the subliminal instincts of generic values still flow in the veins of these Sussex stalwarts as we entered the 20th century? Did a new tolerance dawn? With the repeal of the Witchcraft Act in 1951, the Old Ways rose to the fore almost overnight, as Sussex overtook surrounding counties in the number of people who returned so swiftly to their Pagan past. Within a couple of years after the repeal of the Witchcraft Act and the new found freedom of worship, the Lord Cernunnos, the God of the Woodlands, and Ceridwen, the Goddess of the Moon, had come into their own - restored into their rightful place in Sussex folklore as they were worshipped of old.

This, then, is the story of the yeomen and women of Pagan Sussex, a hardy breed who had never learned to bow the knee to either invader or religious zealot. Sussex is a unique county, which over the centuries had acquired a reputation for religious tolerance, while all around them, their neighbours were persecuting, torturing and murdering in the name of their God on an unparalleled scale. It was here that a fugitive who was fleeing from religious persecution could cross the border to safety and disappear. Contrary to reports that I have seen in books, the infamous Mathew Hopkins, the Witch-finder General, never entered Sussex in search of victims, but kept his depredations mainly to Essex, where he was eventually denounced and disgraced. It was there that he eventually died of tuberculosis - Nemesis having finally caught up with him.

Which county that fell to the new ways could boast to allowing dogs in church? In Sussex, those Shepherds who made a rare attendance in church would never have dreamt of coming along without their faithful dogs. In this ever-Pagan county, this was accepted. Xtian Priests raised no objection when relatives opened the coffin of a deceased shepherd and placed a small piece of sheep's wool inside. This indeed is an old Pagan custom. I find myself smiling with wry amusement at the thought that, if a Priest asked why the relatives did this, they told him that the shepherd had wanted God to know his calling on the day of judgement and to forgive him for rarely being able to leave his flock to attend church on a Sunday!

I feel it appropriate to record some of the old language here – a relic of the Celtic tongue that was used for counting sheep:

CELTIC NUMERALS	
One	Yan
Two	Tan
Three	Tethera
Four	Pethera
Five	Pimp
Six	Sethera
Seven	Lethera
Eight	Hovera
Nine	Dovera
Ten	Dick
Eleven	Yan-a-Dick
Twelve	Tan-a-Dick
Thirteen	Tethera-Dick
tcetera...	

Lest we Forget

Witchcraft is not just a memory in the twenty-first century, because from 1951 onwards a renaissance has swept the country. The entire history of the Craft before its resuscitation can be seen in Sussex, the Isle of Man and Cornwall.

There have been three museums dedicated to the Old Religion in the British Isles - all in the 20th century. One of these was most appropriately in Sussex. These are the Museum of Witchcraft founded by Gerald Broussec Gardner in the Isle of Man, which was known as the Witches Mill. For the record, this museum was founded while the craft was still outlawed. It no longer exists, but a large quantity of the exhibits that it once contained can be found in the only surviving museum in England, which is at Boscastle in Cornwall.

The owner, Graham King, lovingly preserves those precious mementoes of yesteryear. He has established a vast library where scholars may study the history of the original religion of England. The stories he could tell are legion and he is an expert on all the Old Ways. The rituals, spells and magic of the past are his special subjects. If you should meet him, you would find him a warm character, who is never happier than recounting tales of ancient Witchcraft. You will find an address and contact for him at the end of the book.

The other museum is now closed due to Xtian intolerance, but in its heyday, it was a great attraction. It was the "Museum of Witchcraft, Folklore and Curiosity", and it was situated in the old fort at Newhaven. Every summer, crowds would flock in from miles around to see the exhibits, hear the audio transmission of the history of old days, and how the original religion of this country was so cruelly suppressed in the infamous burning days.

The museum was very carefully planned in its layout. On first entering, visitors walked through an area that resembled a Chamber of Horrors, which depicted all the inhuman practices that our Pagan ancestors endured at the hands of the infamous Inquisition. It was a saga of pure horror, and the immediate reaction of those who saw the instruments of torture was, "Oh, those poor Witches! How could they do that to old women – and children too?"

Then there were all the artefacts that public would expect to see, such as poppets with pins in them, impaled sheep hearts, human skulls, piles of old bones and hands of glory. All these were false, of course. Placards told the story of how this false depiction of the Witch had come about, and how all these stories of their activities had been obtained by torture. The museum showed the methods that had been used, along with a history of how the Inquisition, as a tool of the Catholic Church, became so powerful.

We have been lucky enough to obtain an original transcript that told the story of an elderly woman who had fallen foul of her neighbours and who, as a result, had been "put to the test".

She had survived the traditional Witch-ducking and she had been condemned to death for having floated. However, her inquisitors required a specific charge other than that of "Being a Witch". It appeared that somehow the accusers had not discovered any specific incident worthy of accusation, so it became necessary to fabricate a charge to substantiate the "swimming". It turned out that a village boy of some thirteen summers had gone missing several days beforehand. To her persecutors it was all they needed, and it did not take these brutes long to choose to say that the old woman was responsible. This she vehemently denied, so she was tortured with hot irons - and in no time, at all she confessed to killing the boy. This did not satisfy them, as they now wanted to know if this was the first time she had kidnapped and killed children, and again she was "put to the question", a euphemism for torture!

By nightfall, she had confessed to killing a further twelve, making thirteen in all, counting the original one that had gone missing. I gather that this pleased the accusers no end, as, according to them, the number thirteen was one that could be expected of a Witch. The poor woman further admitted that she needed the body fat to make her devilish brews. Now thirteen young men is a fair bag for anyone to capture. It did not occur to them that a frail old crone who had to walk on two sticks and who could scarcely bend down to pick up an apple - let alone overcome a healthy farm boy - could capture these boys. It seems that, at that point, someone queried these disappearances. The fact was that there was only one missing lad, and that enquiries covering a wide area around the village could find no reports of any other missing persons. There was a missing horse though, so this was promptly added to the charges!

The accusers were deciding whether to burn or hang the poor old soul, when, lo and behold, the missing boy who had started all this by running away suddenly returned home. He came back, completely disillusioned, after joining a fair that had come to the village. At this stage, they reduced the charges to twelve and put her to the question yet again, because a somewhat bemused interrogator wanted to know what she had done with the corpses of the victims.

This time no amount of torture could make her reveal what she did not know and could not answer. The old crone in her agony agreed with everything they said, frequently contradicting herself because she could not invent a convincing enough story to satisfy them. Her end is not recorded but in a flash of inspiration, they ended her torment when she admitted to poisoning all twelve lads and eating their bodies "bones 'n all". When you think back, it is beyond our comprehension that anyone should have believed these incredible stories.

If one walked further around the museum in a large arc, the exhibits were beginning to depict to visitors how the popular image of the evil Witch in history had been fabricated by those who were out for revenge, personal gain or reward - or uppermost of all, religious persecution. Next came woodcuts and depictions of the burning days and the fallacy of the beliefs at the time. Then the story drifted very gently into modern day Witchcraft and the truth of the Old Religion. This showed that the Wisecraft was the original religion of England and that Sussex roots were inextricably entwined with their past.

We who cared for the museum had obtained some beautiful mannequins from a large department store that had closed down, and we put them into a wonderful woodland scene. One, depicting the Goddess surrounded by handmaidens, was set in a glade full of animals, butterflies and birds. This was the central attraction. Another showed thirteen Witches gathered in a forest setting and working on a healing ritual. Around these exhibits were posters explaining what was happening and demonstrating the significance of each artefact, such as the besom broom and cauldron. Local newspapers lauded the museum and published articles extolling its virtues as a tourist attraction. It gave birth to many newspaper articles praising and re-appraising the Old Religion.

So much publicity brought a storm, and when it broke, it brought a local Newhaven Evangelical Church, which took up cudgels into the fray. They berated this "House of Satan" in their midst that was threatening the God-fearing citizens of Newhaven. I only heard at second hand of the diatribes that the priest issued, but they came very close to urging the locals to drive us out physically. The museum's windows were broken every single week - always after we had locked up. One day, the vicar himself turned up on our doorstep. Purple-faced, and with a Bible in his hand, he demanded that we close the museum down, stating that it was "An abomination in the eyes of the Lord" and that we were all destined to go to Hades and to endure everlasting torment.

He was greeted civilly and invited in for coffee and we offered him a tour of the museum. We wished to explain that we did not believe in the Devil, and that the people of Newhaven had nothing to fear from us. His response was almost to strike me with the "good book", shouting, "Will you close this sink of iniquity down NOW! Yes or no?" Once more, we invited him to sit down and talk in friendship, but he had arrived literally shaking with temper and was by now almost apoplectic with rage, so much so that we feared he would break a blood vessel! Then, as suddenly as he had arrived, he left - still shouting invective at us. We never saw him again, but it was a chilling reminder to us all of what our forebears must have endured, for we had witnessed pure unadulterated fanaticism.

This was not the end of the matter. His ravings from the pulpit grew in animosity each Sunday as he urged the congregation to evict us. From the gossip that floated back to us, he even told his flock how they should do it. Following a break-in at the museum one Sunday evening, we had no alternative but to call in the police.

A plain clothes officer attended the church the following Sunday, and as a result of what he heard, the church was cautioned as to how far they could go in verbal onslaughts. He also told them that any incitement to violence and damage would contravene the law. The following Sunday, the Minister told the assembled congregation what the police had said, and he withdrew his statements as to the action he had advocated. He then added venomously, "It is therefore up to your own consciences as to what you do about this evil in our midst; I have no more to say - you all know my feelings on this matter."

To our chagrin, this religious zealot did actually succeed in closing the museum, because the insurance premiums for the building and the continual smashing of our windows forced the insurers to withdraw cover for the breakages. The endless outlay in repairing the damage exceeded our income; and so, sadly, we closed. Not long afterwards, the local council took control of the fort and increased the security. I found it strange that within weeks of our leaving, dog patrols and a full time security guard were found overnight by Lewes council. However, I have nothing but admiration for the Newhaven police.

So now, we have only the Museum of Witchcraft in Boscastle in Cornwall left to tell the history of our people. It is thriving, despite some nominal opposition locally from staunch churchgoers. However, Xtians succeeded in closing down the beautiful "House of Elves", condemning it as an "iniquitous pit of evil" for showing fairies and elves. Given a little power and authority, it would take but a spark to bring the persecutions back. The church is ever watchful, but the clock has moved forward and it will never be allowed to happen again.

So mote it be.

The Goddess Wakes

"She is not any Common Earth,
Of Water, Wood, or Tin
But Merlin's Isle of Gramarye
Where you and I will fare."
"... Unluckily the Hills are empty now,
and all the people of the Hills are gone.
I am the only one left.
I am Puck!
The oldest Old Thing in England,
Very much at your service if - if you care
To have anything to do with me.
If you don't, of course you've only to say so,
And I will go."

These famous and strangely prophetic words by Rudyard Kipling (from Puck of Pook's Hill) could so easily have been exclusive to Sussex, which was his home county and where he lived and died. From his home in Rottingdean, he could see the rolling hills of Sussex that had been a stronghold of the Old Religion from time immemorial. Here, within its secluded valleys, ancient Pagan rites had survived the burning days or the days of the hempen rope, but essentially in secret. The ways of the Witches and their Craft were still outlawed at the time of his death in 1936.

Why did Kipling pay such attention to Puck in one of his most famous poems? Puck, Pan, the Green Man, Herne the Hunter or the old Horned God. They were all synonymous with the God of the Witches, so he was outwardly referring to the same entity - who in theory had disappeared from the Sussex scene aeons before. Two decades were to pass after his death before the ways of the Witch could be practised openly once again, and it was Sussex and Hampshire where the first stirrings occurred after the repeal of the archaic and onerous Witchcraft Act in 1951. Sussex finally threw off centuries of persecution.

Practising Sussex Witches, together with their brothers and sisters of the Craft of the Wise, or the Wisecraft, as it came to be known, knew that the Goddess of old, together with her consort, the God Cernunnos, had merely slept. They could be awoken at the Witches call, just as Kipling had indicated. Dead to the world and to ordinary mortals, but ever ready to come back to the beat of the drum if summoned, and the drums were about to beat as of old.

Over the years, the Old Religion had been driven almost to the verge of extinction, and the few fragments that remained had been driven underground. Outwardly, the Old Gods had been abandoned by the common people, but they were only in primordial sleep. The old ways were not gone. They were still here - and they could be readily awakened and resurrected when called. This was known to the few existing practitioners, who secretly called upon the Gods and Goddesses of yesteryear, usually from behind drawn curtains. Hence, the prophetic words of Kipling, who must have gazed out at those green hills that once were home to the Sussex farmers and workers who would gather on the full moon and new moons to invoke prosperity for their crops and livestock. He chose the mischievous Puck to represent the focal point of the poem that ends with such sadness and poignancy, depicting him as symbolic of a benevolent, wise and beautiful religion that was once practised openly by our forebears, and which was the original religion of England, with Sussex as its stronghold. How can an essentially Pagan soul fail to respond to the haunting words that he wrote of Puck's lament: "Very much at your service if... if you care to have anything to do with me? If you don't, you've only to say so, and I will go."

Well the Craft did survive. Fifty years on, Witchcraft is one of the fastest growing religions in Britain, Europe and the USA. (In some areas, Islam is another major growth area as far as religions go). The Goddess has returned to the people. In a wave of euphoria, all that is green is suddenly in vogue. The populace avidly supports green issues. Conservation groups abound and the cry is for a return to a healthy way of life, as they demand organic foodstuffs. In the wake of this movement, people found the Old Gods and the old ways once more. The Goddess of the land, the Eternal Earth Mother, had returned and was once more being worshipped, as of old. From the few survivors who had been driven underground prior to 1951, a completely new era has blossomed. A friend once remarked, "The white man nearly exterminated the North American Bison, yet from the handful that were saved they now roam the prairies as of old. Don't you sometimes feel that we also have come back from the point of extinction and are now counted in our hundreds of thousands?"

The number of covens openly practising in Sussex as at 2004 is legion, and the largest individual groupings are to be found in this secular county. Throughout the length and breadth of Sussex, each meeting of Witches and their adherents is well attended. The Sabbats are the equal of those that took place in the past, and the covens who boast a mere thirteen in their membership are very rare, because the average gathering in reality starts closer to the twenty mark.

Broomstick rallies and moots are now a frequent occurrence in Sussex. Psychic fairs abound wherever there is a strong Wiccan presence. There are esoteric gatherings and Witchfests, not to mention the massive gatherings at the Green Man Festival that takes place in Hastings each May Day. Over the years, the Witchfest has grown, as countless thousands of pagans flock to Hastings castle every first of May to participate and watch the Rites of Spring. From all over the country, Morris dancers descend to show their dancing skills and enact age-old Morris. They dance - group after group - throughout the entire day, to the delight of the thousands of watchers. People bring picnics, children play and a good time is had by all.

The whole of Hastings is drawn into the festivities as the people await the great procession. Along the procession route, people put out green bowers and foliage. Sprigs of oak are tied to garden gates and flowers abound. I have never seen a town that has so closely embraced such an essentially Pagan event as Hastings has. On the seafront, Witch covens gather, together with Pagano/Wiccan groups, green conservationists, and countless fellow travellers and sympathisers to the old ways, all dressed in a merry assortment of costumes, embracing an essentially "green" theme.

Animal costumes and heads predominate, as do horns and foliate masks. Women and girls spend hours painting their faces in intricate floral patterns, while men seem to go for old Celtic designs. Then, to the throb of drum and tambourine, the great march commences around the old town part of Hastings and slowly wends its way up the step hill to the castle. Revellers search the streets and alleys looking for victims who have not been "greened". To walk the streets of Hastings on this day of days is to court attention, and a completely white face will stick out a mile. Instantly, a tablet or stick of green greasepaint will be produced and the perpetrator greened, usually just a token marker on the cheek or brow; no-one refuses, because marking someone on May Day is considered lucky, and this should bring good fortune in the coming year. At the head of the winding column is the Jack, a ten-foot high effigy of the Green Man, complete with a strong male consort within, who dances and whirls as they traverse the streets. "Jack" is happy and carefree as he dances his way to his ritual slaying when he reaches the amphitheatre. There, as the ceremony reaches its climax, he is destroyed and his body parts clamoured for by the frenzied crowd. No one departs from the Green Man Festival without a piece of the Jack o' the Green. Even if it be a mere leaf!

May Day was celebrated before the coming of the Xtians and now it is once again accepted in Sussex. Although a fertility symbol, strangely enough it has survived in many other counties too. The diminishing of the Mayday rites owes more to Oliver Cromwell, who condemned both the festival as well as the Maypole itself as "a heathen abomination", but with the Restoration, the Maypole came into its own again.

The early followers of the Old Religion were extremely promiscuous on this day, as the fertility rites were followed, and none looked askance as couples paired off to slink into the woods. This Pagan practice of what passed into Wiccan history as the "Great Rite" was performed at Candlemas (February 2nd), the Spring Equinox (March 21st) and Beltane (on May Day or May Eve). Hallowmas (October 31st) was celebrated as an intense reaffirmation of the life-force. Up until recent years, it was enacted between Priest and Priestess on these days or consenting adults within the coven, and at elevation to the Third Degree. With the advent of Aids, the old fertility rites have all but passed into history.

The coven - in fact, the entire village - eagerly awaited the outcome of these couplings, and all prayed that a child would be born to a Witch because of them. It was known as "The Child of Promise" and was honoured and raised as a coven child. Every member of the coven accepted the baby as their own and contributed to its support and maintenance, as would the local villagers. Here again, in Sussex the baby was honoured and was "child of promise", but it was called by the wondrously descriptive noun of "Merrybegot", and it was a blessing from the God and Goddess. Everywhere the Merrybegot was welcomed, because this progeny was considered lucky.

Within old Alice's "book of rite", I have extracted a page as an indication of the Craft of yesteryear. It is dated the 6th of May, but the year is not recorded. It runs as follows:

"It is the 6th of May and the May blossom at last is in bloom. Tonight the young men and women will gather in the branches for the ritual. Tomorrow at 'dawn break', James and I are to be handfasted, and together we will jump the broom. I hope I am able to get through ritual - such is my excitement. I have a gown of blue, which mother and Ada have made. I will carry primroses and wear some in my hair, and I will be allowed to wear my hair up. I have been told to stay after the ritual, as the Magister and Lady wish to speak to me before I can go home to change".

The sheer simplicity of this extract gives an insight into a balanced and gentle way of life that we are all the poorer for losing. Well, so much for May.

In recent years, the formation of the now renowned Occulture Festival attracts countless numbers to its seminars and lectures. This has become a major player on the Pagan scene. Outside of its emphasis on the occult, it embraces social issues in the investigation of Eastern religions and doctrines. It is not afraid to raise social, political and ecological issues. In June 2002, it raised the issue of Tibet, the Tibetan people's religion and beliefs and their subjugation under Chinese communism. However, for now, let us return to Sussex and let its history stand as a microcosm of the story of the Old Religion in the country as a whole.

Roots

Here within these pages, we will show how Witchcraft survived in Sussex and how Sussex became a hallowed county, when its relatively clean record is compared to its neighbours and to the atrocities that were inflicted throughout Britain as a whole.

By far the largest coven in Sussex is The Order of Artemis. This was founded in 1959, eight years after the repeal of the infamous Witchcraft Act, but its roots commenced in 1951. I tried desperately to hold to the old hereditary ways, but with the upsurge of Gardnerianism in the new age, the Old Ways were dying. When the Craft was finally free of outward oppression, to the best of our knowledge, only five hereditary families were left, in addition to a handful of solitary practitioners whom we traced over several years. This search was given high priority between 1951 and 1958. The Craft had survived, but it was diminished, so now these people needed to be found. It turned out that there were more solitary practitioners and small groups in existence than had formerly been realised, and they tended to be grouped in specific areas. This was most heartening.

Cornwall and Devon proved exceptionally rich hunting grounds, for in these counties there was a greater proliferation of Witches, Wise Women and Cunning Men than we had realised. The Isle of Man also proved a rich hunting ground. I feel that it was no coincidence that the two major Witchcraft museums that still existed in Britain were situated in Castletown on the Isle of Man and at Boscastle in Cornwall.

At that point, The Order of Artemis set out to try to trace the remnants of the alleged famous "Nine Covens" founded by Old George Pickingill, the last descendant of Julia the Wicce of Brandon, who was killed in 1071. There were contrasting results. We concentrated on Sussex, as it had been the last bastion in resisting the Witch-finders. This was also the last county in Britain outwardly to accept Xtianity, so we felt there was a fair chance of success. We hoped that the first discovery would lead to others.

It was by a quirk of fate that the first turned up following an advert in the Sussex Evening Argus. In the personal column, we found an insert announcing, "Witch wanted to remove family curse." It had been inserted by the aging and impoverished Duke of Leinster, who was a friend of mine and a distant relative. A local Witch responded - and within weeks, the first of the "Nine Covens" had been traced to the village of Storrington in Sussex. Subsequent research determined that at least two of these covens were known under different names, but were one and the same group. This alone reduces the famous nine covens to seven.

The four members were all elderly and they kept strictly to the Old Ways. A rapport was established, and after well over the traditional year and a day, I was initiated. They knew that the Willingdon coven practised on an ancient site at Seaford and that it had Pickingill connections. To my dismay, the members of this coven also were all elderly, the youngest at the time being their High Priestess of seventy-two summers. They had not initiated anyone since before the Second World War! Two of the oldest covens in England were on the brink of extinction, but what they could tell us was beyond all our hopes.

They combined to help the old Duke of Leinster, and with the aid of magic, they were able to overcome many of his problems. However, the family estate and his major problems were beyond their means. There were not enough years left to the ageing nobleman to revive his fortunes and solve the legal problems that he had inherited. Apparently, he had received another two letters from Sussex Witches in response to his advert, one from someone whom he was not sure about but another from someone who, as he quaintly put it to me, was "the real McCoy". He engaged in correspondence with them, but regretfully he died before passing on the full information about what he had found - or their identity. Thus, another contact had irrevocably been lost, and time was running out.

There was a strange side effect to this. I was a private investigator in those days, and I had received a highly confidential instruction from a firm of solicitors in Brighton who were acting as agents for an eminent firm of lawyers in the City of London. This requested me to investigate certain "occult" activities in the Brighton area. The solicitors arranged a meeting with their client, who turned out to be closely associated with the Royal Family. He was concerned at the activities of a certain woman within Royal circles who was taking a more than usual interest in Witchcraft activities in the area. He also had a certain interest in the Duke of Leinster. The Argus advertisement had been noted and forwarded to the solicitor by a local lawyer who also acted for a Royal on property matters in Sussex.

I swiftly realised that after making preliminary enquiries that I had a conflict of interest in the case, so I had to decline it. I assured them the names of the parties would never be revealed and that their clients were safe in the knowledge that I would not ever disclose their names. Years later, the same solicitors contacted me with regard to a certain woman who had been purchasing certain esoteric magazines such as *The Cauldron* and *Pagan Path* through an intermediary. I watched her progress for many years through the press and was delighted to know in my heart that she was one of us, but her untimely and sad death robbed and saddened both Xtian and Pagan alike.

The last Priestess of the Willingdon coven, Ceridwen, passed to the Summerlands in her late 90s in 1977, having bequeathed her artefacts to The Order of Artemis. I had dearly wanted to join their group as well, but they felt they were too old to accept anyone by that time. I did join them in occasional rituals, because, by this time, I had been initiated into the Storrington Coven and was thereby "accepted". These were rare but wonderful occasions. A most odd little group would occasionally join us, which rejoiced in weird and wonderful names. I never knew what happened to them, as they faded away like snow in the Sahara.

It was from here that much of the research into Pickingill's progeny commenced, for, by this time, "Gardnerianism" was the rage and the New Forest coven in their turn had accepted Gerald B. Gardner into their group. They were the third of the "Pickingill covens" that had survived, dispersing the fallacy that Gardnerianism and the Pickingill traditions were separate entities. They were not. Gardner's roots also went back to Julia the Wicce via the New Forest practitioners, and it was from here that Gardner subsequently "hived" and formed his own new concept of the Craft for the 20th century.

It was difficult after a lapse of so many years to uncover the full background to what happened. There was much discussion amongst old practitioners when Gerald's book, "High Magic's Aid" was published, in which he sailed perilously close to many old secrets, but it seemed to pass.

It was only when "Witchcraft Today" was published that the fat was well and truly in the fire. Old Dorothy Clutterbuck had passed to the Summerlands over three years earlier, so she was in no position to rebuke Gerald. Rosamund, who could well have been High Priestess, or at least the Maid of the coven, died at the age of 83 in 1948 – three years before the Witchcraft Act was repealed. By all accounts, she held a position of some authority within the coven, and she was certainly an elder.

It was at this point (approximately 1954 to 1955) that the New Forest coven - or to be more specific, that particular one - disappeared from history, never to return. Their existence cannot be denied. Old Dorothy Clutterbuck and the inimitable Dafo were, of course, real, but phones rang and there was much disquiet at the time, despite the renaissance. Many old Witches decided to go on keeping their heads low.

I feel it is no coincidence that, with the upsurge of interest in Witchcraft, those covens with extremely elderly populations, such as Storrington and Willingdon, went into sharp decline. It is highly likely that all the New Forest practitioners could also have been elderly, for it is a fact that many of those had been severely depleted of young members during the Second World War, when only the elderly were left to carry on from 1939 to 1946.

If only Dorothy had survived for another five years, we could have rewritten the whole history of those eventful years. Dafo – Edith Woodford Grimes – went public on just one occasion and gave an interview. However, by all accounts, she was clearly disturbed at being in the public eye, for afterwards she "went to ground", never to raise her head again. I think that, at about this point, she probably resigned from the coven, as she had become a *"cause célèbre"*. Visitors were turned away and she became completely incommunicado. She died in 1975 at the age of 88, taking the secrets of the New Forest coven to the grave with her.

What happened to them? Did they disband or did they die out? Alternatively, are their descendants still out there, meeting secretly? My feeling is that the secret may soon be unlocked through an old Romany Gypsy now in his dotage, who knows every inch of the Forest and what goes on there. I shall be meeting him and I hope to answer some of these questions in my next book.

My feeling is that one of the other covens that still exist in the area may know; or they may have absorbed the remnants of Gerald's groups or their progeny into their own groups. When one realises that the old Hereditary Witches, such as the Kingston people, were still undiscovered until the 21st century… but more of them later in this book. They kept a low profile for many years and they still wish to do so.

And why not? With so many secrets and practices of the Craft being openly sold, and with so many established practitioners who have sold their souls to Mammon and broken their sacred oaths, it is little wonder that the old covens are saying "enough is enough". I have been careful to avoid giving any rituals in this book (other than a tongue-in-cheek love spell at the back), but I am sure that most are readily available in some DIY Witchcraft publication.

I feel that much of the conjecture and legend of Pickingill and his nine covens has been misinterpreted over the years, so the time has come to set the record straight. Firstly, there never were nine covens. The most that had been known at any one time, in fact, was seven. The indigenous coven would be common knowledge in a certain area, but it would also be known to villages and local folklore by the name of a second area. For instance, the Willingdon coven held their outdoor meetings at Seaford, which was some considerable distance away. When the weather was bad, they descended on a very large and rambling house in Willingdon for their rituals. Over the years and by various means, including rumours of occult activity in the area, they were referred to as the Willingdon coven. In the meantime, some twelve miles away, when they worshipped in moon rituals on the old sacred site at Seaford (now, sadly, built upon), there the locals referred to them as the Seaford coven. This gave rise in Sussex folklore to the existence of two quite separate covens practicing within a few miles of each other. This was not so - for the Seaford coven and the Willingdon coven were one and the same.

The same concept applied to my own coven of those days. Within Storrington, our activities were common knowledge - village gossip being as it was: although the finger of suspicion as to whom the Witches were, or who was a Witch within the village, pointed in completely the wrong direction; the main suspect was a somewhat eccentric old woman who lived in what they called the "crooked cottage". The cottage was a local house with a wall that had subsided so that the whole building was out of alignment. The poor old soul had no connection to the Old Religion, but she constantly held conversations with her cat! She was regarded with awe by the villagers, although none gave her offence.

Although having a delightful abode in which to meet and conduct rituals on the village outskirts, the Storrington coven actually performed its rituals in nearby Bramber when the weather was fine. This included the ruins of Bramber castle itself, again giving rise to rumour of two covens operating in the area; for example, a Bramber group of Witches and a Storrington coven. Again, this was not right, for the Bramber coven and the Storrington coven were one and the same.

Since the 1950s, occult activity has been more open, so even Artemis has become identified with separate covens operating within a specific area. This has been largely contributed to by local newspapers over the years. Within this period, we have shifted our activities to a number of different houses. If a member sold his house, we would move to another member whose house was large enough to accommodate the numbers. Often, this was to the residence of the reigning High Priestess or to my own house. Because of this, along with newspapers often following up a story, we have been reported as the Brighton coven, the Hove coven, the Portslade coven and the Littlehampton coven. Since I moved to Shoreham by Sea, we have become known as the Shoreham coven - but these are all one.

Our sacred coven site is near Warnham, which is over twenty-two miles away. Our activities, which include drumming, giant balefires and frequent musical accompaniment, are legend there. Thus, we are referred to there as both the Kingsfold coven and the Warnham coven. This has given rise to the rumour that seven covens are in operation, through the activities of just one, notwithstanding the substantial numbers of practitioners within the boundaries of Brighton and Hove that practise independently of us.

Pickingill - Myth versus Fact

Ceridwen, who was High Priestess of the Storrington coven at the time, had met Old George Pickingill, as had the Priest and Priestess of the Willingdon coven. However, there is no evidence whatsoever of Old George ever having ever written, telephoned or to my knowledge, having ever corresponded with them. Pickingill was not a literate man! On the other hand, his knowledge was legendary. I understand that his memory of old lore that had been passed down to him in a verbal tradition through his ancestors had no equal. Old George Pickingill was a walking encyclopaedia, if you were accepted by him and he was prepared to talk to you. One could go to him, but he did not come to others! As far as I know, he rarely ventured far from the village of Canewdon.

Old George welcomed these overtures once you were accepted by him. He often referred to such referees as "my people". From the information that I have dredged up, it appears that he never ever founded a single coven in his life, but he was the mentor of at least seven covens, including the New Forest coven from which Gardner originated. George was their Guru, and he dispensed his knowledge only to those with sound roots. Little did he realise the controversy that would follow after he entered the Summerlands - although Gardner was strangely reticent on this issue.

Ceridwen was in contact with a coven in the New Forest during the Second World War, and I presume that this was the group that initiated Gardner, although there is no reason to believe that the vast sprawling wilderness housed only one coven. There seems to be evidence of a number of Witches being in communication with Old George Pickingill in the early days of the War. This culminated in the famous ritual on the White Cliffs of Dover where, I understand, a practitioner died at the climax of the ritual, in what was regarded as the supreme sacrifice. Who knows what secret ritual Old George imparted to them that helped save England in 1940?

The only other knowledge I can shed on the other covens with whom Pickingill was associated also came from Ceridwen. This was of a connection with two groups in the West Country, again regretfully not recorded. This accounted for five of the seven covens...but were two of these the same? Somewhere out there the answer still lies. Therefore, in finishing, I can state that Pickingill, in referring to "his" covens, was in fact referring to them as a father would refer to his children. Yes, they were his covens. They were his followers and he was their Guru - but he did not found them.

In the latter days of Doreen Valiente's life, the background of Pickingill was discussed at length with John Belham-Payne, who inherited the artefacts that she bequeathed to his Centre for Pagan Studies. After consultation with John, I am pleased to be able to state categorically that my theory on Old George Pickingill and the famous nine covens was also Doreen's conclusion. So let us finally put to rest the Gardnerian heresy and the mystery of the now infamous and alleged nine covens. These matters must be recorded before they become lost in the mists of time.

So, for the records of our American brothers and sisters of the craft, and their creation of the dreaded "puppy papers" that are now so dear to them, the Witches in England before 1951 had common roots. Few written traditions existed because verbal lore was a safer way of broadcasting information in the days of persecution. Did anyone have the temerity to ask dear Gerald for his puppy papers? I think not.

Gardner's ideas became part of a new renaissance of the Old Ways, and it was realised by The Order of Artemis that they had to reappraise their traditions. The Order of Artemis decided to keep the old laws and adapt the 162 laws Gardner had devised. They ran a close parallel to the sparse "Hand of Rite" (hand of write) documents that were still in existence. They amended the fertility rites, whereby they invoked power for their women-folk to be fertile and bear many children. Some 80 per cent were on the pill and trying not to conceive, so they altered these rites to bring fertility to crops and animals instead. Thus was born the "Traditional Witchcraft" that was henceforth to be the middle way for many followers. No longer holding to outdated traditions, yet still maintaining the Ancient Secrets, such as the passing of the secret names of the Goddess at the Third Degree. Now that we are in the 21st century, how many Witch covens have been heard of – let alone known by their secret names?

Witch Blood and Witch Ways

In 1978, The Order of Artemis was reformed, and by then, adherents were flocking to the new tradition. Members eventually reached their Third Degree and "hived" to found other covens in their turn; and so continued the tradition. At the last count in 2002, covens had been founded in the USA, Canada, France, Ireland, Scotland, Wales, Australia and Spain.

In the same year, my wife Audrey took a gigantic step forward and decided to be initiated. Close friends ran a large Gardnerian coven in Brighton known as the Acorn coven. This coven was her choice, for at that stage, Audrey favoured New Age Wicca. Audrey's initiation was a cause for great celebration, because Audrey was "Witch Blood", her mother being Alice Kemp, whose grandfather founded Kemp Town in Brighton.

Regretfully, this interlude did not last more than two years, as the High Priest and his partner of the Acorn coven divorced. The group dispersed to other covens and so Audrey's path led to The Order of Artemis, where she embraced traditional practices. During this period, The Order of Artemis worked closely with Mabs and Tom Penfold, who were eminent local Gardnerians. They had previously "hived" from Rae Bone, who had initiated Tom, and whose High Priest had initiated Mabs. Tom was a police officer and Mabs an official at the Strand Law Courts in London. Ray Bone had been one of

Gerald Gardner's initiates and had worked with him for many years before "hiving" and further perpetuating and expanding the Craft.

The Kempe ancestry embraced two famous Witches, along with an Archbishop of Canterbury and an Archbishop of York. One Witch was "Nan Kempe", the famous Lewes Witch who had been executed at Kingston in Sussex in 1610. The other, Ursula (Ursley) Kemp, the Witch of St. Osyth, had been executed in 1582 and she was buried at a crossroads nearby. Her riveted body was subsequently rediscovered in 1921 when the road was widened. It was placed on display in a local labourer's hut for viewing at tuppence a time. After this, a Mr. Barnum purchased the body and placed it in his travelling sideshow at sixpence a peep.

Ursula eventually was "rescued" and placed in the Witchcraft Museum in Boscastle, where she remained for many years, but mysteriously, she was missing when Graham King purchased the museum in 1996. She was subsequently traced to Plymouth and eventually ended up in a private occult collection.

Frequently, the Artemis and Penfold groups joined together. On great Sabbats, we were joined by the Coven of Arachne, the Willow Coven and the Coven of the Green Man, along with others. Mabs often invited me to become a Gardnerian, but initially I declined. She swore that she would bring me in if it were the last thing she ever did. Looking back, I'm sure that she bewitched me, for as promised, she eventually succeeded to the merriment of all, including Audrey, who was also delighted.

Mabs threw a great Full Moon celebration the following year, and thus I endured a second initiation! The union of the two groups was a great success, and we worked even closer together from then onwards. Both Mabs and Tom accompanied us to Egypt in 1992 when Audrey sought to lay at rest the recurring dream that she had had since being a schoolgirl. The dream was of being at the Temple of Hatshepsut at Luxor.

Mabs in particular was fascinated with old lore, and within a year, she and Tom reciprocally joined Artemis. They were a great asset and they helped me in my investigations into the paranormal, time and again. Tom had an analytical approach to all investigations, owing to his police training; as Mabs also had, in view of her legal background.

Over the years, I was consulted repeatedly regarding the paranormal and I became known as the "ghost hunter". Whenever psychic activity was detected, I packed my case and departed with my kit. For years, I investigated haunted groves, hostelries and houses, and many, many castles. The most haunted of all has to be Huntingdon (now Clonegal) Castle in Ireland.

The police would often contact me to investigate what appeared to be satanic activity in the area, in case there had been any criminal activity, such as animal sacrifice. I am happy to report that most activity was nothing more than the work of brain-dead vandals who were playing a very dangerous game. In fact, I am happy to say that the number of genuine cases of black magic was so few over a span of 50 years or more that I could count them on the fingers of one hand. It is a subject that often comes up when I lecture on the early days of the Craft.

One thing that saddens me is the rise of the so-called "puppy papers", so prevalent in the USA. I recently met many leading American Wiccans during my 2003 lecture tour. They seemed to think that all Witchcraft was Gardnerian, and if one's roots could not be traced back to Gardner himself, then they could not be recognised as Witches. To their credit, when I told them of the old Hereditary Witches who still existed in country areas, and who were most certainly not Gardnerians, they saw the fallacy of this new craze.

For over fifty years, I have seen covens rise and die out, old Witch families disappear and all traces and records become lost. Many have been deliberately destroyed by Xtian relatives after the Witch has gone to the beloved Summerlands. In those early days, there were few records kept by the hereditary

Witches, so Traditionalists and Gardnerians ranked side by side.

Many practising Witches from all three of these persuasions did not recognise the Alexandrian movement, because this courted so much negative publicity and wrongful depictions of the Craft at the time. Having said that, many good Witches have since emerged who started out as Alexandrians. The Farrars, Lindfields and others who are closer to Gardnerian and Traditional practice have since become eminent.

Both my wife and I were fascinated by ancient Egypt. Audrey has believed since childhood that she had a previous incarnation in ancient Egypt. Since she was less than five years old, she had been haunted by a vivid dream about a previous life there. She had vivid recollections of being inside towering Temples - always seeing herself in that period as an Oracle. This is a vision that had persisted and dominated her life for over forty-two years. By the time she was nine, it had become a dominant factor in her life, yet she had never ever even read a book on Egypt, and there was no television in those days!

The fates took a hand once more, and this time the path led us to the Honourable Olivia Robertson at Huntingdon Castle in Clonegal, Ireland and Lord and Lady Strathlock, who were the heads and founders of the Fellowship of Isis. I had been enrolled in the Fellowship some time before. In 1978, I was ordained a Priest of Isis at a Holy site used secretly by Isian followers at Clapham woods, near Worthing, in Sussex. The supreme accolade, however, was reserved for Audrey's initiation, which was privileged to be held in Huntingdon Castle at Clonegal, County Wexford in Ireland, three years later. In 1981, we travelled to Eire as guests of Lord and Lady Strathlock, where we spent six weeks happily exploring the countless hauntings within the castle and its grounds and learning all we could of Isian ceremony.

Audrey was ordained by Lord Strathlock (affectionately known as Derry) that year, during our sojourn at Huntingdon, together with Lady Strathlock, equally affectionately known as

Poppy, and with the Honourable Olivia Robertson as the Maiden. Derry arranged for many local Druids to attend, together with Witches and Pagans, so it was a grand occasion.

Robes of every hue and colour dominated the scene. Unfortunately, I had not brought any garments along that were suitable for the occasion, but a smiling Derry presented me with some old Chinese Mandarin robes to wear. Chinese silks blended in with Audrey's green robe, interspersed with the blues and reds of the Witches and the white of the Druids. Derry and Poppy appeared in the full and ancient garb of the High Priest and Priestess of Ancient Egypt to conduct the initiation ritual.

My simplistic ordination in Clapham Woods three years beforehand paled into insignificance at the splendour. A great welling of pride emerged as I beheld the elaborate preparation that had been organised to induct Audrey into the hidden mysteries. So that she would not be too nervous, a beautiful Irish girl by the name of Grainne, pronounced Grainya, was also to be ordained that day. Beautifully decked out with flowers, the two women entered the chamber for the final part of the secret rites after a moving outdoor ceremony.

In a separate ceremony the next day, Audrey was taken even deeper into the very bowels of the old castle, and there in the deepest chambers, she was initiated into the inner mysteries of what was known as the "Rite of the Black Isis". The word "Black" in this instance merely referred to a Nubian Isis of legend. It was wondrous to witness one of the most fascinating rituals I had ever beheld, as my wife went through the old Egyptian mysteries.

Olivia spent much of her free time tutoring Audrey in the Egyptian mysteries. I listened intently as Audrey described the rituals that she had subliminally remembered from that earlier lifetime. However, many years were to pass before the final mystery of her life in those far-off days was to be revealed. In 1992, we travelled to Egypt to unravel the final mystery - but more of this later in this book.

Sadly, both Derry and the ever-gentle Poppy have departed this life and they are sorely missed. They have now fearlessly embraced the final adventure of death itself and gone to what we know as the beloved Summerlands, secure in the knowledge of the life hereafter. They were probably the leading Magi in Egyptian magic in their day, together with the Right Honourable Olivia Robertson. The mantle of power now lies firmly on her shoulders. Olivia now runs the Fellowship of Isis. In her capable hands, this has continued to further and expand its cause worldwide.

Our next stop in Ireland was a visit to Stewart and Janet Farrar. We spent time as their guests, and while sleeping in their Temple, we experienced further occult adventures, but I will go into more detail of our time with the Farrars later in the book. We then visited old Neolithic barrows, cromlechs and castles with them, culminating in a memorable visit to New Grange with Janet and Stewart, where they recounted an old Irish legend that said a troop of ghostly horsemen rode into its dark chambers every full moon! A delightful companion of the Farrar's accompanied us on the tour. This was Ginnie, who was a new initiate into the craft. All five of us spent time exploring the inner depths of New Grange and learning its history.

Upon our return to England, we founded the "Temple of the Goddess of the Many Forms" within the framework of the Fellowship of Isis. We set up a centre in Sussex and set many upon the path of the Goddess Isis, but this was really Audrey's scene, and I devoted my time to the Wiccan mysteries and the furtherance of the Craft in this County.

In March 2003, I initiated my hundredth Priestess, so furthering the expansion of the Craft and The Order of Artemis. The Covens emanating from them in a span of some fifty years are countless. However, at the age of seventy-five, I feel that I am the last of the old school.

Woodland Magic, "Jack's Patch" and the Fight against Evil

Sussex has long been a stronghold of the Old Religion. At the height of the great persecutions, in what has now passed into history as the Burning Days, Sussex miraculously escaped almost unscathed. Of course, there were isolated incidents of Witches being seized and tried, but the total was only eighteen. There are records of some being acquitted, so largely the majority escaped. This lucky situation was exclusive to Sussex. Loved, respected and revered by the local people, the village Wise Women, healers, midwives and charmers were spirited away when the Witch-finder arrived to seek out his prey.

Even those who were not practitioners of the Old Arts were hidden, for at the height of the hysteria that swept Britain, no woman (or man) was safe. A wart, a gob tooth or a cast in the eye, was enough to send you to the inquisition chamber and ultimately the gallows or the funeral pyre. Church doctrine was clear, "Let there be no possibility of an accused Witch escaping justice. Do not allow the possibility of doubt to enter your mind, for 'tis better to hang an innocent than let a Witch escape." These terrible words were fact. In one notorious massacre of innocents that occurred on the Continent, the slaughter was so horrendous that a clergyman voiced his doubts at the mass killing to the overseeing Priest. His superior waved him away with the chilling words, "Let the slaughter continue. God will recognise his own."

So, Sussex was (and still is) a hotbed of Witchery. Here in the County that was the home of the *"Suth Seaxe"* the "South Saxons", the area name was born. For *Suth Seaxe* evolved into the Sussex we know today. Here, many of the old traditions survived and memories of the Witches of yesteryear are still passed down from mother to daughter and father to son in the outlying villages, and locals speak fondly of their local Witch covens.

I know well one village that has a long history of local Witchcraft. It is here on the nights of the full moon that you can still hear the throb of drums and their singing and dancing as they bring up the power. Have a drink in the local pub, "The Wise Old Owl" and listen to the comments as the rituals echo across the landscape. They sip their beer and murmur, "Witches be in the woods tonight" and then whisper, "Cows will yield good milk, corn will grow high and crops will prosper". This is the reason the Witches were protected - and still are.

Scarcely a stone's throw from its boundary, lie about six or seven acres of scrubland that was once known as "Jack's Land". This is sometimes called "Jacks Patch". It is a secluded area, and it was once heavily forested. It used to be left as a retreat for the God Pan and in later years, to allow solitude in which the Green Man could recline. This was the home of "Jack in the Green", hence "Jack's Land". None would venture there and disturb the God. Tracts of forest and wild land like this abounded in England throughout history. These "no-go" areas were etched on faded and crumbling maps. Areas that were inaccessible at the time would often carry a warning to travellers with the caption, "Here be Dragons".

The God Pan or Herne the Hunter undoubtedly did reside in this glade. The locals knew this for certain, because he had been seen on many an occasion. Undisturbed by trespassers, hunters or poachers, the secluded little area had become a nature reserve, in which wildlife proliferated. Here at night, the locals shuddered at the blood-curdling cry of a vixen on heat crying out for a mate to sire her. To their superstitious minds, this became a demon on the loose. This would be followed by the cry of the puck bird (nightjar) announcing to all who heard it that the mischievous Puck was in the woods that night. Of such happenings are legends made.

One can imagine the scene, where in the calm of evening, the horns of a stag would be seen silhouetted against a canopy of green. Occasionally a glimpse of the God himself would be revealed, as a shaggy head came into view for a fleeting second. In the rutting season, the God could be heard echoing his challenge to all-comers as he defended his territory, and the great God Pan's voice could be heard echoing across the landscape. Combine this with the scream of a vixen in heat and the call of the dreaded Puck bird echoing eerily at eventide - and is it any wonder that "Jack's Patch" was a place to be avoided at night!

Locals will tell you of a local farm that welcomes the "Hidden Children of the Goddess", as Witches are known, onto their land. They know that the old ways are re-enacted there as they leap ever higher over the Balefire. Chanting an ancient adage, "High as we leap, the corn will grow as tall. All Hail to the Goddess, the Goddess of us all." for it is an old tradition that the corn will grow as high as the highest leap made by a female Witch.

Here, within a secluded glade, they cast their spells and make Magic, helping, healing, and invoking the horned God, Cernunnos, and the great Goddess, Ceridwen. With the God and Goddess in polarity, you would find that the matriarchal influence would dominate. The Goddess will be worshipped in many forms: Aradia, Isis, Astarte, Bride, Aphrodite and Arrianhod, to name but a few. Here they will summon Pan and Herne, invoke the Green Man of the Forest and call to Selene, the Moon Goddess to appear.

One of the most amazing incidents that ever took place there was on a Sabbat, when the coven expanded on this particular occasion into a Ritual Magic Ceremony. Ritual Magic, quite unlike ordinary magic, has to be undertaken within strict guidelines as it is rarely practised. The *raison d'être* for using a supreme ritual at the site was to reverse and return the dark emanations of a sinister group of amateur "black magicians" who had started a satanic group in nearby Sompting.

Although ill trained, this group was still dangerous, and their presence in Wiccan territory was considered a threat. Bad press from the church and some lurid newspapers continued to pour out vile propaganda that was not even remotely associated with Witchcraft. Almost all their so-called "evidence" was based on fifteenth and sixteenth century Witch trials. Three hundred years later, this was still the basis for church dogma and attacks upon the Old Ways.

Satanists and practitioners of the truly black arts are fortunately very rare indeed, and Witches are constantly on the lookout for any signs of them. This is for the very simple reason that any evidence of their abominable practices would undoubtedly be laid at the Witches' door. Finally, the popular image of the Witch has started to be dispelled. As the Craft gained momentum, people began to see that practitioners did not violate virgins, dig up graveyards or enjoy the odd snack of unbaptised babies. They did not engage in a continuous orgy of sexual frolics, during which "Old Horny" would appear, lift his tail and invite all and sundry to pay homage to him with the infamous "kiss" that was so frequently given in evidence at Witchcraft trials (*osculum infame*.)

Confession to this was an absolute must in the bad old days; the only exception being if you were a woman and were prepared to give the avidly listening priests all the details of copulating with the devil, including descriptions of his penis. Was it forked? Was it ice cold inside you? Did his semen freeze your womb? In addition, just for good measure, "How big was it and "did it come out through your mouth!" In the 1600s, no confession was complete without this rubbish. An ancient edict runs as follows:

"Dixit enim Diabolum in forma leonis (ut putabat) domum intrasse, et secum concubuisse corpus foedissime subigitando. Que cum fecisset tam uiolenter cum pudents suxisse et pro dolore magnos se edidisse clamores."

Anyone accused, particularly women, had to confess to delivering unto Old Horny the infamous *"osculum infame"* mentioned above (the obscene kiss). Apparently, so legend says, the village Witches would line up as Lucifer obligingly lifted his tail so all could pay homage!

So, imagine the reaction of Wiccans who find a batch of brain-addled weirdoes on their doorstep. They are probably sacrificing the local tomcat, leaving black candle wax on the odd gravestone in the local churchyard and leaving condom packets to show that they have had sex with the local trollop on the Minister's doorstep. Who gets the blame? The nearest coven, that's who! Repeatedly, the vicar calls the police and the local paper and the evening edition the headline will scream, "Satanic Rites in local churchyard!". By the time a journalist has turned up to get a good photograph of the scene he swiftly realises that there is precious little story there. Black wax on a gravestone does not come out very well on a black and white newspaper photo! There is not much news in discarded condoms, after all this is a trysting place for local youth. There is no sign of the tomcat but he needs a story - so what does he do? Well, he probes!

Within five minutes, he has found a couple of fallen headstones. (Pushed over by Witches, of course.) The first rule is to avoid checking with the vicar, in case he tells the journalist that they fell over years ago in a great gale. Best to assume it was Witches. Better still, he will find a broken gravestone. This is usually no problem in an old graveyard. As long as he overlooks the moss that shows the crack is a hundred years old and he is happy to ignore the subsidence that could have cracked it, he is in with a chance.

Now he has to find a sunken grave where a fox or badger has been digging. Ah, there are clear signs that the local coven has tried to dig up a corpse. It is best not to photograph that, as the local poacher may write in anonymously and indicate that a badger sett is established in the churchyard, along with a fox lair and that the place is overrun with rabbits. Therefore, he simply includes what he wants to find without allowing the truth get in the way. When the story eventually hits the press, does the vicar issue a statement correcting it? No chance! It is all good, anti-Pagan material and good propaganda, so let it ride.

As an occult investigator for well over fifty years, I have found genuine signs of black magic attempts. Invariably these are amateur and childish, and they bear more relation to the books and films of Dennis Wheatley than they do to genuine satanic ritual. Nine times out of ten, these are nothing more than sheer vandalism.

We fear the incursions of any group that will afford us a bad press. To Witches, all practices of evil are anathema. People who love and revere the earth and all things in nature regard these interlopers askance. Whenever they are found, they must be dealt with, in accordance with the Wiccan creed of "An' ye harm none". We are not allowed to hurt others, but we are allowed to invoke either of two laws of return. Therefore, if one finds that a person or group has invoked evil, bad luck, or cast a spell, we are allowed to send it back to them threefold.

"Three times happy, three times sad, three times good or three times bad."

This is the "Law of Retribution", which states that one can turn evil back upon the perpetrators threefold. If they do not learn, then multiply it by three times three and perform the "Call of Nine" ritual. The spell is safeguarded, as it sends everything back threefold, so if it happens that good vibrations have been sent out, these will also be returned in triplicate.

The Witches Return to their Land

Returning to the Great Sabbat, some forty Witches were gathered at the farm at the time and the ritual was painstakingly performed, the Cone of Power was raised and the fire started to swirl upwards like a tornado. Real power was being generated. As the ritual reached its climax, the Summoner gave out three blasts on his horn, while I recited the call to Pan. "Come, O come, to the heartbeat's drum. Come to us who are gathered below while the broad, white Moon is climbing slow, etc." The drums reached a crescendo, the Words of Power were uttered and then, to everybody's surprise, the Horned One himself slowly and majestically walked into the centre of the circle and stopped just in front of the balefire.

You could have cut the silence with a knife! There before the coven was the Horned God himself, majestically gracing us with his presence. Horned head, beautiful goat-like eyes. There before us with cloven feet, was the old depiction of Pan! Shepherd of the Lea. Lo, Herne the Hunter himself! Then he gave a little snort, bowed his head and slowly, oh so slowly backed away.

It was only as he turned with a backward glance towards us that we realised that what we had been looking at was a stag that had entered the magic circle. When it was facing us directly, we could only see two legs and two feet at the time. The great horns that towered resplendently against the full moon were nothing but an illusion. That evening is still a talking point in the coven to the present day!

Yet this incident is itself wreathed in mystery. Firstly, deer and stags are shy creatures that shun humans. Secondly, even the most inquisitive would never have approached so many people at one gathering. Thirdly, surely the beat of the tom toms would have scared any herd away. However, the most puzzling factor of all is the presence of the balefire, which all wildlife avoids. None of the facts added up to a king deer entering the circle. He was a large male animal, so perhaps he had a herd nearby that he was protecting? My experience of deer is that they would move out en masse. I suppose we will never know the answer to this rare phenomenon, but we still like to think that we had been graced by the Old One himself. Who knows? Perhaps this little copse was once "Jack's Land". Local legend certainly says it was.

Artemis is much envied by other covens inasmuch as it has its own land to hold its rituals on. This has been the case for well over thirty years, but things were not always this way. The land is steeped in tradition and it has been used by Witch covens since time immemorial. The old barns that stood there were honeycombed with secret hideaways in which the local Witches could find refuge. Fie on the Witch-hunters or Witch-finders who dared to cross the border into this Pagan county, for they could expect little cooperation from the local populace. No! This was Sussex: the last county to fall to the Xtian invasion - and a county that had never accepted the new doctrines that came with these strange men who preached death and sorrow as opposed to the Pagan ways of love and mirth.

Sussex men and women were wary of the newcomers who spoke of a God you could not see, but who was able to create miracles and who would take your sins away. They found the doctrine of a virgin birth anathema to their own fertility rites. They considered this a highly patriarchal Middle Eastern teaching that was at variance to the cult of the Goddess and the worship of woman. The Xtian God they spoke of was invisible and could not be seen. The answer to every question they put to the newcomers by way of challenge was to the effect that you must believe and that you must have faith, but all this without proof. They spoke of a God who had died and come to life again, a virgin who gave birth and a man who walked on water. Yet when they asked to see this happen, or asked, "Show us how you can raise the dead", they were always informed that this was true and that they must have blind faith.

The yeomen of Sussex were made of sterner stuff than their neighbours were. They decided to pay lip service to these newcomers and go about their own ways regardless. They loved their Wise Women who cured their ills, who delivered their wives' babes and who worked their magic to make the land rich and the livestock fertile. When the Witch-finders came searching, they said, "There are no Witches here" and the persecutors' searches never revealed any Witches.

Thus, it was that the two Old Dutch barns came to become a refuge for these oppressed women. A lasting monument as to how deeply the Old Religion was engrained in this County is the startling fact that there was not one case of betrayal. The old barns survived with their hiding holes right into the 1900s. In fact, when you compare Sussex with the rest of the country over a 200-year period, you will find evidence of eighteen Witch trials in the whole of this period.

The years passed, the Witch-seekers came and went and the Old Ways were celebrated openly in a sacred circle at the little farm where the coven site was. This was always undisturbed. Every coven still maintained the "War-look" - the man whose eyes continually scan the countryside, looking for those who would seize its members if the opportunity arose. He was the lookout for enemies. His name has come to be erroneously confused with a male Witch who is frequently referred to in literature as a "Warlock". The War-look or War-lookout was not really needed here, because local eyes would warn of the coming of these interlopers well in advance.

Even so, vigil was maintained as a matter of principle. It is a sad fact that a vast percentage of those taken, tried, and ultimately executed in other less fortunate counties were not Witches at all, but unfortunates who had been seized by the Witch-hunters for the reward that the arrest of a live Witch would bring. Some had been denounced by jealous neighbours in hope of a reward, or by those who had old scores to settle. The traditional craft that we practise so openly nowadays was performed secretly then, and woe betide those who were found to be in possession of the implements of the Witch. You all know of the infamous cauldron so beloved of the traditional Witch, not to mention the even more famous birch broom that was to the Witch what the motorcar was to the motorist! Well, joking aside, the cauldron and broom are an integral part of the fully-fledged Witches' itinerary to this day, and they were two objects that should not raise suspicion; Every house had a cooking pot, for that is what they are, and every abode had a broom with which to sweep the floor, so these objects did not excite any particular interest.

However, what of the other magical instruments so necessary to work magic? If you were found in possession of these, then Jack Ketch (slang at the time for a famous hangman of the period) would surely be waiting for you at dawn. The most important item of the entire Witch's armoury was the *"Athame"*; the black-handled knife used in the casting of the magic circle and so essential in the making of spells. This instrument had to be carefully engraved with the secret magical sigils of the art, without which the magic would not work. If this was discovered it, would lead to the gallows. Kitchen knives and their handles came in all shapes and sizes, so the Witch would select a large black or dark handled knife and use chalk to inscribe each magical symbol on it. The symbols had to be carefully memorised. Then, if there came that fateful knock on the door of the Witch-finder accompanied by the local priest, a quick wipe with a damp cloth obliterated the evidence in a split second.

The situation with the pentacle was similar. Tradition says it should be made of copper or brass and engraved with magical sigils. However, the enterprising Witch would make a circle of beeswax or candle-grease and engrave the secret signs on it. In times of danger, it could be flung into the fire that was kept continuously going in every peasant home. In seconds it would be gone – a complete destruction of the evidence. Thus it was, with each implement used. Ingenious means were engendered to disguise them and to render them back into ordinary household tools in an instant.

Outdoor meetings where a number of Witches gathered, could also court attention, and the early craft once more was equally ingenious in combating this problem. Inquisitive eyes would carefully appraise what a group of villagers might be carrying into the woods. Only those who had been born of noble birth were allowed to possess a sword, and owning such a thing would bring the person a short step to the gallows if discovered. Off they would go, armed with an array of agricultural implements such as hoes, spades, rakes, shovels and forks to cast the magic square! Not circle. It is not generally known that in the early days of the persecutions the Witches worked in a square. They summoned and stirred the traditional four quarters, and marked the boundaries of the magical area to be worked in with pitchforks, hoes, rakes and spades and so on.

Returning to the story of our piece of land, Sussex was unique; there is not one recorded instance of a square ever having had to be cast, such was their confidence in not being taken. At our spot, as in the remainder of Sussex, the ancient tradition of the casting of a circle of pure Magic was upheld throughout. The old circle where they worshipped still remains within a circle of trees, carved with the signs of the adored and holy God and Goddess, plus copious pentacles.

Over the years, old trees have fallen and we have planted new ones to replace them in the cycle of rebirth. These now reach towards the blue canopy. These in turn had to be ritually anointed and engraved by succeeding generations of Witches. When the covens ceased to meet there, the old circle became overgrown and it swiftly reverted to woodland. I have recorded the extinction of other covens over the years, but this spot remains a mystery. I have no indication as to when it ceased to be used and have had to rely upon what I have gleaned from the farmer who owned the land, who subsequently bequeathed it back to the Witches for posterity – along with local legend.

All we know is that it fell into disuse - probably in the late 1850s. Each succeeding owner of the farm knew of the little grove with its curiously carved trees, and understood that it was a holy and sacred place, to be revered. The farmhouse itself and the two barns were also blessed. In fact, the Witches countless years before had engraved an old beam in the main barn with luck and prosperity symbols as a lasting blessing and protection to their old benefactors.

Some time after 1900, the little farm changed hands once more and it became prosperous. The new owner was ambitious; he wanted to expand his land holdings and the ancient barn was the fulcrum to his plan. This same barn housed the sacred luck beam. His plan was simple - arson! Insure the barn heavily and then fire it. Therefore, on a hot summer's night, flames could be seen licking skywards as the ancient hiding place of the Witches was consumed by fire. Nothing could save the old building and in the early hours of the morning, it gave up the ghost and disappeared forever in a cloud of sparks.

Dawn the next morning saw the charred remains still smoking, but miraculously, the scorched and charred sacred beam survived, still distinctly bearing the old sigils! Subsequently, an insurance claim was submitted - and challenged. Investigators moved in and arson was discovered. Within months, the farm was sold and passed into the ownership of the people who were later to give the land back to the Witches.

With the destruction of the barn, luck melted away from the farm. The old protection was gone. It seemed as if the complete reverse had been achieved, so that the jewel of the area was now blighted and nothing the new owners could do ever worked. Within weeks of their acquiring the holding, the water mains blew up and the farm had no water. Days later, a tree crashed onto the farmhouse, causing great destruction and expense. No calves were born that year, no sheep lambed and the crops failed. To the innocent new owners it was a catastrophe.

Local farmers were swift to react and offer help, saying that the land would never prosper until Witches returned to the farm. Others wisely affirmed the local legends and stated, "Only Witches can help you. Bring the Witches back, because they will know what to do." Thus, a desperate and near-bankrupt farmer set out to find a Sussex Witch coven. By a series of astonishing coincidences, the trail led him to my doorstep and to the Order of Artemis.

I could devote a whole chapter to this episode alone, but what matters is the outcome. The coven was called and the farm was examined. Not far from the ancient site, the debris from the barn was discovered, complete with the sacred beam still intact. Power saws had started to reduce the remains to firewood and logs, but for some strange reason they had ignored this particular beam.

The coven swung into action and a ritual of cleansing was performed. There was no doubt that once the ancient protection had been removed, malign forces had anchored themselves there. There was undoubtedly a malign force present. After consultation, the Elders decided to do a full exorcism upon the premises and restore the beam to the farmhouse itself. Weeks later, the old beam was ensconced in the newly decorated kitchen of the house just above the fireplace; the ritual was a complete success. The following year there were bumper crops that surpassed all the neighbouring farms, cows calved, sheep lambed and the corn ripened. It has been a story of continuing prosperity for the farm ever since. The farmer, in gratitude, severed the section of the land and gave it to the coven for posterity, and it is there that the Order of Artemis has enjoyed peace and tranquillity to conduct its rituals ever since.

It was not long before tongues wagged and the return of the Witches became a topic of village gossip - particularly at the local pub. Its progression from there until it reached the press was but a matter of time, and while the coven desperately tried to keep a low profile, it was not to be. The press were not hostile, in fact, they loved the story and the subsequent reports did much to enhance a new image of Witches and their craft. Following on from there, three Witchcraft programmes featured the farm, and the press conducted interviews with both the farmer and his wife, in addition to a number of local farmers and citizens. Everybody was glad to see the Witches back and there was not a single negative response. We were invited to conduct our rituals on the surrounding land as well.

9

Ḫumour, Positive Publicity and Continuing Superstition

Over many years, a number of television overtures have been made to The Order of Artemis, and we cooperated as long as our strict criterion was observed that the craft be viewed in a positive light. However, for every overture that we accepted, at least two were rejected. The Order participated in programmes such as South Today, Meridian News, Day by Day, Focus and The Friday Report.

These were swiftly followed by French and other continental stations, and even some American ones. The Japanese Denen Kobo TV Company (which is to Japan what the BBC is to Britain) came over in 2002 to make a programme on the occult and the Order of Artemis. They brought along a beautiful Japanese actress to present and take part in it. Normally, there is a small crew for such programmes, but to my surprise when I looked outside; the whole of the close was full of TV vehicles, crews and a vast array of equipment. There were Japanese men and women busy setting up generators, laying cables, dollies and tracks up to my house – it took us completely off guard! Within the hour, the bedroom had become a dressing room, the kitchen was the make-up department and my little office was now a changing room. They left a fine vintage Chateauneuf du Pape behind as a present, because they were surprised that we refused payment for doing the programme. It is a strict rule of Artemis never to accept money for anything we do: and that includes helping, healing and rituals such as exorcism.

Over the years, programmes were also made for Hexagon Productions, Hammerwood Films, Angelique Productions and many more. In January 2003, Hart Ryan Productions in association with Channel Five arranged to make a one-hour documentary, centred on Artemis and following the lives of some of our people as they go about their everyday chores. The current year promises to be busy, as other companies wish to make documentaries, while the Craft surges forward.

Channel Five's idea was to show the world that Witches are everyday-folk going about their business in a variety of professions. Its intention was to show that we are ordinary hardworking people who are neither zealots nor eccentrics. We share a common interest of a love of the Earth Mother, a respect for womankind and a love of nature, animals and all things green. Hart Ryan looked at the lives of a script and book writer, a theatrical costumier, a solicitor, a chartered accountant, a supermarket assistant, a lady of independent means, a fishing boat proprietor, a woodsman and forester, a hypnotherapist, a charity shop worker, and, last but not least, an Income Tax Inspector. (Perhaps this goes to show that there is some good in people - despite their dubious professions!). Regretfully some people such as police officers, magistrates and social workers cannot be seen for professional reasons.

Over the years, many members of the group have reservedly given interviews, mainly to local radio stations at such times as Halloween (Hallowmas) and at Yule. I find it particularly sad that only those who do not fear dismissal from their jobs are able to participate in these interviews. There are many eminent people within the structure of Artemis who could shed an even greater mantle of respectability around us (and around Witchcraft as a whole) if they could only speak openly.

Amongst the hierarchy of Artemis, there are many eminent people in positions of power. Among these are leading police officers, doctors, surgeons, nurses and those from the legal profession, including magistrates, judges and barristers. Added to this, we have masons, a member of parliament and local councillors. This should be proof enough of the purity of the purpose and aims of Witchcraft. What other organisation could possibly attract this cross-section of society, including so many members of the medical profession? It is the helping and healing in which Artemis specialises that attracts these people, and we are proud to welcome them to the Old Religion and the worship of the Old Gods of this sacred land. We have had a few brave souls who were prepared to stand up and be counted, including a police officer who went on television to expound his beliefs. I am pleased to report that there was not one iota of repercussion from their superiors (many of whom followed the Old Ways), although there was a great deal of leg-pulling.

There is an amusing tailpiece to this, because a female police officer, to whom I will refer as "J", was given a very good administrative job with a very senior Chief Inspector. Her boss was a droll man who would merely raise an eyebrow when he knew that J had been seen on the television, but he never spoke of it. She went down to Glastonbury one weekend and brought back a little witch on a broomstick, which she hung in the office where she worked. It happily sat there for months. Eventually "J" married a Scottish police officer and moved to Edinburgh.

You can imagine my surprise when, days after she had moved to Scotland, I received a phone call from her old boss. He asked if I could do him a favour and he said that he would be delighted to invite me to lunch in the Police canteen. His was an extremely simple request, to the effect that he would be most grateful if I could see my way clear to removing the little cloth Witch on her broomstick from the window where "J" had left it. I duly obliged, took the little Witch home with me, enjoyed my free lunch and earned his gratitude. Even here, in a modern police station, a primitive fear of touching such an artefact existed, lest the person becomes "blighted". I phoned

"J" the following day and we had a quiet chuckle. She informed me that on her last day in his office he had pointed the figurine out to her, saying, "Don't forget your little friend up there" to which she had replied, "No. She is there to keep an eye on you!"

A few years ago, the farmer who was our benefactor died and the farm changed hands once more, but we were not to lose the farmer's wife. She converted the remaining barn into a dwelling and moved in, but the coven worried about the new owners and wondered what they would be like? The farmer's widow swiftly solved that one by telling each potential buyer, "Oh by the way, the farm comes with its own indigenous Witch coven." Even the local estate agent had been instructed to inform all enquirers that Witches came as a package with the land!

It was not long before the farm was sold and we all met the new owner. Witches! She loved them! She expanded the woods and created an even larger circle in the trees for us. This was after we had to create two circumnavigating magic circles when we tried to cram 71 people into the sacred area. She supplied logs for our balefire and she laid a new road down to the coven site. Surely, the Old Ones were smiling on us!

Since then, she and her family have attended the Summer Solstice gatherings there. The Solstice festival is one of the Sabbats that outsiders may attend and participate in – as long as they are conducive and sympathetic to the Craft. In 2002, the woods were thinned out, allowing more light to enter through the canopy, so in Spring the bluebells and wild daffodils came into their own again. The final gesture that the new owner is making will add to the coven's comfort. She has felled some timber and built seats and benches for the coven to sit on and she is planning making a great log table for the famous love feast of the Witches, the *Agape*.

Attitudes towards us have softened over the years. The vitriol that was poured out against us in previous years proved to be baseless. Witchcraft has come to be recognised as the gentle Earth Mother-orientated religion that is devoted to helping, healing and to all manner of green issues in the worship of the Goddess Ceridwen and her consort, the Horned God, the Lord Cernunnos.

In 1951, the infamous Witchcraft act was repealed. Witchcraft became known as Wicca, and an overnight renaissance of the Old Ways emerged – with Sussex once more to the fore. Within a decade, Witchcraft was growing fast. This was boosted by the ecological movements and those conservationists who readily embraced the original religion of Britain. The religion had survived the dark days, and it has always been strongly identified with Mother Earth. So here - ready made, so to speak - was a religion that worshipped all things in Nature, loved animals and all things green and worshipped the Earth Mother in all her glory. The time was right it seemed, because the developed world at least began to value our ethos.

There are far too many covens to list here, but the main ones that dominate the Sussex scene outside The Order of Artemis are as follows:

The Willow Coven
The Coven of Arachne
The Andelaine Coven
The Coven of Selene of the Moon
The Order of Ishtar
The Avalon Coven
The Followers of Hermes
The Coven of Astarte
The Arrianhod Coven
The Followers of the Goddess Diana
The Order of Tanith

Many of the followers of these and numerous other groups are also members of "The Followers of the Goddess of the Many Forms", which is a branch of the "Fellowship of Isis".

Naturally, this is in addition to the covens interacting with each other.

By 2003, it has been estimated that over 1,200,000 Witches, Pagans, Druids and fellow travellers are established in Great Britain, and that Wicca is now the one of fastest growing religions in the world. This was the principal topic on ITV Meridian's Focus programme, which we recorded in June 2002. Once The Order of Artemis had received guarantees as to the content, it participated fully with the television station. The programme revealed the following facts:

In the USA, Witchcraft has reached momentous proportions.

In 1967, Witchcraft was officially recognised and protected as a religion by statute. Witches are accepted in Britain, but they have yet to achieve official status.

In the last census, vast numbers openly declared their faith. The census office has been slow in releasing official figures, but they have published a Declaration of Comparison showing that the previous census revealed 9,000,000 Xtians declaring themselves, and that the latest figures reveal a decrease of 33 per cent, as only 6,000,000 were recorded.

With the re-birth of Witchcraft and Paganism in the 1950s, we saw the emergence of a new giant on the scene. Gerald Broussec Gardner founded a modern brand of the Wicca, which came to be known as Gardnerianism. Originating from a famous New Forest coven, his roots were strongly entrenched in the ancient lore of Old George Pickingill, at whom we have looked in detail earlier in this book. The last great gathering that the coven members attended had been in 1940, when the Witch Covens gathered on the white cliffs of Dover. (White is symbolic of purity of thought. Additionally, the area was the closest point to France). There they worked their most potent magic spells and invoked negative thoughts against Adolf Hitler, beaming out danger signals and chanting, "Danger, do not invade".

An identical ritual was held after the covens returned to their respective homes following this rite, and they continued to

Humour, Positive Publicity & Continuing Superstition

work against the possibility of invasion. I do not doubt that numerous other Witches throughout the British Isles also worked independently against Hitler in those dark days. The cliff-top ritual held at Dover by the massed covens became widely known. The authorities must surely have been aware of it, but it suited their purpose, so they turned a blind eye. What is surprising is that the Witches were able to avoid the gaze of the media and conduct the ritual without being observed.

The rest is history. At the time of going to press, the Government has at long last set up a department in Whitehall called "The Faith Community Unit" to outlaw prejudice. The reason for this is the current prejudice against Muslims and, to a lesser extent, Jews, but it looks as though any new laws of this kind should help Witches as well.

So mote it be.

Witchcraft, Masonry, and the Dawn of the Aquarian Age

The old Willingdon coven used to meet inland on a site at Seaford in Sussex – as previously explained, the Willingdon and Seaford covens were one and the same. In 1969, Ceridwen, the last remaining High Priestess, passed over into the Summerlands. She bequeathed the Great Sword of Power and other ancient artefacts to The Order of Artemis, on the condition that they still upheld the old ways in Sussex. They still faithfully adhere to this command to this day.

Other new covens were subsequently founded following the repeal of the Witchcraft Act, many of whom have "hived" from Artemis over the years. Sadly, some of the old ones started to die out, and amongst these were the Bramber coven. The Bramber coven had sprung up in 1952, being founded by Astarte, who had left the Storrington coven shortly after the repeal. I did not know her well, but leaving the coven created a great sense of loss. Astarte was intent on starting a new Sussex upsurge of the Craft, so she swiftly gathered acolytes and neophytes around her and by 1953, she was running a successful group.

Astarte took with her many old and ancient artefacts that had survived the years. She could do so because they were her own private property. She was still extremely secretive as to her groups' activities and she did not mix with the "nouveau

Witches" who were eagerly taking up the Old Ways, as they found a new freedom to worship in the new (Gardnerian) way. In the eight years of this group's active life, I received only three or four invitations to join them in a Sabbat - then there was complete silence.

I knew Astarte had moved and presumed that her group went with her, but whatever actually happened remains a mystery. Within a decade, the coven had disintegrated. After the death of Astarte, her relatives had sold her ancient artefacts and these had disappeared into local antique shops. All that was ever recovered was a delightful carved head of Pan as the Foliate God. I recognised this, as I had seen it during one of the rare occasions that I had worked with the Astarte group. This was a find indeed, for I knew the head had a false back where spells had been hidden. I purchased the carving and opened the back but it was empty. I have bequeathed it to the Museum of Witchcraft at Boscastle when the great call comes.

Gardner's particular persuasion of Witchcraft took off. He revised the Craft and brought it into the 20th century - "Blowing away the cobwebs" as he put it. This move was highly unpopular with hereditary covens. Hereditary covens that had survived the burning days had not escaped unscathed, but at least they had held on to the old ways... but this was the modern age and some things had to change. However, Gardner had gone too far in popularising the increasingly secular version of the Craft and by going public.

I am often asked as to how much Freemasonry was introduced into the new Gardnerian movement by Gerald, because many of his rituals bear an uncanny resemblance to Masonic practice. Gerald Gardner was a freemason, so I do not doubt that his Masonic background embellished much of the new practice of the Craft that he advocated. As a freemason myself, I have scrutinised Gardnerianism closely and there can be little doubt that the speculation is true.

Let us reflect for a moment and turn the clock back to the very first Masonic Lodge, which was founded in 1717. It cannot be a coincidence that the same year saw a resuscitation of Druidism, which itself had been extinct a thousand years or more. John Toland formed "The Stonehenge Druids" and "The Druid Order". This was followed up in 1781 by Henry Hurle, who formed "The Ancient Order of Druids", to which the great English wartime leader and Prime Minister Winston Churchill belonged.

(Churchill became a member of the Ancient Order of Druids, Albion Lodge, Oxford on the 10th of August 1908.

Ieuan Hopkins, Archives Assistant, Churchill Archives Centre. www.chu.cam.ac.uk/archives)

Ten years later in 1791, Edward Williams promoted the *Iolo Morganwg* (Autodictact), promoting the Welsh Gorsedd, which demanded that all rituals should be in the Welsh language.

In 1717, Witchcraft had survived the worst of the persecutions, although they were not metaphorically speaking out of the fire for quite a while to come. The relaxation of intolerance towards esoteric religions allowed such interests as Druidism to return. Wiccan practices were fairly well known to the common people. They no longer accepted that Witches flew on broomsticks or took animal form if they wished, or robbed graves. Druidism was a completely new issue though, for it was suddenly realised that with the great massacre of the Druids on Mona (now Anglesey) by the Roman army under Paulus Silentarius, little was known as to true Druidic practices.

Initially, the Romans had nothing but good to say about the Druids, and Julius Caesar wrote copiously about them. They bent the knee, paid their taxes and were no trouble. In fact, the Romans were fascinated by them and loved to watch them performing their beautiful sun and moon rituals. Then suddenly everything changed, and the next thing we know is that they were on the end of a vitriolic propaganda campaign in which they are accused of human sacrifice, "wicker-men" offerings of massed animals and child murder. Once the

Romans turned on them, they fought back bravely, but the writing was on the wall. Roman armour, superior weapons and sheer weight of numbers eventually told, and the Romans performed a genocidal slaughter on Mona that left no trace of the Druids. Long after the last Druid fell, the legions were stationed on Mona just to cut down the sacred groves. Druidism was dead.

We will never know what caused this *volte-face* by the Romans. History does not record it. The only accounts that now exist are scant and from the Roman side, for does not the victor write history? However, the following extract from Tacitus is revealing:

"On the shore stood the opposing army with its dense array of armed warriors, while between the ranks dashed women, in black attire like the Furies, with hair dishevelled, waving brands. All around, the Druids, lifting up their hands to heaven and pouring forth dreadful imprecations, scared our soldiers by the unfamiliar sight, so that, as though their limbs were paralysed, they stood motionless and exposed to wounds.

Then, urged on by their general's appeals and mutual encouragements not to quail before a troop of frenzied women, they bore the standards onwards, smote down all resistance and wrapped the foe in the flames of his own brands. A force was next set over the conquered, and their groves, dedicated to inhuman superstitions, were destroyed."

Sussex was more enlightened. The first Masonic Grand Lodge was founded in 1717 and it seems far more feasible that ancient Witchcraft practices were incorporated into Freemasonry rather than vice versa. Therefore, when Gerald Gardner rewrote Witchcraft rites in the 1950s, he tinged it with Masonic practices to bring it into the 20th century. He may or may not have realised it, but he was simply reintroducing the ancient practices of the Witch cult of yesteryear back into the present. In fact, an article by Kyril Oakwind and Judy Harrow in the spring/summer 1989 issue of FireHeart suggests that Gerald synthesised his system from various elements, including Masonic ritual and French Mediterranean Craft.

While on the subject of Freemasonry, many Witches are Masons and some have reached high rank within the Masonic orders. I personally have attended at least three Masonic Lodges where the Grand Master is also the High Priest of a Coven. In fact, I am always amused when I look upon a particular group photo, which hangs proudly on the wall at a certain lodge. Every single person – man and woman (it was taken at a ladies' night event) - is a Witch of high rank in both orders.

Eventually Gardner and his doctrine were accepted, and a new age of the "Craft of the Wise" (Wisecraft = Witchcraft) emerged. The old ways were revised, old laws were examined - and after lengthy debate, they were incorporated, as the new Gardnerians themselves sought to follow suit and prepare for the Age of Aquarius. The bad days of the Age of Pisces were dying; an age that had seen over 17,000,000 people accused of Witchcraft throughout the continent of Europe and condemned to death. An age that had seen not only themselves condemned as heretics, but their Xtian neighbours, Jews, gypsies, agnostics and all who dissented from the Roman Catholic Church's overpowering doctrine. In less than two centuries, the Waldensian nation was wiped out in France, alongside the Albigensians and Manichees. Cathars also suffered terrible genocides, as did Lollards, Pelagians and Gnostics.

The Xtian crusades introduced slaughter on an unimaginable scale in the Holy Land, and saw the Conquistadors commit genocide on a near helpless people, as the Aztec, Inca and Maya civilisations fell before the Xtian swords. These people brought the Xtian faith of love and forgiveness to the bewildered natives in a welter of bloodletting. When Xtians could do this to fellow Xtians, what would they dare to do to non-Xtians such as our people? History has answered that question on our behalf.

When Columbus discovered the Americas, he seized the land in the name of God and King Philip, and erected a giant cross on the shore. He also erected a gallows alongside it, to hang all those who refused to convert. Small wonder that only five hereditary Witch families had survived in Britain, in addition to the remnants of the Pickingill covens and a mere handful of solitary practitioners. This was a hard core of just over 120 souls. These were later to be the seeds, whereby the old ways would re-emerge into the Aquarian age and grow into healthy trees with solid roots based in the past.

It is not possible nor is it allowed for the "Laws" to be published or read to those who are uninitiated, although it saddens me when I see so much of the Old Ways available in bookshops nowadays. So much that is published is spurious, but an indication below will help the reader to see how the Traditionalist persuasion was born in the wake of the birth of the Gardnerian tradition.

Archaic laws so necessary in the infamous burning days were swept aside. Such ancient dictates like "No Coven shall know where the next abideth" were vitally necessary 300 years ago. Thankfully, the followers of the Art Magical now call each other by phone and are summoned to the Sabbats by email and fax.

The old fertility rites whereby country folk and Witches worked for their women to be fertile and to produce many children were swept aside. We were no longer living in an age where retirement leaned heavily and dependently on one's offspring. It was hardly appropriate when ninety per cent of the female Covenors were on the pill and trying not to get pregnant! So now, to the farmers' delight, they work for fertility of cattle and crops instead.

Well, so much for history. Although this book is essentially on Sussex Witchcraft, the background to the Craft as a whole is essential if we are to show the development of modern Paganism. Not long after the impact of Gardner, the Traditionalist persuasions were born out of hereditary roots here in Sussex. Therefore, Sussex spawned what came to be known as "Traditional Witchcraft", while another that flared and died was Alexandrianism.

Another newcomer had appeared on the scene and leapt to fame…or should I say infamy overnight. A showman by the name of Alex Sanders obtained a copy of what came to be known as the Witches Bible, the "Book of Shadows". He promptly rewrote it to conform to his own ideology and a new citadel of Witchdom was built on sand. This book was based upon many ancient laws and traditions that were devised by Gardner. He had carefully written down all the oral traditions that he had learned during his years with the New Forest coven, plus a mixture of Masonry. The "Hand of Rite" (write), which comprised sparsely written traditions, usually held by the one who was called the Summoner, became known as a "Book of Rules" held by a Magister.

What Gardner had done was to formalise everything he had learned, revamp it, add to it and evolve a true conception of magical ritual that was safe and that worked. The method of sanctifying and consecrating the magic circle was based on Solomonic and Hebrew magic (The Clavicle of Solomon.) The Rituals and degree structure had many parallels in ritual magic, but without the need for geometric accuracy - so it worked.

Sanders took the Book of Shadows and adapted it to what was now to be his own particular brand of the Craft, adding minor and invented rituals to give it an "Alexandrian" flavour. His particular brand of Witchcraft took off, attracting young and old alike, and he swiftly emerged as the new boy on the block. He became the darling of the press and media, for whom he would perform instantaneous rituals, invariably with nubile young women in the "altogether". He protected his own modesty with a small pouch. For a quite lengthy period, he was lauded in the press, appearing in magazines and periodicals as his flame burned bright. Then a series of nebulous and futile appearances, where money seemed to dominate, extinguished the Alexandrian flame overnight. In one specific instance, he hired an old cinema and claimed he would raise a particular demon as a demonstration of his power. Many old Witches nodded their heads gravely and cast doubts as to whether he could perform such a task. They also wondered what this had to do with Witchcraft and the worship of the Earth Mother and associated elementals.

Fame seemed to have gone to Alex's head. Here was a Pagan and self-professed Witch who was unable to substantiate his background and initiation into the Craft of the Wise. He preferred to refer to his grandmother, who had passed on and was thus unable to substantiate her grandson's claims. He said that she had inducted him into the Wicca as a young lad and allegedly had nicked his private parts with a ritual knife. The sages of the Craft nodded their heads wisely and searched the ancient manuscripts for any trace of such an archaic ritual. They concluded that this was another invention, further substantiated when no trace of grandma's Witchery could be traced either.

Alex Sanders was a showman who delighted the press with his antics until his bubble burst and the entire Alexandrian movement collapsed. In 1988, Alex passed out of this world and into the Summerlands. Occasionally a remnant or splinter group raises its head and announces itself to be of the Alexandrian persuasion, but this is a fast dying race. While the world watched Sanders, the Gardnerian movement quietly gathered momentum. Gardnerianism was here to stay. So what good did this showman do? His antics caused many an upturned eyebrow and gave the established churches a new basis with which to attack the practice of Witchcraft. Sanders had given them the ammunition. In the end, the answer was that he did little other than create a negative impact and discredit the Craft in the public's eyes.

The seriously inclined reporters, along with a number of highly reputable magazines and periodicals, set out to find the truth of the ancient practice of Witchcraft. If they had not done this, a jaundiced view of Witches who had already experienced hundreds of years of Xtian persecution and a biased and evil would have suffered a renewed campaign against them, this time from the modern media.

Strangely enough, with the demise of Alexandrianism, the knock-on effect on Witchcraft took on a positive aspect. With its passing, thousands of followers sought new fields and were quickly absorbed into the Gardnerian movement and the ever-expanding Order of Artemis. This had grown into more than 60 covens; it was now laying down their roots as far afield as Germany, Austria, France, and Belgium, and had established covens in Canada, the USA and New Zealand. Covens from the Isle of Man, Jersey, Guernsey and Ireland were also in regular communication with this Sussex organisation, and they worked closely with it. The Order of Artemis was here to stay, along with its Brothers and Sisters of the Gardnerian movement.

Within the space of two years, many local Gardnerian covens in Brighton, Hove, Eastbourne, Shoreham, Bognor, Lewes and Littlehampton were all working together with Artemis. They mingled, shared rituals and spells and attended each other's meetings. It was a good union. Many practising Gardnerians sought further initiation into the mysteries of the Traditionalists belief and we in turn learned much from them.

I had worked alongside Alex Sanders for a short while, but I found his version of events incompatible. The two groups did however respect each other while differing in their outlooks, and they remained loose friends right up to Alex's passing. I did establish a firm friendship with two leading Alexandrians (who also subsequently converted to the Traditionalist/ Gardnerian craft) by the name of Ray and Lynda Lindfield. These two were destined for eminence in the world of Sussex Witchcraft, and they now lead a major and large coven in Eastbourne. They also arrange mega gatherings and moots throughout East Sussex.

It was not long before I, as the head of Artemis, was invited to become a fully-fledged Gardnerian Witch. Therefore, in 1982 Herne was brought in at the hands of Tom and Mabs

Penfold, the leading Sussex Witches in their day. They had been joined by Audrey in their coven some time previously. Mabs (Feronia) was a leading official at the Law Courts in the Strand in London, and her husband Tom (Faunus) was a leading police officer. Tom and Mabs Penfold retired from work, after which they frequently appeared on television because they were no longer afraid of the stigma that could have affected their formal careers. They were direct descendants of Gerald Gardner, having been initiated by Rae Bone, Gardner's High Priestess. Sadly, Tom passed to the Summerlands early in 2003 and Mabs moved away. Rae Bone is with him in the beloved Summerlands, where they await their rebirth.

As I travelled the world, both persuasions of the Craft expanded further. The next esoteric movement to appear on the Sussex scene was the "Fellowship of Isis". This was a great influence, which was readily accepted. Their art was heavily involved with the ancient Egyptian mysteries and their knowledge was awesome. Its membership began a meteoric rise, soon embracing over 40 countries.

For many years, we had planned to go to Egypt, and in 1992 in the company of Feronia and Faunus, we commenced the trail to ancient roots, the target being the Temple of Hatshepsut, to which Audrey was inexorably drawn. The Director of Antiquities in Luxor (Old Karnak) was intrigued. By the long arm of coincidence, he turned out to be a fellow member of The Fellowship of Isis and knew the Honourable Olivia Robertson well. He sent a guide to open up areas of the Temple that had been closed since the early 1900s by torchlight to see what Audrey could recall. To him it was an interesting experiment of the occult, for there were no records ever published of the area we were about to explore, and there were mysteries he also wanted to discover.

When confronted with the outside of the Temple, Audrey was overcome with emotion. She sobbed as she told how much had been destroyed. She recalled vividly the exotic colours that had graced the rooms, the friezes and tableaux that were fast crumbling away, and glancing up the long slope that led up to the Temple itself, she recalled the pure white staircase that had existed thousands of years before.

As we entered chamber after chamber, she recalled vividly and in detail what each new section would reveal. The pictures, the depictions and everything: for it was here that, under the great Queen Hatshepsut, she had once served. It was here that she had spent most of a previous life. Later, taking the traditional ritual of tea and coffee with the Director, she told of how three great doors had once stood at the entrance to the inner shrine. The first inlaid with gold, the second with silver and the last bastion of solid cedar wood. The director smiled and said that years before, archaeologists had in fact found the rotting hinges of three doors exactly where Audrey had pointed them out. Old papyri showed them to be gold, silver and cedar! Egypt was a great experience and a few months later, we were to return as the desert called us – a haunting and subliminal imprint that had reinforced our Wiccan belief in reincarnation.

11

Dark Secrets, Mystery and Murders most Foul

Audrey had been born into a strict Xtian family, dominated by her mother, who was a "hell-fire" type born-again Xtian. Religious instruction and regular attendance at Sunday school had been her lot in her early days, plus enrolment into the church choir. A practising Baptist at the time, she was baptised by total immersion and became a leading Sunday school teacher. An unhappy marriage followed. She had been press-ganged by her staunchly Xtian mother to marry despite her grave misgivings, only to realise within weeks that it had been a terrible mistake. Divorce was inevitable, and all the hell fire and damnation beseeching of her mother fell upon deaf ears, for she had now met the man she truly loved. The first cracks in her Xtian upbringing had appeared.

Audrey's family had suppressed a terrible secret that undoubtedly had led its 20th century descendants into becoming the rigid Xtians that they now were. Theirs was a prominent Sussex family, for they were descended from the Kemps who had built Kemp Town in Brighton, which bears her grandfather's name to this day. They had many roots in Sussex, but there were two dark episodes in the family history that spanned over 300 years, for the Kemps were a Witch family! Nan Kemp had been hanged for being a sorceress and a Witch in a public execution in 1610 at Lewes. Known as the "Witch of Lewes", her fame in the practice of what was then called "The Black Arts" was notorious. Eventually she was seized and tried for the practice of Witchcraft, and the verdict was a forgone conclusion.

Nan Kemp appeared to have been genuinely guilty of the crimes of which she was accused. This was a rarity, because 99 per cent of those convicted were completely and utterly innocent of any crime at all. However, the Kemp family unearthed a real can of worms in trying to establish the background to her hanging. Research suggests that the parish and parochial documents of the period seem to have become confused. There was a Nan Kemp executed at Lewes in 1679 for infanticide and for the murder of her husband. Apparently, she cooked and ate their bodies. Every detail of Nan Kemp coincides with what is known of Nan Kemp, Witch, also of Lewes. The comparison is even closer, for both lived in Kingston, scarcely a stone's throw from Lewes Town, and every historical reference overlaps. The method of execution is contradictory though, including what happened to Nan Kemp's body. The contrary records state that she was executed and that her body was buried at the crossroads at Juggs Way (nearer to the Ashcombe Hedge), where the crossroads fork.

Such a burial in the centre of a cross was always reserved for Witches, fearful that the Witches spirit would haunt the area and continue to work malevolence upon them. Therefore, by placing the corpse in the centre of a crossroad ensued that the dead would not rise. Another indication is the following quote: "The bodie was staked". Driving a stake through the heart was further proof that she was a Witch.

This ritual was not exclusively reserved for Witches, for those who broke the laws of God by the sin of suicide were also afforded the same fate – of burial in the centre of a crossroads, because they were banned from consecrated ground. Now here is the rub, there is a record in the same year of a Nan Kemp committing suicide and of the authorities ordering her (as a suicide) to be taken beyond the parish boundary and to be interred at the crossroads at Juggs Way!

Even this is not the end of the story, for the Kemp family history stated that she took her own life after being sentenced to death, which meant that she cheated the gallows and was subsequently buried at Juggs crossroads. She may still have been hanged, for the authorities would not have wanted to be cheated, so they were more than capable of ordering the corpse to be hanged as a warning.

So, is this the end of the Nan Kemp saga? Not a bit of it... a further record states that she was walled up, presumably alive. At least her body was, in what is now known as Holywell Cottage by the entrance to Gows Croft in Kingston. This may be true, because when the cottage was demolished in the mid 1800s, the bones of a female were discovered secreted in the wall. These bones were subsequently believed to be those of Nan Kemp. So, was she buried at the crossroads at Juggs Way? Local and recorded legend states that, years after her interment at the crossroads, her bones were dug up by the Kemp family and hidden in the wall of a cottage named Holywell, owned by the Kemp family in Kingston, at the site of what was originally a holy well. Her remains were rediscovered and reburied at Juggs Way, where they remain to this day.

Certainly, the ordinance survey map shows that this was not the burial place, and the grave is clearly marked outside the town rather than outside the Jugg Arms. In fact, this site is one that still attracts interest to this day as an alleged cure for warts! This suggests a Witchcraft slant, for Witches and wart charming go hand in hand. The legend says that if you have a wart, you must rub a piece of meat on it, take it to Nan Kemp's grave, walk around it three times and then bury it above her body. If you do have warts and you want to try this cure - go ahead. Whatever you do, don't lose count of how many times you walk around the grave, because legend says that if you walk around her grave twelve times, Nan Kemp will come out and get you; dare to do it at midnight and the Devil himself will join her!

Further research also shows evidence of a newssheet of the time indicating that the people of Kingston village rose up and lynched Nan Kemp. They seized her and bricked her up alive in the same oven in which she had roasted the mortal remains of her late husband and child. How long the body remained there is not indicated, but records once more speak of the discovery of the skeleton of Nan Kemp subsequently being uncovered during renovation of the cottage. They say she was taken and buried at the crossroads, once more at exactly the same spot that all the other records indicate. This legend includes the traditional "stake through the heart" routine - or perhaps through the ribs, as by now all that would be left was a skeleton!

Other records indicate that she was left bricked up in her oven just long enough for her to die of thirst and starvation or lack of air. Then the oven was opened and her corpse staked and buried at the Jugg Arms. This Jugg Arms scenario is the only common factor in the Nan Kemp saga, so the story remains a mystery. I think we have to conclude that she was a Witch and not a very nice one at that. That is the trouble when you dig into your family history - or in this case my wife's - you never know what you are likely to find – the skeleton in the cupboard so to speak – or in this case, in the wall!

Right up into the early 1900s, people would visit Nan Kemp's grave as a cure for warts or toothache. At the turn of the 20th century, children would dare each other to run around the grave twelve times to invoke her spirit, then run away screaming in case they lost count and went beyond eleven. Early maps show the burial at the southeast corner of the crossroads, but a later map depicts the site at the northwest section. We visited the area to try to solve the mystery, but we found that a post-Second World War house had been built on the original site. The other one is now in a private garden and is covered by a garden shed. No longer will there be small boys raising poor old Nan, as those days are receding into memory and they will soon be lost forever.

Nan Kemp was not the only Nan that we found. There is Nan Kemp's corner and Nan Tuck's Wood. Nan Tuck was also a Witch who committed suicide, like her counterpart. The circumstances of her death are sad; and strangely enough, there are many versions as to her fate. Two Witches in one area? Two suicides, maybe - but there is only one ghost. Locals tell of a woman who walks forlornly towards the east corner of the lane from the crossroads. One man was driving his daughter home late one night from a party when he was confronted by the apparition of a woman standing in front of the car and forcing him to brake sharply: then the apparition then disappeared. It was an unnerving experience, to be sure. One thing I did manage to discover is that church and ecclesiastical records of suicides were well recorded in Sussex, and there is no church record of either suicide!

As an example, when the notorious murderer, Robert Blinkhurst, committed suicide in his cell by poisoning himself in 1679, he was refused a Xtian burial. The ecclesiastical authorities in Lewes insisted that he was buried at the cross roads at Spittle (now Spital Road). A newssheet of the time gives the following chilling report of the ritual that was enacted:

"On Monday afternoon, being the eighth day of December, a dung cart was provided, which, being littered with straw, the bodie of the murderer Robert Blinkhurst, in its wrap, without any coffin, was cast into it: thus with part of the face and the feet bare, it was drawn through Lewes town, a ghastly spectacle to the beholders. At a fair crossway at the Spittle, a grave was ready digged lying north and south into which the bodie was put by two fellows; their hearts failing them for that other service, a third fellow was prevailed with to drive a stake through the suicides bowels, the earth then being cast in upon him, a fair bulk was raised over the grave and covered with green turf, the stake being left visible above it."

He is there to this day, because no one has ever dared to remove his bones. His ghost has been seen on many occasions as well. Lewes is a mightily haunted place!

Nan Tuck's end is a sobering lesson of the lack of mercy of the church at that time. She lived at Buxted in Sussex in the 1700s, a time when Witch hysteria was abating. She was only a teenage girl, and from reports of the period, it is obvious that she was mentally deranged, and an object of ridicule and abuse from the villagers. Disease suddenly struck down the local livestock, and overnight, ridicule turned to hatred. The locals came to the guilty conclusion that this was some form of retribution for their persecution of "Mad Nan". As they muttered amongst themselves, further disasters struck. Crops failed, wells dried up and the corn and wheat were blighted. They became convinced beyond any doubt that the village was bewitched, and the culprit was the deranged Nan Tuck. Arbitrarily, it was decided that there would be no trial for Witchcraft and that Nan must die at once. Within an hour, a lynch mob had gathered and set about hanging the unfortunate girl. We do not know her exact age except that she was a young teenager. Age mattered not to the enraged mob, because surrounding counties had hanged children, so this teenager would be no exception.

Old records state that they caught and beat her through the village as she was dragged to her execution. Then she broke away screaming through the village, pursued by the murderous mob. She ran through the narrow streets and apparently escaped them temporarily, but the search was on and they would not be cheated of their prey.

Apparently, she had made it to the local church, because despite her mental retardation knew she could claim sanctuary and protection of the church. Arriving at the church she threw herself upon the mercy of the vicar, who, seeing her racing ahead of the mob, turned her away and locked the church doors. If she had gained entry to the church, theoretically, he could not evict her, but to his mind, prevention was better than cure. The doors were slammed shut and the vicar placed himself between them and her. Her tears had no effect upon him whatsoever. He remained unmoved. The mob was closing in and the hysterical Nan took to her heels once again, succeeding in making it to the local woods. Whether the mob did catch her we will never know; presumably so, for her battered body was found swinging from a tree the next morning. Nan Tuck was dead.

Local records record her death as a suicide, and accordingly, she was buried at the crossroads. The woodland where the poor girl met her unhappy end was thereafter haunted by her ghost, which sadly wandered the woods, sobbing. It is known as Nan Tuck's wood to this day, and it is still avoided after dark by the locals. How another human being – let alone a "man of the cloth", could be party to such an atrocity is beyond comprehension today - especially where a young and mentally retarded teenager was concerned.

However, Nan Kemp was only one of the family secrets, for there was an even more sinister one that predated the unfortunate Nan Kemp's hanging by a hundred years. An even more notorious ancestor was Ursula Kemp (recorded in history as Ursley Kemp), the infamous Witch of St. Osyth. Her misdeeds, which were clearly fabricated in the hysteria of the period, were said to be legion.

Ursley was a noted healer of cattle, and her skills in healing sick cows earned her a reasonable living. This, in addition to scrying (fortune telling) and other magical gifts, helped spread her fame – or as it later transpired her infamy. One day she was approached by a trader leading an obviously sick horse. This man was looking for Ursley Kemp to ask her for a cure for the sick beast. Ursley apparently tried to send him away, crying out that she was a healer of cattle and not horses, but the man would not be deterred and he insisted she examine the animal. Grumbling to herself, Ursley took no more than a cursory glance at the animal. (Later, at her subsequent trial, she was alleged to have given the horse the "evil eye".) She then announced to all and sundry that, "The animal would die that night". And die it did! Ursley's fate was sealed, and she was falsely accused of bewitching the unfortunate beast. Her subsequent trial was held at Chelmsford assizes amidst great publicity, because she was famous in many counties. Apparently, she was a much-respected local character who was loved and yet feared.

Initially it looked as if there would be little evidence of bewitchment at the trial, because the evidence was purely hearsay. It was clear, though, that she was indeed a Witch, and in those days, that alone could send her to the gallows. However, Ursley was renowned as a healer and she was much in demand locally for her services, so outwardly the trial would be touch and go. Old records show a number of witnesses coming forward and testifying. One woman gave evidence that misfortune had overtaken her after an altercation with Ursley.

Ursley was "examined" and later confessed, after one John Thorlowe's wife had accused her of bewitchment, that she had in fact sent her grey cat to torment her. Upon further interrogation, she then confessed to "bewitching to death" the child of one Annis Letherdalles. This child had been poorly since birth and its stomach and genitals had swollen up enormously. His mother said that, as she had carried him past the Witch Ursley Kemp's cottage, the baby was said to have exclaimed three times, "Wo, wo, wo". After which, it raised its arm in the direction of Ursley's cottage.

This evidence was damning. Particularly when a relative of Ursley testified that her child overturned its cradle, fell out and then died of a broken back. Upon further interrogation, Ursley admitted she did have more than one "familiar". In fact, she had four of them, named "Tyffin", "Tyttey", "Pigine" and "Jacke". She also confessed to having control of these four evil "*sprytes*" that she used to kill and lame those who had crossed her. These were referred to in old documents of the time as "two hees and two shees". The two hees did the killing and the two shees were used to lame and disease. These, Ursley declared, were in the form of a hee, which was a grey cat (Tyttey), another hee, who appeared as a black cat (Jacke), a shee, which was a black toad that came when she summoned it (Pygine) and a white lambe that was a final shee (Tyffin).

Now the floodgates really opened and mass hysteria erupted. Soon, numerous other charges were laid at her door. In addition to being a Witch, she was a whore and harlot. She had also worked evil with another local named Elizabeth Bennett, who confessed to having two spirits. These were a black dog, named "Suckin", and a dog that was "like unto a Lyon and was redde", who answered to the name of "Lyerd". Soon, more locals stood accused, as neighbours attributed every misfortune that had befallen them upon Witchcraft.

Before the hysteria had abated, sixteen women were incarcerated in Chelmsford Jail and the Judge – Darcy (the Lord of the Manor) was determined to gain esteem as a Witch-finder. It is clear from old records that, without confessions, there was a fair chance of acquittal, despite the Biblical adage of "Thou shalt not suffer a Witch to live". Under ecclesiastical law, that included anyone even remotely accused of Witchcraft.

Ursley was a great healer, midwife and herbalist. She had a reputation of being able to "un-hex" or "unbewitch" anyone who was afflicted. She could lift a curse when milk soured (a sure sign of Witchcraft abounding in the area) and prevent beer from fermenting and souring in the vats, or bread burning in the ovens. She also plied a living as a wet-nurse, and at the trial it was said that she "did give her body freely", but the accusers failed to mention whether this was actually free!

Darcy now played his ace, offering to exercise clemency to the two accused in return for a confession. By now, both Ursley Kemp and Elizabeth Bennet were thoroughly frightened. They agreed to confess and a deal was struck with the treacherous Darcy. The other fourteen women accused would have none of this and refused to confess. Triumphantly, Darcy arraigned the two women before the court and a mandatory sentence of death was accordingly passed upon them. When the case was referred to Darcy for the clemency that he had promised, he reneged. The two wretched women both went to the gallows on their own voluntary confessions, while the remaining fourteen were spared. (See historical footnotes in the later chapter on Witch trials).

Within hours of the hangings, there were dark mutterings around the village, particularly as Ursley had been strangled to death slowly. They swore she put the evil eye on them all as she suffered. They gathered swiftly to discuss her burial, deciding that it should be in the centre of a cross, which would restrain her from rising from the dead and haunting them. They rapidly decided that the crossroads nearby would be ideal and a pine coffin was brought forth. However, something about Ursley, even in death, disturbed them greatly – so they feared her body as well as her ghost.

They decided that it would be better to take the corpse to the local blacksmith and have him bind and rivet her in iron for their own safety. In their hearts, they had shown cowardice by declining to come to her aid, and some had added vociferously to the clamour of the Witch-hunt. Besides, were not smithies magical? Surely, the blacksmith could protect them from the wrath of a disturbed spirit; smithies wrought iron into horseshoes to repel Witches and it was known that iron had magical properties. Without further hesitation, they transported the already stiffening corpse of Ursley to the village Blacksmith.

The result was that Ursley Kemp, now bound in iron rings, was duly and without ceremony, buried at the nearest crossroads – and in a final indignity, an iron spike impaled her. There she remained until 1921, when a local council road-widening scheme uncovered her bones. She was still riveted but her mouth was wide open as if in an everlasting scream. The worker who found her bundled the decaying coffin onto his handcart. He took her home and installed her in his garden shed where for two old pennies a time, the curious could view the mortal remains of a much-feared Witch! Subsequently a travelling showman bought her and put her in his sideshow, where she was exhibited at six old pennies a time, until she landed up for a while in the Witchcraft museum in Boscastle, Cornwall.

Now some 500 years later, Audrey Kemp can practise the Wise Craft in Sussex with no more than the occasional upturned eyebrow. Nan Kemp is at peace, but controversy still reigns around Ursley's bones. Part of the Boscastle collection of Witch paraphernalia was sold to America. Cecil Williamson, who owned the museum before Graham King, was alleged to have sold Ursley Kemp's body as part of the deal. When challenged he retorted, "Ah, but was it her body? For who knows what I have in my cellar still!" and he would say no more. Eventually, Graham King discovered her in the cellars of Plymouth library! Overtures are now under way to give poor, misjudged Ursley the peace she deserves in death, that she was not afforded in life.

So much for the past. Old Witches bequeath their secrets to the zealous followers who will become the practitioners of tomorrow. Doreen Valiente was as much the mother of modern Witchcraft as Gerald Gardner was its father. Sadly, they have both passed on to the Summerlands, and the world is less rich with their passing. Our loss is the Old Gods' gain.

I was privileged to be one of the selected few to attend Doreen's funeral, and I was invited to deliver an oratory on her life during the service. I later contributed articles to the book of her beloved poetry, entitled "The Charge of the Goddess". Witches from as far away as Canada and the USA attended the ceremony, including Professor Shelley Rabinovitch, who subsequently published "The Encyclopaedia of Modern Witchcraft and Neo-Paganism" in 2003.

Doreen was cremated at the Bear Road Crematorium in Brighton, and her ashes were subsequently collected by John Belham-Payne, who founded the Centre for Pagan Studies at Maresfield in Sussex. In accordance with her instructions, he scattered them at a secret glade that was much loved by Doreen.

In accordance with one of her last wishes expressed to John, her book of poetry has been published by Hexagon Hoopix, and designed by the well-known art director John Hooper of Eastbourne. Doreen Valiente was a prolific writer on Witchcraft, and the books she wrote are probably the finest on The Old Religion known to date, but she was most acclaimed for the magic of her poetry. Famous poetic rituals to raise the Power and dedicate it to healing the sick and afflicted became regular coven practices worldwide. Hereditary, Traditionalist, Gardnerian and New Age Witches incorporate her rituals in their ceremonies - because they work! The mark of great Witches lies in the heritage that they leave behind, including the rituals they wrote or invented, which have proved to be practical. All Witchcraft practices were evolved by someone, somewhere, but it is only the exercising of the Art Magical and spell-casting in rhyme that builds up the power - and at this, Doreen was a great adept.

One fine example was the famous Witch's Rune, which I will record here to give an example of her work, and as a guide to future Witches who may buy or read this book. Normally we do not disclose what is recited at coven meetings, but the Witch's Rune has passed into history and entered the realms of public domain. We secured copyright permission from John Belham-Payne of the Centre for Pagan Studies to reproduce Charge of The Goddess here. He had inherited Doreen's artefacts and poems.

The Witch's Rune has been broadcast on radio, seen on television, written into countless books worldwide, sold on calendars and Witchcraft diaries, and it is obtainable on illuminated manuscripts, because it is Doreen's legacy to the world. Doreen's works were for the benefit of everyone, so the verse is widely used by Witches and Pagans worldwide, and it is reproduced below by permission of John Belham-Payne.

We are grateful to Doreen for the most popular of all the invocations, and again, this Witchcraft gem originated in Sussex, as it was evolved by Doreen, Sussex's most famous Witch. Probably the next most powerful invocation Doreen ever wrote was the Charge of the Goddess, and next to the Witch's Rune, it is probably the most frequently used. I have never ever attended a Sabbat as a guest, where the great Deosil dance is not performed in conjunction with this "Charge" on the special occasions known only to the Craft's followers.

In my opinion, it is too powerful to print here, so I have declined to do so. However, to give an indication of the superb magic that Doreen was capable of conjuring, I have published the Witch's Rune in part, below. This is so that the reader can get the feel of a Witchcraft ritual.

Darksome night and shining moon
East, then South, then West, then North
Hearken to the Witch's Rune
For here I come to call Thee forth
Earth and Water, Air and Fire
Wand and Pentacle and Sword
Work ye unto my Desire
Hearken ye unto my Word
Cords and Censer, Scourge and Knife
Powers of the Witch's Blade
Waken all ye unto Life
Come ye as the Charge is made
Queen of Heaven, Queen of Hell
Horned Hunter of the Night
Lend thy Power to my Spell
And work my Will by Magic Rite
By all the Power of Land and Sea
By all the Might of Moon and Sun
Then as I Will, So Mote it Be,
Chant the Spell, and be it Done

At this point, the words of Magical Invocation are used to seal the power within the spell. I will not include them here in case untrained readers should try to dabble in the Art Magical.

Unless you have experienced a night of sheer Witchery under a full moon, you will never understand. You must have danced the old dances to the throb of the drum, leaped the bale fire, and when the Gods are pleased, heard the haunting music of the Pan pipes as the great Horned One echoes his pleasure o'er the haunted hill with haunting music for all to hear.

O I have heard, at still Midnight
Upon the Hill Tops far Forlorn
With Note that Echoed through the Dark
The Winding of the Heathen Horn.
And I have seen the Fire Aglow
And Glinting from the Magic Sword
And with the Inner Eye beheld
The Horned One, the Sabbats Lord
So runs part of the Witch Ballad...

Because a Witch normally recites this incantation, I have only published two verses in full, which is enough to give a tantalising insight into Wiccan ballad and verse.

Judge the Witch by what they bequeath to the world. Doreen left her encyclopaedic books and poetry. Gerald Gardner his early introductions with such books as High Magic's Aid and Witchcraft Today, plus the teachings of Stewart and Janet Farrar, Eleanor Bone, Rae Bone, Pat Crowther and Paddy Slade, to name but a few. They have all bequeathed us a fine and honourable legacy.

Secrets Unlocked and Witchcraft Trials

Let us examine what was known to exist in the case of occult and esoteric books before the repeal of the Witchcraft Act. Hypocrisy and contradiction ruled what was allowed. Sir James Frazer's The Golden Bough was forbidden in its original form: it was only published in the 19th century after much debate, and then only in an expurgated form. Other books followed in the late 1800s, and a kind of black market arose for unexpurgated books, in particular The Golden Bough.

Dion Fortune was a prolific authoress and a brilliantly gifted writer of the esoteric. Had she been born later, the secret doctrines and knowledge that she had would have ensured that she rose to great prominence. We will never know the source of her knowledge, but what we now refer to as the Great Secret was tucked away in her numerous volumes, awaiting its discovery in years to come. The Great Secret was a Tantric ritual of great power. This concluded with the union of the God and Goddess or High Priest and High Priestess in their role as the God's representatives on Earth. The world was not ready for this yet, but why? Dion Fortune wrote, "All the Gods are one God and all the Goddesses are one Goddess, and there is but one initiator".

This form of Tantricism was better known as The Great Rite and it had been practised as part of ancient fertility rites amongst Hereditary and Traditional Witches for years. This had also been embraced by both the Gardnerian and Alexandrian cults. It was clear that this ancient practice would have been roundly condemned at the time, and most certainly would have been the subject of prosecution. By the start of the 21st century, The Great Secret would turn out to be the perfect substitute for The Great Rite, as the Craft evolved into the Aquarian age and the old ways were dying. The Great Rite was becoming obsolete. Now the Tantric ritual would come into its own as the perfect substitute in the 21st century. This would enable the supreme power to be passed between woman and man. With the hidden time bomb of AIDS in the New Age, the ancient practice was well and truly dead.

Years before, sexual induction was introduced at initiation in what was a complete reversal of the degree structure of one, two, three. This had now become three, two, one in the tri-gradal system. These were the days of the hangman's rope, and if a coven was discovered and decimated, if there was only one survivor, then at least that survivor had the Power, and the Craft would survive. Knowledge would come later. On a historical note, some of the oldest practising covens such as The Jarretts operated a bi-gradal structure. Today we have embraced the original ways, for we have no fear of being taken and killed, so the one, two, three initiations and elevations are once more in existence.

Had Dion fortune foreseen the future and hidden The Great Secret carefully amongst her works so that it might be discovered in easier times? This thought intrigued me greatly and I set out to unravel it, but years were to pass before the books finally gave up their secrets. I started with works such as The Goat Foot God, The Sea Priestess, The Winged Bull and Moon Magic. Before the repeal of the infamous Witchcraft Act, anything published was liable to lead to a prosecution. Even though this Act was rarely used in the 20th century, it was occasionally invoked.

Dion Fortune had secreted what is probably the most powerful spell/conjuration within the pages of numerous books. Once we were free of the fear of prosecution, these were unravelled. The task was like a giant jigsaw puzzle, with fragments skillfully woven out of sequence and threaded through all her works. A book would contain part of a line with the next line appearing out of order in a later page.

The result would be that out of the 33 secret verses (approx 150-160 lines), a typical book would juxtapose - say line 131, followed by 7, 93, 17, 77 and 111. It would have been wonderful to have a computer in those days. The only way to create an orderly database in those days was by spreading nearly 200 scraps of paper around a room and trying to put them in order and to unravel the mystery. This daunting task took years of hard and laborious work, but it ultimately came to fruition.

Isis (Carol), one of the Witches in the Artemis coven, was intrigued with the research. Often, she had been present when the near complete ritual had been performed at Brighton and in Hove, in Worthing and in Littlehampton, as well as at Eastbourne. Each time it was performed, the success increased, because the ritual was good! However, the full power was still not being raised.

One day, Isis asked me about the obstacle. I explained that a death-like sequence had been incorporated into the ritual by Dion Fortune, but this was not compatible with a ceremony of implicit love and adoration of the Old Gods. There is an old practice within the Craft to include what we call "letters of confusion" into a word. This ensures that the codes cannot be deciphered if they should fall into the hands of outsiders. So why not inject a false line or lines in this case?

After pondering for a while she exclaimed, "It is strange, but I did not interpret that section as a death sequence, but of a deep somnambulistic trance-like state". Eureka! At that point, I revised that particular section and looked at it in a new, enhanced light. The story was the descent of Persephone into the Underworld, so then the full implication dawned upon me: Dion was referring to the "Sleep of Persephone" in legend. It had been staring me in the face all the time, and I had failed to read the true significance. Now after several years of research, the complete ritual could be amended. Ecstatically we called the coven together, mustering everyone for a full moon ritual the following week to try it out.

Even then, we realised that something did not gel. It was now virtually 99 per cent perfect, but one small hiccough remained and we could not work out what this was. We went back to the drawing board and examined it from A to Z. Once the error was analysed, the ritual could be completed - and it was perfect. Until recently, this has been one of the most jealously guarded secrets within Artemis, but we have now started to dispense it to other covens. All it took was a small change in the order of the lines to solve the final riddle. Thus, the most powerful Tantric ritual of high magic had unfolded. Now, in the 21st century in Artemis, it has replaced The Great Rite itself in elevation to the Third Degree. Over the years, Carol went on to attain the supreme accolade of Third Degree herself, and took it "in true". She now runs a thriving coven in California.

When we look back, we can see within our own lifetimes that we still feared the possibility of being denounced for practising our ways. We can see this later when we examine two famous Witchcraft trials that took place in 1930 and 1944. Although the last trial for Witchcraft (in theory) took place in 1712, when Jane Wenham stood trial accused of sorcery and bewitchment, this only heralded the end of the persecutions. Jane was in fact undeniably a Witch, and she was consulted as such by many. Hers was the last trial in England whereby the death penalty could be invoked, but it was certainly not to be the last trial! Jane Wenham was convicted on the most outrageous allegations. These were so preposterous that the Judge, one Justice Powell, was appalled. He actually had the temerity to say so, for as we entered the 18th century an age of reason had begun to dawn. During the summing up, he addressed the jury with the words, "Do you really find her guilty on this particular indictment of being able to change into a cat?" He then continued with a note of incredulity in his voice, "And as a cat she did converse with the Devil himself?" "Aye," the foreman replied, "We find her guilty of that."

Earlier Justice Powell had referred to evidence given by a local farmer, who testified that one of his sheep "did skip", and that he had seen it "stand on its head" with his own eyes. Naturally, this was sure proof that the sheep had been bewitched, When the Judge asked him why he suspected Jane Wenham to be the culprit, the farmer replied that he had refused to give her a turnip when she was starving and that he had sent her away. Therefore, he was sure she had bewitched his sheep. "Do you think this evidence is sufficient to take this woman's life?" snapped the Judge. The foreman nodded once more, "Aye, we do Sir".

Justice Powell's patience was fast running out, particularly when the prosecution called upon the local vicar, the Reverend Strutt, to test her. This test involved asking Jane to perform the Xtian test of reciting the Lord's Prayer absolutely perfectly. Poor Jane, who was only semi-literate, stated she could so recite it and commenced to do so, but fumbled her words when she came to "Lead us not into temptation, but deliver us from evil". Under the stony gaze of the Reverend Strutt, she tried many times more to complete the prayer. However, she became completely unnerved as he pushed her to repeat it. The climax came when he urged her to say, "Lead us not into temptation and evil" but, by now thoroughly confused, Jane blurted out, "Lead us into temptation and evil". Triumphantly, the prosecutors said this was damning proof she was guilty, and once more demanded the death penalty be inflicted. "And what does that prove?" demanded Judge Powell, "Other than that she is a poor, uneducated and ignorant woman who knows not the niceties of English grammar." He then dismissed the evidence.

Undismayed, the prosecutors gave evidence of her being seen entering her cottage, but when they called at the cottage, there was no sign of her. However, they found her on the doorstep – and, as they said, "She lay in the form of a toad". Another told of how he saw a vixen leap away across the fields from near the back door when he approached. The door was open, but there was no sign of the Witch. This was because, "He had see'd her make her escape." The Judge become exasperated and he made his feelings obvious to the Jury.

Then another witness was called, and this one swore that he and others had personally seen her change shape before his very eyes. The Judge listened as he testified that she had been seen in her house, but that moments later they had entered, only to see a mouse scuttle under the sideboard. "Did you look further for her?" Powell demanded. They confirmed that they had, and that she was not to be found anywhere in the cottage. "And where do you think she was?" asked a somewhat bemused Justice Powell. "Under the sideboard Sir, like where I seen her go." The man replied.

Later the judge heard of an incident when Jane Wenham was seen to pass by the window of a Mrs. Harvey. The woman glared at Jane in the box and shouted, "Why don't they take her out and hang her out of the way now". At that point, Justice Powell summed up the case and sent the jury out again to reach a verdict. The Judge became exasperated when the foreman assured him the jury were already agreed on a major piece of evidence. This being, "That as a cat, she had cohabited with the Devil." However, he agreed to reconsider the remaining indictments after lunch. When the court resumed at three o'clock in the afternoon, they unhesitatingly returned verdicts of guilty on all counts. Justice Powell shook his head in astonishment, and placing the black cap upon it reluctantly, pronounced sentence of death as prescribed by law upon the hapless woman, expressing his extreme displeasure at the verdict.

Jane Wenham was lucky. This level of hysteria would have sent her to the stake a hundred years beforehand. Although it had now abated amongst the well educated, mob hysteria and lynch law still simmered just beneath the surface amongst the peasantry. The Jury's verdict was incredible, but twelve "good men and true" had been gathered from the highly superstitious country folk and they had reached a lawful conclusion.

Judge Powell sent a strong plea for clemency to the Law Lords and it was immediately granted by them. Jane was released and given sanctuary with a Colonel Plummer, so that the enraged mob could not wreak their brand of vengeance upon her. She lived under his protection until she died from natural causes some eighteen years later. She was the last witch in England to be sentenced to death, but a further 200 years were to pass before the Act was finally repealed – in 1951!

Tides of the Air, Tides of the Inner Earth
The Secret Tides of Death and Birth
Tides of Men's Souls and Dreams of Destiny
O' Isis veiled and Rhea, Binah, Ge
Sink down, Sink down, Sink Deeper and Sink Deep
Into Primordial and Eternal sleep
Sink down, Forget, be Still and Draw Apart
Into the Inner Earths Most Secret Heart
Drink of the Waters of Persephone
The Secret Well besides the sacred tree.

This poem ran into many pages of intense Tantric ritual – thirty-one verses in all. It is highly prized by the followers of Artemis; a highly mesmerising ritual that transcends time as it is intoned. It enables many members of the coven to reach a trance-like state long before it is completed, and there are nearly 300 lines to be recited in strict order to obtain the power.

Artemis is now the largest coven in Britain, numbering over 100 members and with a backlog of hopefuls eagerly awaiting initiation. However, the rules of the Order of Artemis are strict and a "wannabe" Witch has to attend open meetings each fortnight; meetings in order to ask, and be asked just why exactly they seek the "Hidden Path of Witchdom". This process is designed to eliminate those who seek power for material ends and who may well nurture a hidden agenda.

Out of all whom I have initiated over the years in Artemis, and by invitation to adherents in other covens, I have made three mistakes, and they were most unhappy ones. Fortunately, in each instance, these miscreants left and we all sighed with relief. Luckily, they were all initiates of the First Degree. Each left within months, long before they became eligible for elevation to the Second Degree. When the real power is passed, the wisdom of the Old Gods comes into view, and when they turn against a wannabe Witch who transgresses, the Witch soon leaves.

By the very oaths that they swear to, Witches cannot work adversely or against anyone, lest it be for a very good reason. In such an instance, the High Priest and High Priestess together with the entire coven would also have to approve. One such extremely rare occasion was the gathering of the Witches at Dover in 1940 to blight Adolf Hitler and put a barrier across his mind that would make him fearful of invading. I doubt that anyone apart from a religious fanatic would disapprove of that particular exercise!

Witches are benign creatures who are mainly dedicated to helping the sick and using their magical arts to cure the afflicted. To cross this narrow line is to invoke the "Law of Three" that would turn against them. This is the Law of Cosmic Retribution:

"Three times bad, and three times good," so an old adage runs. "Do good and the Witch is rewarded threefold, do bad - then beware the law of three."

There are exceptions to the rule and these are part of the training. In extremely rare cases, the law that works for "*benefice*" of the coven may be called upon to work a "*malefice*". Such would be the case (and has been) for example, when a paedophile is loose in the area. In this case, a legal curse could be placed upon him. Witch logic in perpetrating such a "*malefice*" is that it will save innocent victims, and so indirectly perform a far greater "*benefice*", but it is rarely invoked.

The purity of Witchcraft, their ways and practices, are much misunderstood. Xtian suppression over hundreds of years and false propaganda have depicted those who follow what was once the original religion of England as wicked and evil. Evidence is based upon the false confessions of those whom they tortured so inhumanely and sent to the stake.

"Evidence", if that is the word, was obtained from mainly old, afflicted women. Invariably, these were peasants, with no education or learning, who could be coerced or tricked into making a confession. Failing this, the use of the red-hot iron, the breast crusher, the crushing of the feet in a hot boot and the rack could obtain the same results. The degradation and wanton cruelty that certain members of the Xtian church descended to in order to obtain a conviction will forever remain a blot on the Xtian community and the purist teachings of the gentle Messiah.

One infamous torturer by the name of Sanson was so skilled in exquisite cruelty that he had a 100 per cent success rate. He once boasted, "I swear to God that such is my art, that give me the Pope himself in my chambers for but the passing of a day, and I swear to you that I would make the Holy one himself confess to being a Witch and sorcerer". Chilling words. This kind of thing is the basis of the evidence against us, of having confessed to blighting crops, laming children, causing horses to throw their riders, turning people into toads and frogs and so on. Let us not forget to mention that we have also been accused of being lyncanthropic werewolves and of turning ourselves into black cats at will!

The Holy (Unholy?) Inquisition was a disgrace in that so many devilish and demoniacal instruments and methods of torture could possibly be devised by the inhuman mind. Some of the instruments and their purpose defy description and are so vile in the application that I cannot bring myself to depict them here. All I will say is that only a twisted mind could envisage such diabolical cruelty - and all this in the name of a gentle and loving man by the name of Jesus, who gave his life for his fellow man. Clearly, this has nothing to do with Jesus or with Xtianity as such, but only to do with the devilish mindset and behaviour of certain people.

"By their deeds shall ye judge them". So the Xtian Bible quotes. Witches adhere by the same principles of love as did Jesus, and Witchdom practices what it preaches. It cannot be denied that, wherever the Xtian faith has ventured, persecution of the "unbeliever" has followed in its wake. The term "unbeliever" does not mean that their victims did not have a belief, but to the Xtian mind, indulging in a different belief was criminal heresy.

One day, when lecturing in Brighton, I was heckled by a local hell fire and damnation priest who screamed at me, "You are evil". I asked him directly how many Witches in the infamous *"Auto da Fé"* had his church indulged in over the years. How many had been burned, who had not only been Witches, but those who did not belong to what they called "The True Faith". These unfortunates had been publicly burned en masse in their own country. This included children and babes in arms, whose crime had been that their mother had been declared a heretic. "We have no accurate numbers," he retorted, but he agreed that it would account for millions over the centuries.

"Tell me," I asked, "how many Catholics or Protestants have been put to death for their beliefs by Witches over the years?" He hesitated and then replied tartly, "I know of no recorded instance." I retorted, "On your own word, you admit that your church has fiendishly put to death untold numbers of our people, yet we have never killed a single one of yours: and you call us evil!"

The priest sat down and there were no further interruptions from him. At the end of the lecture, he came up to me and apologised. He said my remarks had made him think. The outcome was to my meeting him at his church the following day, when he presented me with a large donation of candles and incense for the coven's use. What a surprising *volte-face!*

The two of us remained friends for many years, and on one occasion when we were unable to find a secret and large enough venue for a particularly important and large Sabbat, he allowed us to use the old Crypt in utmost secrecy for our ceremony. He explained that the church had been built on an old Pagan site many years ago, in what was to become known under church doctrine as "replacement theology". This was the superimposition of Xtian doctrine upon existing Pagan beliefs. In the basement of this church, the Witches had secretly returned for a day.

This replacement theology was designed to adapt or adopt all Pagan beliefs and incorporate them under the mantle of the church. An obvious instance is the transposition of the great fertility Sabbat of the Goddess Eostre into Easter on the same date. It is interesting that to this day the date for Easter is still set by the moon. This kind of alteration was imposed upon every known Pagan practise and it was absorbed into the church. The exceptions were that the church held no fertility rites or Goddess worship, other than the Virgin Mary, who became a Goddess substitute.

Xmas was imposed upon The Yule Sabbat (December 21st) and the Candlemas Sabbat was absorbed (Feb 2nd) into the church. The Harvest Festival replaced the Pagan Gathering of the Fruits, and so on. In fact, all the practices other than total love, were incorporated into Catholic ritual and ultimately into Xtianity in general. The holy water, the wine, the incense and candles were all originally Pagan – not to mention the chalice or cup...

It was nice to befriend a priest who had a conscience. Mischievously perhaps, we thought we might well convert him, but it was not to be. The Catholic Church has become a rich hunting ground for converts to our ways and probably over 50 per cent of our members are lapsed Catholics. He continued giving us candles and incense and he very kindly made us a gift one Xmas of a set of blue glass candle-burners plus a red one, stating the four blue ones were for the four quarters of the Wiccan circle and the red one was for the old devil himself!

His church boasted a sealed up north door, which was a clear indication as to its Pagan past. He did not know why the old church had its north door sealed up; all he knew was that it had been bricked up two or three hundred years earlier. He had been told by the previous priest that it was called the "devil's door". We opened a bottle of communion wine and I enlightened him. I explained that when England was a Pagan country, the early Xtians had been instructed to build their churches and cathedrals on Pagan holy sites and places where the populace had previously worshipped the God Cernunnos and the Goddess Ceridwen.

I explained that the Xtian philosophy was simple. It said, "Build your churches on the sites where the Pagans worship and they will have to enter a Xtian church to stand on their sacred land. Give them a few generations to forget the reason and allow the children to absorb Xtian doctrine, and eventually the Old Ways will be but a memory". This worked, because within the space of 50 years, the Xtian Church was established in England.

Originally, the churches were split into two sections. The north was where the Goddess effigy was established and revered, for the north was associated with the Old Religion. The East was for the new religion. Each religion had its own doorway and entered the church by their respective entrance. The Pagans were in the north and Xtians in the east.

For years, this arrangement worked. The two sides lived in harmony and worshipped in the same church. Eventually the Xtian religion took hold and became the religion of the upper classes. On one hand, there were the Xtian ministers with all their panoply of grandeur, rich robes and grand processions. On the other hand, the simple Wiccan priests who lauded the Earth Mother in all her Pagan simplicity. The Lord of the Manor would be a Xtian, while the common people who worked so close to the land would worship the Green Man of the Forest and the Goddess.

Then came the fateful day when Xtianity had grown to be the majority religion. Xtian services swelled and Pagan attendance diminished. Were the people of the country abandoning the Old Gods in favour of this strange sect whose emblem was a man in the extremes of agony? This contrasts to the religion of love of all creatures and the singular commandment, which was a simple *"An'ye harm none"*.

Build on their Sacred Sites

The swing towards the new religion had been carefully contrived. Establishing churches on old sites, within standing stones and in the groves of oak and yew, was only the beginning. Children were targeted, for these would be the Xtians of tomorrow. This process would show results within twenty years. The introduction of educated and schooled monks who could read and write put them above the illiterate peasantry. It became impossible for even the simplest form of commerce to take place without written evidence or bills of sale.

It was no longer possible to buy or sell land, a barn or a house without deeds. Marriage had been as simple as jumping a fire with your beloved before witnesses and being hand fasted by the local Wise Woman. Now it required entry into parochial records and verification. The Xtian newcomers now controlled lives and commerce. Ecclesiastical law replaced old and sometimes strange laws, which had governed the populace for over a thousand years. Without these written papers, you could no longer exist. Clergy would only draw these for Xtians, so country folk were turned away if they were not churchgoers. By "church", that meant sitting in the right section in the east!

Outwardly, the people paid lip service to those who now controlled their lives, while they worshipped the Old Ones in secret. Nevertheless, the established newcomers were now in commanding positions and the fateful decree was now given. "Leave our church, take your altars away and go worship your Gods in the woodland, anywhere but not in our church".

For the first time since the invidious encroachment of these newcomers, the gentle and largely pacifist populace now rebelled and gave a resounding refusal. "No!" they cried. "You have built your churches on the sacred sites where the Goddess has been worshipped since time immemorial. It is the Goddess's land and we will not take our altars away from where they have been erected since time began." The Church carefully considered its position and compromised; they knew they were strong enough by this time to force the issue, but they sought to avoid confrontation.

The issue was that the old altars must remain on the sacred sites or there would be trouble. A compromise was reached. The altars would be buried beneath the church floor, thus being returned to the bosom of the Earth Mother and the Pagans would leave. This seemed a reasonable compromise, so the altars were buried, and over the passing of time, their memory faded. Even the exact locations of the old altars were lost and became just a memory of yesteryear. Occasionally one is found, and it makes a paragraph in the press, but most go unreported. There was an exception some years ago, when the magnificent, elaborately carved frieze in solid oak at Notre Dame in Paris was found to be rotting. Dry rot and woodworm had taken their toll over the centuries and a new surrounding needed to be carved. It was decided that the old one should be preserved and placed in the Louvre in a glass case. When the old casing was removed, an ancient stone altar dedicated to the Lord Cernunnos was revealed! Fortunately, being a more enlightened age it remained there, preserved for posterity.

To return to our story. The burying or covering of the altars was not the end of the tale. Where the Goddess of England was once worshipped in the church, her effigy was removed and replaced by the Virgin Mary. A new sanctuary was created that was now called the "Lady Chapel".

Then the door where the Pagans had once entered to worship the religion of their ancestors was bricked up. This order went out via the Bishopric across the land, and within the passing of two or three years, the bricked up north doors could only be seen from the outside, while inside the old entrance was plastered over and painted with a Xtian fresco.

Sussex is rich in these churches. There is an excellent example at Steyning Church opposite the village museum and library, close to the site of Martyr's triangle, where the old Catholic pastime of burning heretics was carried out. When you find these churches, stop and then ask the vicar the question, "Why is the north door of the church bricked up?" Invariably he will retort, "Ah, that is what we call the 'Devil's Door', where the Infernal One used to come in years before, when the church allowed heathens to enter, but we stopped that a long time ago." Oh dear!

Our friendly and enlightened Catholic priest did not know the full story of his Devil's Door. However, with the passing of time at least one Witch coven had returned, albeit temporarily, to its Pagan roots and worshipped once more in a Xtian church on the original land of their forbears. The priest is no longer there and another now preaches in his pulpit. Beneath the ground in an old church in Brighton, there is a consecrated area, which will be forever Wiccan. We have buried a little casket of artefacts as a lasting memento to an enlightened man. Maybe long after we have passed on, there will be the pleasant surprise of finding the casket. In addition to its contents, we have placed a shiny new silver coin of the year in which it was buried there.

Well, with the passing of time, the original religion of this country came to be known as the "Old Religion", as the "New Religion" took over. The tide is turning now, as Xtianity declines, and The Old Ways are in the ascendancy once more. "So Mote it Be." Hasten the day.

Let us now return to a profile of those Witches that dominated the Pagan scene in Sussex since legalisation of the practice of the Old Religion entered the scene. We will refer in muted form to many eminent Wiccans, whose position in society forbids their "coming out" and openly declaring themselves as practising Witches. These include many doctors and surgeons who enact their ceremonies in secret with us, and whose patients would undoubtedly throw up their hands in horror to think that they had been operated on by a follower of the "black arts", as they would call it.

These medical practitioners are all the more skilled owing to their Wiccan training. Because, as they perform their operations, they know the secret healing words that they can utilise as they use their skills. Why should they be afraid of openly declaring their religion, you may well ask? The answer is that, if all goes well, they would be acclaimed, but oh, if it goes wrong, watch the sparks fly. Just imagine the scenario. Great grandma lies beneath the doctor's hands at the ripe old age of 98. She is clearly about to meet her maker, as her time on earth is spent. However, her mother made 100, so there is no reason why great grandma should not follow suit, particularly with all the skills of modern science at the doctor's disposal. Great grandma's tired old body has other ideas, and with a smile on her face, she crosses the great divide. What would happen if the family were to discover that the doctor was a Witch! An investigation. A hospital inquiry. Wow! The press would have a field day! Imagine the headlines, "Devilish Doctor Drama as Patient Expires. Is the doctor part of satanic ring in Sussex?" The world is not quite ready to accept openly a return to the ways of our ancestors.

No High Court Judge could afford the publicity of "outing" himself as a Witch. Senior police officers are in the same boat. However, as I said earlier in this book, a number of intrepid souls have come forward and faced the television cameras. Some police officers have appeared in uniform and declared their belief. One extremely brave soul, to whom I will only refer as "Dave", announced to the world on television that he was only one member of a large Kent coven that included high-ranking officers who went all the way to the top! The coven verified it, and in this case, their strength in numbers meant that none was ever chided. Witchcraft was well established in the force in Kent, far more so than here. Dave, who was High Priest, was an ordinary police constable; yet his position in the Craft afforded him the respect of both high-ranking fellow Witches and police officers. These Kent people regularly "crossed the border" to work with Artemis in Sussex, as we did with them in Kent.

Countless covens have sprung from the loins of Artemis. Witches progress from neophyte to acolyte and are then initiated into the First Degree of Witchdom after a year and a day, if they have progressed well. Once they have learned to cast a magic Circle, are adept at spell making and casting and have learned to raise the Power, they are truly eligible. Then they can take the next step up the ladder and be elevated to the Second Degree - something for which every initiate strives. Ultimately, the goal is to achieve the Third Degree, the supreme accolade in Witchdom.

Once a Witch has acquired the Third Degree, ancient tradition expects them to leave the coven and to do what is known in Wiccan circles as "hive". This means, to be like a queen bee and found another colony, or in this case found another coven whereby the craft might be promulgated. Within Artemis, the Tradition has not always been adhered to, as the camaraderie that has always been enjoyed (with a few exceptions) has meant that Witches of great occult ability have been reluctant to leave and start another coven. The result is that Artemis is now over a hundred strong, not counting the multitude who have "hived" and started new groups.

Those who left have trained other Witches to the Third Degree. These in their turn have founded further covens. The result is that the Artemis tradition is practised by over 200 covens worldwide. We have exceeded the 117 covens that followed the Alexandrian tradition in its heyday. These have disappeared like snow with the rising of the sun.

Now let us take a break and examine some tenets, not only of Sussex Witchcraft, but also of Witchcraft as a whole, as we go into the realms of folklore and old beliefs.

Witch Trees and Fond
Reminiscences

Witches revere nature, and as we know, animals such as the stag and hare are of particular significance. We will come back to animals, birds and insects later. However, no book would be complete without a reference to the various trees that are held in such reverence, not only for their magical properties but also for their curative ones. Wiccans call the willow "The Tree of Enchantment" and it is sacred to The White Lady of the Moon. The leaves of the willow contain salicylic acid, which is a constituent of aspirin. In modern times, this tree has become known as Witches' Aspirin, because long before the modern drug was synthesised, willow bark was used for headache, toothache, migraine, heart problems and rheumatism.

The old village wise women were already aware of the healing properties of the willow, and they used this in conjunction with an extract of leaves from the foxglove plant for heart problems. We are now aware that foxglove leaves provide digitalis, which - in moderation, under professional supervision, as it is otherwise a deadly poison - slows the heartbeat. Meadowsweet was used as a cure for headaches and migraine, as this was another rich source of salicylic acid. Research has since shown meadowsweet to be even richer in this substance than willow. Salicylic acid is also common in many plants such as broccoli, peppers, curry, cucumbers and raisins, but to a much lesser extent than in the willow.

The willow therefore ranks high in Witchcraft esteem. It was also held sacred by the Druids, and it was considered it to be one of the nine sacred trees of the Irish, who cultivated groves of them. Willows were adored by Priests and Priestesses for their magical qualities. They would troop to the enchanted areas of the white willow, to meditate and communicate with the spirits of earth. This enabled them to gain insight into future events and to make prophecies. They would mix thyme and juniper berries to create hallucinogenic incense and obtain vision. They would also pluck catkins and bring them into their dwellings to bring luck for the year. The catkin gathering, which was prevalent in Sussex, was an old custom amongst country folk that traditionally took place on May Day.

Every nation seems to love the oak. Woodworkers adore its toughness and it looks wonderful when it has been polished. The oak endures well over many lifetimes. It made fine war shields (spear shafts were made of holly), so oak was indeed the "King of the Trees". Oak was considered magical, and Priests listened to the rustle of the leaves for messages from beyond. Acorns are the fruit of the oak and they were considered to hold magical properties. They were used in fertility rites. These oak galls were called serpent's eggs and they were considered powerful charms. Oak wood and leaves were used in spells for success, strength, healing a weak heart and protection - to name but a few.

Trees that were venerated by Witches had been established in both British and Sussex folklore for over 2,000 years and they date back to the heyday of the Druids. Kingley Vale near Stoughton in Sussex has always been associated with Witchcraft, although no written records of this have been discovered. The yew forest there is virtually untouched by time and it dates back literally hundreds of years. It is said that many of the trees in that area are centuries old. The ancient association with Witchcraft lingers on, and I have been told that even now, nobody will spend the night there.

According to local legend, a little village called South Heighton had a row of trees that had been there since the beginning of time. These were particularly revered by the villagers, who said that a curse would befall anyone who ever felled them. Apparently, the farmer on whose land they stood decided to ignore the entreaties of the locals and cut them down. Soon afterwards, people reported a "strange presence" moving around the farm and no one would go near after dark. The ultimate fate of the farmer is not known, except for one reference that "he prospered not thereafter".

The oak and ash, apple and alder, juniper, rowan and the elder and pine were all associated with magical powers, but the greatest of all was the magical mistletoe, which is a parasite that grows on sacred trees such as the apple. The Wise Ones added the holly, birch and hazel to the list.

No treatise on The Old Religion would be complete without at least a single reference to All Heal, as mistletoe (*viscum album*) is better known. Sir James Frazer's book on all things magical was aptly named after another of the ancient names for mistletoe, The Golden Bough. The magically endowed plant ruled the winter solstice, and tradition states that it could only be cut with a golden sickle - iron was particularly forbidden. All Heal was particularly revered in March, it was always cut on a new moon and was not allowed to touch the ground, so the people used a white sheet to catch it as it fell. It would be carefully handed to a Druid, who in turn would pass it to yet another Druid, but if it touched unhallowed ground, its powers were considered lost. The word mistletoe has its origins in an Old Saxon word "*mistan*" meaning "glue-twig". *Mist* was the ancient word for glue and *tan* was the ancient word for a twig.

The customs associated with mistletoe are legion, particularly in Sussex. It made women fertile if carried, it cured disease and it repelled evil spirits. One old custom was that the last man born in a household cut the mistletoe and ornamented it with brightly coloured ribbons, nuts and apples. It would then be hung near the entrance on a pulley or string. When a girl entered the room, the men would lower the sprig, she would pluck a single berry and then they would kiss her. Afterwards the berry had to be thrown over the girl's left shoulder. This custom gave rise to the modern custom of kissing under the bough at Xmas, but how many people know of its Pagan origins?

The mistletoe bough would then be left as a protection against evil spirits and goblins. In some places, it would be ceremonially burnt after a year and immediately replaced with a fresh branch. On a final note, if you fear Witches, do not throw your mistletoe away, but keep it. Take it down on Twelfth night, save and dry it; then burn it a year later under your Xmas pudding, and we will not come near you!

In Sussex, in ancient times, a great ceremony was traditionally held on "The Sixth Night of the Moon". This was held as close as possible to the tenth day of March, heralding the start of the ancient New Year. The Druid Priests and Priestesses in white raiment would lead a brace of white oxen ornamented with flowers and garlands; then they would arrive at a specially chosen oak tree where a large bunch of mistletoe hung. The golden sickle would be ceremonially unwrapped, and the chief Druid would solemnly climb the tree, sever the mistletoe and signal the ceremony to commence. The oxen would then be sacrificed. Ceremonial fires lit and *metheglen* (a spiced mead) would be served in wooden bowls as the sun set. They chanted and sang, and carried the mistletoe to the Druidical Palace in worship of their God, Tutanes. Although mistletoe grew on other trees, such as the apple, only mistletoe from an oak was regarded as sacred.

So much for the past, for, almost overnight, mistletoe completely and utterly disappeared from Sussex. We will never know the true reason behind its decline, but it is believed that it was deliberately culled and destroyed. Some say that, according to ancient Scandinavian and Saxon legend, Loki used an arrow that was made of mistletoe to slay Baldur. It seems that the Danish influence via the South Saxons may have urged the local populace to destroy it. All we know is that it is now virtually extinct in Sussex and all attempts to grow it here have failed. It is said that one must place fertile berries against the sun to see if a distinctive black spot appears. I have tried this, then tried inserting it into apple, oak and hawthorn, and then sealed them in muslin, only to see my experiments fail. The greatest problem was that I could not find the original kind of mistletoe. Apparently, certain berries would only graft on to oak, others would only take on apple, and so on. If anyone reading this does find an instance of mistletoe growing in Sussex, I would love to hear from you. If so, please send an email to the address for the Order of Artemis that appears at the back of this book. The only known sighting was on the famous Maresfield Oak. This was sometimes called the Maresfield Bough or the Mistletoe Bough of Maresfield.

Mistletoe, the Mysterious; steeped in legend for centuries. Let me finish on a poem which was written around 1650 by the famous poet, Robert Hinkley.

Down with the Rosemary, and so
Down with the Bays and Mistletoe;
Down with the Holly, Ivy, all
Wherewith ye dressed the Christmas hall;
That so the superstitious find,
No one least branch there left behind;
For look, how many leaves there be
Neglected there, maids, trust to me
So many Goblins you shall see…

Hazel wood was swiftly adapted by Witches to make *stangs* (forked ritual shafts) and wands, especially when one was needed in an emergency, because the circle of magic could be swiftly cast with a switch of hazel. Probably the best-known use of hazel is the divining rod, which is so beloved of water diviners and dowsers. The Witch's wand had to be cut at a specific time of year, in a certain way and with the correct craft tool. It had to be taken from right part of the tree, which also had to be the right age. No wonder the local covens watched the growth of each tree so carefully!

15

Old Ways, Old Customs and Warm Witch Fires

Druids recognised the power of the hazel, but when it came to magical working, they much preferred ash. They used ash wands for healing, and in Stonehenge, solar magic was conjured with ash wands. Another old custom that seems to have slipped into obscurity is the old "Yule log". This is now immortalised in Xmas cakes, chocolate logs and the gathering of Yule logs that is often depicted on Xmas cards. How many now remember that the traditional Yule log had essentially to be ash, and that one of these would be put in a prominent position in the cottage until the following Yule? It would be the first log on the fire, to be replaced by its successor that had been ceremonially kept for another year.

Three, seven or nine men, or a mixed coven of thirteen, would ceremonially haul this log into the circle, or three men would drag it into the cottage. Single women, widows and the like would obtain a smaller log for their fire at Yule and traditionally request a man to carry it to the fire for them. Once there, it would be paraded thrice round the boundary, then anointed on one end only with wine and honey, and then blessed. Red tallow or beeswax candles would be set upon it. When sufficient wax had run down onto the log, the pieces of tallow would be taken off and placed in the north. Then the other end - the honeyed end - would be placed in the Yule fire so that the sacred, anointed end would stick out into the room or circle. Once it was well ablaze, everyone present would take a run at it and give it a kick with the cry "Luck to all!" Then the coven would chant to the effect that it be "returned times three".

The idea of kicking the log was to make sparks fly. This would symbolise driving away evil spirits. This ancient ceremony had fallen into disuse - probably through the introduction of coal or modern fires, but it persisted for a number of years in remote areas of Sussex, when Xtians would kick a log (without the addition of honey) and try to make the sparks fly, to drive the Devil away. This is yet another example of replacement theology.

This old custom is indigenous to Sussex, but is one of two quite distinct traditions practised in this county. In a similar one, the ash log would have been taken from a male tree. While the log was being hauled in by the men, all who passed it would make obeisance to it - the men by doffing their hats and the womenfolk by bowing or curtsying. Tradition states that refusing to acknowledge the sanctity of the log would result in bad luck in the forthcoming year.

Once the log was brought to the Yule site or cottage, the remains of the previous year's log would be used to start the fire. The Yule fire was kept burning and maintained for twelve days and nights. This is probably where the Xtian tradition of removing all symbols of Yule by the twelfth night originated. The purpose of this ritual was so that the sun (symbolised by the warmth of the Yule fire throughout the twelve days) would shine throughout every month thereafter. Before placing the log on the fire, the male log would have the figure of the God, in the form of Herne the Hunter, chalked upon it. The ash from the fire would later be scattered over surrounding fields to bring fertility to the land. It would take several pages to expound the virtues of every sacred tree and type of wood, so I will just cover the main properties and legends here.

Blackthorn has been used by Witches for centuries to install strong influences on others. It is alleged that in days gone by, dark practitioners used blackthorn with which to impale effigies of their victims. I must, in fairness, comment on a similar Witchcraft practice that could well have led to such stories, and the name itself may well have played a part by being called "black".

The coven member who gathered the Covenors together for the Sabbats and sent out the call to the local covens at the Summer Solstice was known as the Summoner. He was record keeper, scribe and guardian. His symbol of authority and rank was a blackthorn stang and he was known as "Black Rod".

It is interesting to note that this symbol was swiftly usurped by the Church and adopted for use in the ecclesiastical courts – yet another example of replacement theology and symbolism. It was henceforth displayed by them as a symbol of extreme power over the people.

From there, it found its way into Parliament, where it was symbolically carried by the Gentleman Usher to the Lord Chamberlain's department, the House of Lords and the Chamber of the Garter. This honour derived from another old Pagan custom, based on the Witch's garter worn by a High Priestess of the Third Degree, high on the left leg, to show her rank and authority.

Soon the powers that be decided that the simplistic stang of the blackthorn was not good enough, as it was all too common, so they decreed that henceforth, it should be made of pure ebony. Now, that's what I call progress!

In Wiccan healing rites, one creates an effigy of the sick or afflicted person that looks as much like the person as possible. Hence, whenever such poppets, as they are generally known, were found, the so-called "victim" was easily recognisable. The Witch would isolate the area of pain or disease and insert a silver pin in it, or when a pure silver pin was not obtainable, a silver coloured pin would be used.

Iron was another metal with magical qualities and this was frequently used amongst the often-poor village wise women unable to afford silver pins. Horseshoe nails were also frequently used. This done, the power would be raised and the blue healing ray or cone of power would be focussed on the pin, which would be used to convey the magic direct to the afflicted organ.

It does not take much imagination to foresee the reaction of the clergy and in their wake, the Witch-finders, when such a poppet was discovered in their search. Outwardly, the evidence to those ignorant of our ways was damning. For one thing, the person the Witch was said to be cursing was recognisable. The poppet depicted the person's sex and such features as a beard. The person assumed that they had been blighted and that curse had been effective, for the person so modelled was undoubtedly known to be ill. The fact that the poppet was in fact part of a curative process seemed to get lost along the way. It was of no use for the poor old soul to protest her innocence; that she was a healer and that her pins were a psychic form of acupuncture, or that it was the sick person's own relative who had sought her help. In these circumstances, it does not take long before even those who have sought help take up the cry of, "Burn the Witch!" Even they who knew the score would convince themselves that the crone started it all in the first place, as a means of extracting payment for the work that she did. As the hysteria spread, there was no escape.

So much for Blackthorn and its correspondences. Let us move on to a tree that is universally respected and that is the true giveaway of your local neighbourhood Witch, and this is the rowan. Rare is the Witch who has not planted a rowan tree in his or her garden, to attract the luck of the Gods and for protection. Its wood has always been known as Witchwood and it has been used as a protection against evil. The tree is often sold in garden centres as mountain ash or sorb apple. Country folk and farmers used it as a charm against a number of afflictions. Even today, you may well see a spray of it over cow pens or the arch of the farm-worker's cottage. One of the reasons it is so revered is that the berries carry the Witch sign on them – the pentacle of power and protection. Look at the top of the berry and you will see clearly outlined, the famous "Goblin's Cross". This is the five-pointed star of magic, of which each arm signifies one of the five paths of wisdom. This is also the emblem of the Star Goddess, which is associated with Brigit, who is one of the oldest goddesses in Britain.

The rowan tree was also sacred to the Druids, and like the hazel, its forks are used to divine water. Its fruit is a source of provender to birds in the winter, but the Wise Ones also knew that its berries were deadly to humankind. It was the Celts who gave us the saying that is used by Wiccans as a salutation to this day, "Peace be here and Rowan Tree."

Next to the rowan is the elder, sacred to the Goddess and respected by Witches with unequalled reverence. No Sussex Witch will disturb an elder tree. I believe this particular practice is exclusive to Sussex covens, for outside of Sussex, the wood of the elder is used for a variety of purposes by other Wiccans, such as the making of Panpipes and magic flutes. One thing they all share with each other is strict obedience to the old law that forbids the burning of elder wood. The old adage runs "Now Elder be our Ladies' Tree - so burn it not, or cursed thou'll be". One can hardly say that Witches are not superstitious! Once, when asked on a television programme by an interviewer the question, "Are Witches superstitious?" the retort was, "We invented superstition!" This might be a joke, but you will not find a solitary Wiccan who would knowingly burn elder.

Elder is held sacred by Crafters, but strangely enough, many country people regard the elder as unlucky, mainly due to its association with Witchcraft. Perhaps this is because the handle of the traditional Clan Sword of Judgements was made of elder, and sentences were pronounced beneath the branches of an elder in olden times. In fact, under the Celtic legal system, if you had not been tried beneath an elder branch, you had legitimate grounds to appeal a sentence if it was unfavourable. Mediaeval courts of justice were traditionally held under or alongside an elder. Hence, those summoned to the elder were invariably fearful, not of the elder per se, but the judgements of the court itself. Needless to say, it did not take long for the elder to be regarded superstitiously.

The occult warning is contained in an old *rede* (tale) that describes the various properties of logs. It says that the oak can be burned without fear. However, I do know a few Wiccans who will carve, shape and fashion oak wood unhesitatingly, but they will not burn it. They even go to the extent of burying the sweepings and sawdust.

The old Rede runs as follows:

Beech wood fires burn bright and clear
If the logs are kept a year
Store your Beech for Christmastide
With new cut Holly laid aside.
Chestnut's only good they say
If for years 'tis stored away
Birch and Fir wood burn too fast
Blaze too bright and do not last
Flames from Larch will shoot up high
Dangerously the sparks will fly
But Ash wood green and Ash wood brown
Are fit for a Queen with a golden crown
Oaken logs, if dry and old
Keep away the winter's cold
Poplar gives a bitter smoke
Fills your eyes and makes you choke
Elmwood burns like churchyard mould
E'en the very flames are cold
Hawthorn bakes the sweetest bread
So it is in Ireland said
Apple wood will scent the room
Pear wood smells like flowers in bloom

But Ashwood wet and Ashwood dry
A Queen may warm her slippers by
Tho' Elder be our Lady's tree
So burn it not or cursed thou'll be.

Another old rede from the West Country runs a close parallel to the Sussex one. One notes that oak is not exempted from the sacred balefire, but both redes give dire warnings once more against burning elder.

Oak logs will warm you well,
That are old and dry.
Logs of Pine will sweetly smell,
But the sparks will fly.
Birch logs will burn too fast,
Chestnut scarce at all.
Hawthorne logs are good to last,
Cut them in the fall.
Holly logs will burn like wax,
You may burn them green.
Elm logs like smouldering flax,
No flame to be seen.
Beech logs for wintertime,
Yew logs as well
Green Elder logs it is a crime,
For any man to sell.
Pear logs and Apple logs,
They will scent your room
Cherry logs across the dogs
Smell like flowers in bloom.
Ash logs, smooth and grey,
Burn them green or old.
Buy up all that come your way,
Worth their weight in gold.

Every Witch ensures that even the smallest fragment of dead elder should not go on the fire. The dead wood is always gathered up in Sussex and stacked with logs, whenever possible by a pond as a refuge for wild life, or with garden compost as a refuge and hiding place for frogs and toads and newts. An old Solstice practice (June 21st) instructs Witches to stand under the elder and meditate. Legend says the little people will come to you in your mind's eye - although some Irish Witches swear these are factual. I once stayed with the seventh son of a seventh son in Eire, who swore that the "little ones" really did exist and that they would manifest themselves on Midsummer Day, if you followed this old practice.

16

Fairy Lore - and More

I suppose people will ask, "Do Witches believe in fairies?" This subject will arouse the most sincere debates within a Witch circle. The basic answer is that we do not, but that is not the end of the matter, as there is a great deal of evidence to the contrary. The negative in this context really applies only to the actual physical appearance and sight of the little ones, but the existence of small spirits that can easily be identified as "faeries" is indisputable.

Many whose instinct calls them to the Craft have spent years being aware of certain psychic powers within themselves. They actively seek out a coven. This is not as easy as you think, because covens are not advertised in the Yellow Pages! One of the signs that someone is "fey" is that they see what we know as elementals. These strange, friendly little spirits are everywhere. I would go as far as to say every house has them, albeit only a mere handful. If you have the slightest psychic ability, an inner sense of realisation of the spirit world about you, an affinity with nature or a sense of belonging as you walk in a forest, they will flock to you. Elementals belong to what is known as the *Deva* kingdom. This invisible (or only fleetingly visible) kingdom is inhabited by earth spirits. Ethereal little forces that exist close to the earth and that seem to be particularly attracted to Witches and Pagans.

Elementals can be seen scurrying around the floor like a mass of black beetles, sometimes as large as a mouse although usually no bigger than a beetle. Many a time I have been aware of those who have fearfully observed them and who (if uninitiated) are convinced they are overrun with spiders, mice, beetles or what they describe as "little furry creatures scuttling everywhere". Hoover as much as you like, it will make no difference at all, because they will be back within minutes, happy in what the little spirits find is a happy and welcome environment.

One Witch who joined us many moons ago, and who was previously the High Priestess of Arachne, had inadvertently conjured these up. Her home was literally inundated with these ultra-friendly little creatures, often to the bewilderment of non-Wiccan visitors. In all the years that I have observed these quaint little creatures, I have never seen them in such profuse quantities as within her house.

It is highly probable that the familiars so closely associated with Witches are these denizens of the *Deva* realms, although the creating of a full Witch's familiar, an enchanted creature that has full affinity with the Witch is a completely different matter. This takes great skill on the part of the Witch, and a very special understanding and rapport with the animal he or she has chosen. Nine times out of ten, this is a cat, so this was another indicator in the days of persecution that some old dear may be a Witch.

It is the same with fairies. I personally have never seen a fairy; I do not believe in their physical being, and until one flutters in through my bedroom window and says, "Hi, Ralph!" I will continue to doubt their bodily existence. The existence of fairy elemental folk is a different matter. The existence of an earthly, elemental fairy spirit force that manifests itself in such a way as to be strongly identified with humanity or humanoid form is indisputable. This is part of the invisible *Deva* kingdom, and is said to exist alongside pixies and elves.

The Last Bastion

Once more Sussex stands out, even in fairy lore, for, as the extermination of Witches was systematically enacted throughout Britain, so fairies (perhaps I should say fairy sightings) went into decline simultaneously, swiftly becoming an endangered species. Sussex miraculously escaped the great pogrom. After years of research into old documents, I could only find a grand total of eighteen recorded Witch trials in the whole of the county. There could well have been more, but no record can be found, and records in this county have been well kept. Although the eradication of Witches was factual, by a strange co-incidence, the disappearance of the fairy also took place. Amusing sightings were regularly reported in local folklore, often combined with elves and brownies. These would often be spoken of in hushed whispers by the local men as they supped their cider or ale. They told of how farmer Giles' corn had been gathered in for him by the little ones - usually male. They would always cap the other's story with a tale of their own. One persistent theme that varied little from area to area was that "Old Mother So and So" had failed to thank the wee ones for a service, such as churning her butter in the night, with the result that they subsequently abandoned her. Tales abounded of people being forsaken by the wee folk for failing to thank them.

This propitiation would usually be in the form of a ladle of milk or an oatmeal cake being left out for them. Sure enough, by morning, it would be gone - a sure sign that the little ones had taken it away with gratitude. It never seemed to dawn on our forebears that such nocturnal creatures as hedgehogs and foxes could be the culprits, or that the early bird got the new baked cake…

The story in other areas is the opposite, and it would go something like the following. "Old Jim had seen a group of elves sweeping his floor one night" This occurrence had been puzzling him, as each morning he would find his kitchen floor clean of all the food scraps and crumbs that a lazy old widower like him had left around (mice, one must ask?) Doffing his hat to them, he had thanked them, whereupon they had disappeared, never to be seen again. The moral being that one should never acknowledge to a fairy that you can see them.

Therefore, in the wake of the persecutions, we see the end of the faerie folk as well. Logically, the scarcity of reported sightings during this period would more than likely be because seeing or admitting their presence may well have been interpreted as you being in league with satan's servants, and thus a swift walk to the gallows. So goodbye, little ones, except in Sussex where sightings persisted for some time, but eventually they died out there as well. Harrow Hill at Patching in Sussex is generally accepted to have been the home of "the last of the fairy colonies". Old homes where they were said to have existed in large numbers were Ditchling Beacon, Cissbury Ring, the Devils Dyke and Chanctonbury Ring. At Tarberry Hill, there were reports of a fairy funeral having been seen at Pulborough Mount. This, incidentally, had been verified by the local vicar and curate in the 1800s.

It is amazing that a number of intellectuals and prominent people swear that they have seen the little folk. This leads one to believe that they cannot all have been under an illusion, above all when the eminent positions held by those who have had the temerity to issue these statements is considered. One example I sometimes quote is a statement by the late Leslie Roberts, an eminent Sussex investigator into occult phenomena. He swore that he had seen a fairy on Chanctonbury Ring one Halloween, and that a psychic rapport was established between him and the fairy, without a word being spoken. Apparently, this phenomenon was testified to by three independent witnesses at the time. Personally, I keep an open mind, because I feel that the beings that people identify as fairies are in fact elementals. These are usually no more than about three inches high and they move with great speed.

Roberts reported that the fairy in question eventual grew to three feet tall and appeared to him as a beautiful young girl. True or not, we will never know. However, I do know that before the manifestation, Roberts had carried out a cleansing ritual at a particularly psychically charged area of Chanctonbury Ring. I do not doubt that the figure he describes did manifest as he said; however, in my opinion, if what he did was a pure cleansing ritual, then the beautiful feminine figure that appeared was far more likely to be a manifestation of the Goddess than a fairy. There are a number of Occult rituals known to the Masters, whereby the Goddess can be manifested. We in Artemis have performed this ritual on three occasions over the years, whereby the Goddess or certainly, a female figure, would spiral ethereally from a blazing cauldron.

I have walked at the base of Ditchling Beacon, the Devils Dyke and Cissbury. There are circular areas that locals point out as old fairy rings, which had not been created by toadstools. To add to the mystery, the ground was damp, as may well have been expected. A profusion of the plant known as Lady's Glove was growing. This is usually referred to in the countryside as Milkmaids, but it is usually found in botanical books under Lady's Smock. This plant was sacred in folklore to fairies and to those places where the faerie folk dwelt. Is it not strange, one must ask, that since earliest times in old engravings and in children's books, we see fairies and elves cavorting merrily, flying from bluebells - and lady's gloves! On a superstitious note, this is sometimes called Pigeon's Eye. It is considered very unlucky to pick the Fairies' Flower and unluckier still to bring it into your house.

By strange coincidence, there was a revival of interest in fairies in Great Britain in the Victorian era. This culminated in what is now generally accepted as a great hoax, when fairy pictures taken with a box brownie camera by two schoolgirls called Elsie Wright and Frances Griffiths hit the headlines. This took place in an allegedly enchanted fairy glade in the village of Cottingley, and none other than Sir Arthur Conan Doyle endorsed their authenticity. The discovery caused worldwide debate at the time, but it is now generally accepted as a naughty schoolgirl prank and no more than that. This was further substantiated when the two errant women confessed their outstanding hoax in the twilight of their years. They had concocted this with a book on fairies, a pair of scissors and some glue!

I mentioned previously that Audrey and I spent a happy few weeks in a wondrously haunted old castle called at the time Huntingdon Castle, and which, following the deaths of Lord and Lady Strathlock, subsequently was renamed Clonegal Castle. It was during this visit that we also stayed with Stewart and Janet Farrar and slept in their Temple... but that could take up a whole chapter. One night, a tap tapping on the window awakened us, despite the fact that we were on the top floor! Switching on my torch, we saw a large bat flapping against the window; shades of Dracula had nothing on staying with the Farrars! Stewart and Janet laughed the next morning and explained that in such a rural area, moths were attracted to the cottage lights and the bats had got used to popping round for a free meal.

Each evening, we would go merrymaking, with an emphasis on dancing. Janet adored dancing and Jive in particular, so we "cut many a rug" together, and she was a great mover on the dance floor. The Witch world is the poorer for the sad loss of her husband, Stewart, who was one of the "greats" of our time, and the later loss of Doreen Valiente has further depleted those ancients who have bequeathed so much to modern-day Witchcraft. The Summerlands are now made even more attractive by the thought of one day being reunited with our old friends.

Each day we would sally forth from the castle, often with the Honourable Olivia Robertson, who ran the Fellowship of Isis. She acted as a wondrous guide, taking us to ancient and haunted sites. On other occasions, armed only with an ordnance survey map, we would go exploring. One day, Audrey and I drove aimlessly around the beautiful rolling countryside, descending into one valley after another or heading for a distant set of hills. Arriving at a high point in the hills, a beautiful valley was revealed below. Water tumbled out of a small waterfall and emptied into a narrow stream that meandered through rocks and crevices, at one point going under a little, somewhat shabby footbridge that looked decidedly unsafe.

"What a great place to have a picnic!" Audrey exclaimed, and immediately started to unpack the hamper. Within minutes, we were descending the hillside and tremulously crossing the somewhat archaic bridge. After walking for a while, we picked a particularly isolated but beautiful spot by the stream to enjoy our goodies. We had only just started our repast when we became aware of the most beautiful and ethereal music I avow we had ever heard. To this day, I cannot describe it. It was a mixture of harps and strings, entwined with cymbals and bells and what I can only describe as harpsichord music. All this was blended with a number of flutes. In an ethereal and unreal parody, we dined in the most enchanted atmosphere we had ever encountered. Having finished wining and dining, we decided to try to discover the source of these sounds and to our surprise found that wherever we walked along the embankment the faerie orchestra followed us.

Puzzled we peered under the stream bank and into bull rushes, and then picking up the picnic basket (having failed to discover the source), we headed back to the car, which was quite a distance away - and all uphill. We crossed the old bridge and started to wend our way back, still pursued by our little and invisible orchestra; the music followed us all the way back. As we reached the summit, it started to fade, receding back down the valley as if a little troupe was now marching away, having rendered a final melody. This was one of the most beautiful experiences that we had ever enjoyed.

The following morning, whilst breakfasting with Olivia, Derry and Poppy, Olivia asked us where we had gone the previous day. We produced the map and were able to indicate our route and the area where we had picnicked. When we spoke of the valley, all three of our hosts exchanged glances;

then Lord Strathlock ventured hesitantly, "Was there anything of note you noticed there?" It was then time for Audrey and me to exchange looks as we answered that, we had in fact been exposed to a rather beautiful experience. Straightaway dear Olivia jumped in, "Did you see the fairies there? That's their little hollow you picnicked in." We had to confess that we did not see any fairies but we told them of the music. Lord Strathlock smiled, "Ah, that was their way of greeting you; it means that you have been accepted". I rest my case.

Both Derry and Olivia confirmed they had seen the little ones there while out walking. Poppy (Lady Strathlock) simply nodded in assent. To this day, I have never been able to confirm their physical existence, but in the spirit form, something certainly exists that could well have given rise to the popular image of the fairy. The music and the orchestra were real and the music was not of this world, and the enigma of that Irish experience will forever be with us.

To see the faerie folk, tradition says you must stand under an elder tree on the longest day of the year. If you cannot find an elder, then stand in the centre of a fairy toadstool ring and they will appear. Well, maybe. I have yet to try, but there is constant reference to the phenomenon when you study the old histories of the elder tree, the sacred elderberry or the Ellhorn.

Besom Brooms, Warts an' Old Allen

In some traditions - again, outside Sussex - elder wood or faerie wood is used to make Panpipes and flutes, and these would be cut from the living tree, which is quite contrary to our Sussex customs, as we will never cut the living wood. These covens always offer libations of wine and mead to the spirit of the tree and explain to its elementals the reason they needs its branches, in order to appease the tree. They appease the elder and explain their reasons for taking its wood when they need a branch of faerie wood to create a magical wand to drive away evil spirits, or need to make magical exorcism music to drive away bad luck. Once the tree understands the reason, it will not mind the Witch cutting a branch, provided it is at a single stroke.

In Sussex, no hereditary or traditionalist Witch will even disturb an elder tree, let alone prune it. They would not dream of cutting a wand, pipes or a flute from it. In a traditional Witch's garden, the elder blooms unchecked. I have seen a small garden overshadowed by a spreading elder that has been left alone, for the elder rules supreme. The Witch will accept the fruits and flowers of the elder to make coven wine with the elderflower and elderberry. The exception to this rule is that we have no problem with using elder wood that has died naturally for flutes and Pan pipes, but we would not use dead elder to make a wand; it is not our way. There are many trees that I could write about, but I have concentrated on the most important ones.

So mote it be.

The Witch's ritual broom, the famous "besom", is probably one of the few traditional artefacts correctly associated with Witches. No cartoon of us is complete without a besom broom and a cauldron - the only other essential! Most of the Witches I know are beautiful. They do not have long noses and warts and they definitely do not wear pointed hats, but they do all own broomsticks and black cauldrons.

Traditionally, there are three types of broom used for ritual purposes. Nowadays the broom that decorates a Wiccan altar is the common one that you can buy in garden centres to sweep paths. This is made of birch twigs - hence its name. Traditional Witches always make their own, usually out of three or seven of the nine sacred woods, or freshly gathered birch alone. Certainly, those who attain their Second Degree will seek out three of these woods on a full or new moon, but the broom can be made entirely of birch, and it often is. In some covens, it is constructed of birch (The Tree of Birth), hazel (The Tree Symbolic of Fire, Fertility, Divination and Knowledge) and yew (The Tree that is Symbolic of Death and Resurrection).

Broom or gorse is sometimes called "furze". This plant carries delightful yellow flowers in early spring. It is also called the Witch's broom by country people and it was often used by villagers as a besom broom to sweep away bad influences, a practice they have obviously inherited through the folklore of their Pagan forebears.

All Witches, before the commencement of a ritual or the casting of a circle, use a broom to symbolise the dispersal of evil. Within Witchcraft, it is the intent that prevails, rather than the specific woods that are used. It does not matter whether the broom is constructed of the three sacred woods, of birch or even whether it is made from the plant called broom at all.

Furze (gorse) is identified with the Spring Equinox and is one of the nine sacred woods. Furze was burned for protection and against conflict. Cedar was known as the Tree of Life in olden times. Mediaeval Witches would use it in their brooms to draw earth energy and to "ground" themselves. As a point of interest, they would often ground themselves during a ritual by placing their hands on a cedar leaf end, or by holding the tips of cedar leaves between the thumb and forefinger and meditating.

Silver fir was another sacred wood, its silvery aspects being identified with the moon and, of course, the Goddess. It is a matter of regret that I find that the custom of using silver fir in a besom has fallen into obscurity. I personally feel that it should replace thorn (thorn is not used in the Order of Artemis). On a historical note, I feel I should record that silver fir needles were burnt at the birth of a baby as a blessing and protection for the infant and mother.

Apple wood is also sacred and has been so through the centuries, small wonder that its twigs are used in constructing a Witch's broom. The tales attached to it are legion and its magical properties have been recorded since time immemorial. It usually represents the Tree of Knowledge in the Bible, as in the story of Adam and Eve.

While on the subject of apples, apple fruit was an old charm against warts. You cut the apple into three sections and then rub the cut side of each piece in turn onto the wart saying, "Out, wart, and into apple!" Then, on a full moon you bury it. The theory was that as the apple rotted away, the wart diminished in size and ultimately disappeared. Apples are a sacred fruit as well, and are prolific in love charms and spells; cut an apple across the middle and you will see the five-pointed star or pentacle of the Witches. Eat it and make a wish, but do not use it with thoughts of seduction in mind, for it will rebound on you, and it will be your heart that is broken.

An old tradition that seems to have fallen into disuse in Sussex is the sectioning during rituals of a large ripe eating apple known as "Allen". The origins of the name are regretfully lost in history. The "Allen" would be ritually blessed, then cut up with the white handled knife and distributed to all covenors present, for luck in the following twelve months. There would always be an extra piece cut, to be delivered back to the ground (buried with the drains of consecrated wine or mead from the sacred chalice) as propitiation to the Earth Mother.

Pine is known throughout the world as a wondrously scented wood, and its oil, sap and resin (which ultimately hardens to become amber) is used as incense in a vast range of rituals, as well as being one of the woods used in a broom. It is known by many names from country to country, for it grows virtually anywhere, but the most common is the sweetwood tree and its wood is called sweetwood.

The Irish clans and tribes particularly revered sweetwood and the Druids considered it sacred. The burning of its incense was a means of purification, new homes traditionally burned pinewood and resin mixed with pine needles in equal parts of juniper and cedar to cleanse them. Afterwards, pine nuts and cones would be carried in or scattered on newly weds as fertility charms to ensure they would soon conceive.

No Witch's broom would be complete without the sacred alder in it. Alder flutes were used to conjure elementals of air and to "whistle up the wind". Feronia, a Brighton Witch, was expert at whistling up a wind whenever she put her washing out. She loved to produce her alder flute and to demonstrate her powers, although I have also seen her do it without the flute. We used to think it was sheer coincidence, but she did it so many times to order as we watched that we had to concede that she did indeed have the power to do so.

I will finish with silver birch, which is the final and most important of all the woods in a true besom. Silver is reminiscent of the moon Goddess, and the silver birch is known as the Lady of the Woods, as are white birch and paper birch. I imagine that the name, paper birch, came about from old traditions that advocate the use of its bark to write magical inscriptions on in ritual as well as in spells. The bark of the silver birch is used in most love spells. The petitioner would write his or her heart's desire on the inside of the bark in red ink, red being symbolic of love. Old spells, for example, would run as follows: (First, name the specific Goddess and God to whom the petition is intended), then recite:

Goddess of Love, O God of desire

Bring to me sweet passion's fire

Another way was to remove the tree bark on the night of the new moon (symbolic of new beginnings), then to take it to a pure stream and throw it in, calling out:

Message of Love, I set you free

To capture a love and return him (her) to me"

If you do use the latter, do not direct it against a specific person whom you want, or you will automatically invoke the law of three against yourself. Do not play or meddle with magic. This book is not a treatise on "do it yourself magic and spells" and I have specifically refrained from publishing anything whereby one can bind another. This is but a blowing away of the popular misconceptions associated with Witchcraft, and within these pages, I have tried to show both sides of the coin; both ancient and modern aspects.

Well, we have dwelt upon sacred and revered trees, so let us now revert to the Beltane Fires, when the nine sacred woods are burned - the same as those in the famous Witch's broom and the sacred twigs that traditionally form it. These are ash, birch, yew, hazel, rowan, willow, pine, thorn and apple. Although a high profile sacred wood, oak, the king of the trees is never burnt in the balefire - and as we know, elder is specifically forbidden.

I will end on a lighter note, knowing how everybody - well, nearly everybody - loves astrology. The Druids associated birth times with sacred trees, and specific properties to these and the individuals they believed were under the associated influence. So, which tree are you?

Astrologers will notice that the dates do not link exactly to our western astrology. This is understandable, because ancient Celtic, Saxon and Norse tree astrology used a lunar calendar. In addition to the tree dates, there were extra trees for each of the two Equinoxes and the two Solstices. I mention these at the end of the list. In some cases, the same trees ruled two or more dates. You will notice that the dates roughly fit most of our familiar zodiac signs, and the given characteristics definitely fit those born at the relevant times.

The Birch - December 23 to January 20

For simplicity's sake, we will start at around the time of the secular New Year. This is ruled by the birch, which in ancient times was a symbol of tenaciousness, loyalty and ambition. Many Celtic chieftains born under this sign became great leaders.

The Rowan - January 21 to February 17

The rowan is symbolic of inventiveness and, strangely enough, of eccentricity. The rowan or mountain ash also grows in America and it was held sacred there by specific Indian tribes. Those who were eccentric, and those who were clearly deranged or even mad, were highly revered and were referred to as having been "touched by Manitou" (their God), so no one would ever harm them. According to the Celts, idealism was one of their traits.

The Ash - February 18 to March 17

These were considered sensitive souls who were spiritual and artistic. They were different to all those around them and were regarded as dreamers.

The Alder - March 18 to April 14

These people were regarded by the Celts as a complicated mixture of impatience intertwined with passion and great bravery in battle. Life itself was a veritable challenge to them.

The Willow - *April 15 to May 12*

Willow tree people, they said, had practical qualities combined with resilience and determination. They were noted for being strong willed, although moody at times. Willow people of both sexes have powerful inner emotions.

The Hawthorne - *May 13 to June 9*

The Druids regarded this group as highly talented, albeit somewhat mercurial in character. They were noted for their instinctive intuition and wisdom.

The Oak - *June 10 to July 7*

The oak is a symbol of enthusiasm, combined with determination and optimism. Those born under this sign have noble qualities and great bravery. These people could be intimidating, but graceful in defeat. The Druids had a special affection for them and their perpetual good humour.

The Holly - *July 8 to August 4*

The prickly holly tree covers those born during this period and it endows them with the gift of trustworthiness and generosity. From these, it was believed, came the religious leaders and artists such as writers and musicians.

The Hazel - *August 5 to September 1*

The Witch wand is made from the beloved hazel tree. The wand must be used according to specific ritual and timing, but if I put these into this book, we would find every reader rushing around turning people into frogs! The Celts considered these people very clever, perceptive and idealistic. They always want to be first in everything, and organisation was considered one of the qualities of the hazel person.

The Vine - *September 2 to September 29*

The vine that gave us fine wine and was so beloved of Bacchus is attributed to these people. They are methodical and analytical. They have high standards and they expect this of their partners as well. According to Druidic lore, they are highly sensitive, and they are secret romantics.

The Ivy - *September 30 to October 27*

These people have the gift of artistry combined with being extreme romantics. They are regarded as being highly sociable. Their hearts and heads argue, because they are also highly intellectual.

The Reed - *October 28 to November 24*

Now we come unto the realms of sheer mystery, for the Celts regarded these people as being highly complex and mysterious. They considered them forceful people who have a tendency to be unforgiving, but equally they were noted for their generosity.

The Elder - *November 25 to December 22*

We conclude on the most sacred elder tree, revered by Celts, Druids and Witches alike. This once more shows thirteen to be a mystical number. Elder tree people are very independent, great philosophers and they are very outspoken. They are inconstant because they adore change, and they can be foolhardy and take unnecessary risks. They are among the most eccentric people that exist, as they seem to march to a drumbeat that only they can hear.

Witches believe that the true Zodiac should number thirteen, as there are thirteen moons in a year. Astrologers sometimes try to fit various extra signs of the Zodiac in their calculations, which is why we see some of them trying to add Arachne, Ophiucus, Cetus and others to the list at various times. Other forms of astrology use multiples of thirteen and twenty-seven. This is especially the case in Vedic astrology, which uses the thirteen moons that occur in a year and the thirteen degrees that the moon moves around the ecliptic during the course of a day.

NB: The ecliptic is the apparent trajectory of the sun around the earth, and it is the line upon which the constellations of the zodiac lie.

The extra "tree days" are as follows:

Spring Equinox	21st March	oak
Midsummer Day	24th June	birch
Autumn Equinox	23rd September	hazel (in some Romano/Italian systems that derived from the original Norse ones, the tree for this Equinox was the olive)
Midwinter Day	22nd December	beech

18

Ḫunt Down and Slay the Witch

This book reflects British Witchcraft in general, but it is such a vast subject that, rather than delve into thousands of recorded incidents, I am concentrating on Sussex (the last bastion…), where I was initiated into Sussex traditions and where my wife has her roots. There is enough history here alone with which to fill this volume. So let us now continue to look at Sussex Witches of yesteryear, before we give you an update and profile of those leaders within the Witchcraft scene who are, or who have been, prominent in Sussex to the present day.

Old annals show that two Witches were on the verge of sentence of death for sorcery in the Sussex town of Rye in 1607. Part of the charge against them being that they "brewed spells to gain wealth". The local authorities insisted on their death, but a directive came from London ordering their release. This was rare, but Sussex did miraculously escape most of the persecutions.

At Broadbridge Heath Common, Anne Cruttenden, described as a hag of 80, was sentenced to death. This was for the murder of her husband, who was apparently less than half her age. This was supposedly a heinous ritual murder, after which she mutilated his body. At Horsham Assizes on the 5th of August 1776, she was charged with straightforward murder rather than with Witchcraft. By this more enlightened age, local authorities were reluctant to press charges against so-called Witches. Despite the local ruckus about her being a Witch, the authorities considered it a straightforward homicide.

The Judge, Lord Mansfield, made a profound statement after the guilty verdict was passed. He said, "Let her be drawn on a hurdle to the place of execution and there be burnt with fire until she be dead." The Horsham Diary records her public burning taking place some three days later.

Another case, also at Broadbridge Heath Common, is a murder by one Anne Whale. We find this case listed under Witchcraft, but again the Witchcraft charge was subsequently dropped in favour of a straightforward verdict of murder. The woman poisoned her husband with quicksilver (the old name for mercury). Horsham chronicles read that, "She was led to the stake, her back chained thereto, and then strangled, and after five minutes the fire was kindled, and her body consumed to ashes." At least the poor woman was accorded the mercy of strangulation before her incineration. By this time, technically speaking, nobody had been executed for Witchcraft in Sussex for many years. Jane Wenham had been the last. By now, the authorities were desperately trying to deny the power of Witchcraft, while still recognising its existence.

Note that that this enlightened attitude does not include the ecclesiastical authorities. It is not beyond the bounds that some would unhesitatingly send our people to the stake in the present day, if given the power to do so. Shortly after we entered the new millennium, a vicar in Lincoln, the Reverend Anthony Kennedy, showed his feelings – not about Witches per se, but about women in positions of power. The woman in this case wanted to enter the Xtian Church and become ordained as a minister. His reaction was that all Xtian women priests should be shot or burned at the stake as Witches! Subsequently, it was widely reported in the press that he had been severely reprimanded by his Bishop – not exactly good press for the Church. Once more, it goes to show that the leopard does not change his spots if he can help it.

As late as 1830 in Hastings, in an area known as the Rope Walk, it was said that a Witch lived. According to reports of the time, she was so hideous that none would face her. People would cross the road rather that see her malignant eyes. Her brows were described as "frosted" and with a "mutch" covering her grizzled locks. Apparently, she sported a beard, was "buckled and bent" and could only walk slowly with the aid of a crooked stick. It is written that she cussed, cursed and blasphemed as she traversed the streets. Fortunately, she was easy to spot as she walked exceedingly slow, and what's more, she wore a scarlet cloak and a tall beaver hat. Despite her unpopularity, she was far too fearful a personage for any to dare lay hands on, so she died quietly in her bed at a ripe old age. She was lucky, for mob hysteria would unhesitatingly seize, strip and shave every vestige of hair from a suspect's body while the Witch-finders would search for the "Witches Mark" - an alleged secret teat secreted somewhere on the Witches body, where the Devil suckled. Old records go into detail as to where to look, and invariably they would find it in "her most privy parts". There is little doubt that some sex-starved and lascivious members of a celibate clergy revelled in the stripping and searching of women of all ages, for what was their own personal gratification.

Females would be stripped, hoisted on pulleys above the inquisitor's heads, their bodies bent backwards so that the inquisitors could study their "secret parts". There are many recorded cases of the younger women being raped by their interrogators. One well-recorded instance was the rape of the Maid of Orleans, better known in history as Joan of Arc, by her gaolers the night before her execution.

Age was no barrier to their fiendish deprivations. The infamous *Malleus Maleficarum*, an evil treatise on Witchcraft, emanated from the twisted minds of two Dominican monks named Jacobus Sprenger and Henry Kramer. These two were appointed in 1484 by Pope Innocent VIII to cleanse the country of Witches and Sorcerers. In the same year, he proclaimed a

Papal Bull that was specifically aimed at Germany, empowering the inquisitors to seek out and burn all practitioners of the occult sciences. This included any learned men whose research did not follow the ecclesiastics' ideas. Latter years saw the mass burnings of scholars who dared to deviate from the Church's established teachings. The *Malleus Maleficarum* was ready within two years and it entered the Law books in 1486, although the first edition did not appear until 1489.

This was by no means the first edict to appear. A similar dissertation had been issued in 1464, entitled *The Fortalicium Fideo*. In 902 AD, the *Canon Escopi de Sancre* preceded this. However, the "Hammer of the Witches", as the *Malleus Maleficarum* came to be known, was more far-reaching in its intensity. Furthermore, to ensure that its message on Witch-hunting was continuous, it was subsequently translated into sixteen languages and numerous editions.

I think one should record that the outcome from this diabolical epistle was the near genocide of our people. Kramer and Sprenger are generally attributed to writing and creating this vile book on the instructions of Pope Pius VIII. However, it is Henricus Institoris and Jacobus Sprenger who created the final draft of this evil treatise, alongside what is described as a "Priest of Constance" by the name of Johannes Gremper. From their definition within this tome, I will evaluate how the Xtian priesthood learned to recognise the outward signs that a person was a Witch, and which were enough to condemn any individual.

"A gob tooth, a cast in the eye, a wart upon which hair did grow, a limp or deformity of any kind."

Woe betide the poor wretch who suffered from Downs Syndrome, who was mentally defective, deaf, dumb, blind or crippled in any way, for this was a certain path to the stake and the gallows tree. There is a most hideous case on record, not in Sussex may I add, where a poor Downs Syndrome person, who was further afflicted by being born deaf and dumb was seized by the mob, stripped and lynched in circumstances too vile to describe. We even have a record of the poor soul's name, for he was an orphan who was simply known within the village as "Dumb Jamie".

A prime target was senility. Elderly people who walked around talking to themselves, who had arthritis, were bent or broken or confused, were doomed! Those who had a kindly disposition to animals were also in danger, for the keeping of a cat or dog could equally condemn you to the fire. After all, was it not true that every Witch had a familiar?

A frog in the garden could be interpreted as the Devil in disguise, while a toad was absolute proof, for toads shun light and adore the dark. If you searched a suspect's garden, you could well find Satan hiding there in the shape of a toad. The word was, "be vigilant and do not give up the search, for the Dark One can change into many shapes and may well transform himself into a black cat, a mouse or rat or even a bird, such is his cunning". All the searcher had to do was wait for Mephistopheles to appear. There are countless cases on record where, after torture and having refused to confess, the accused has been left in her own filth for days on end. Meanwhile, the jailor watched for signs of their Infernal Master approaching to suckle. People have gone to a hideous death on the sworn testimony of witnesses who had seen a fly or bluebottle approach them, this being a clear sign of Satan visiting them in disguise.

Children were tortured to give evidence against parents, and even the young innocents themselves were not immune, although Sussex again has no recorded case as such on its conscience. Luckily, such infamous practices were thankfully absent in Protestant England as a whole. However, look to Scottish, Irish and Continental practices, and you have a completely new ball game. The Inquisition and Holy Roman Catholic Church had no such qualms, because boys and girls of five or six were burned alive at the stake, as were pregnant women. In one *Auto da Fé* held in Rome, a mother was chained to the stake and burned alive, and her newborn baby was thrown into the flames with her.

That was yesteryear, you may argue, and such Witch-hunts could not take place today. But they could, and they have. In America, there is the infamous "Kill a Witch for Christ" movement. Already, seven of our people lie stiff and cold in the ground while their self-confessed murderers sit smugly on death row awaiting their turn to die - happy in the belief that they have done God's work as laid down in Exodus XX : II. "Thou Shalt Not Suffer a Witch to Live".

This diabolical edict has sent millions to an unspeakable demise, has been used as a springboard for the Church to launch the greatest persecutions, but it is not even based on fact. The original decree was, "Thou shalt not suffer a poisoner to live". In addition, through mistranslations from Hebrew, Aramaic, Greek and Latin the word for poisoner has been corrupted to sorcerer - and ultimately to Witch. The original biblical word was *kaskagh*, which meant poisoner, but this went through many rewrites to end up with a word like *kasagn* or *kasagh*. In 1584, the historian, Reginald Scott, found that in the Jewish version of the Bible the word *kaskagh* appeared twelve times. Each had a different meaning, but not one of them had any connection whatsoever with Witches or Witchcraft. However, this was enough excuse to wipe out the opposition, and to this day, it has never been corrected by the ecclesiastical authorities.

This false and erroneous edict or quotation formed the base of the persecutions that were perpetrated by those who claimed they were obeying the Lord and doing his righteous work. They called it Holy work, but if this was not enough, they could call upon Leviticus XXI:IX which said, "A man also or woman that hath a familiar spirit or that is a wizard, shall surely be put to death: they shall stone them with stones". In addition, there is Deuteronomy XVIII:X and XI, which said, "There shall not be found among you anyone that useth divination or an enchanter or a Witch or a charmer or a consulter with familiar spirits or a necromancer". The result of this was the destruction of Witches.

How strange that God's infinite mercy is said to accept a deathbed repentance from genocidal maniacs and welcome them into the Kingdom of Heaven, alongside rapists, mass murderers, arsonists and child molesters, whereas a Pagan or Witch who has led a life that consisted of healing the sick and afflicted is destined to hell and eternal torment - and all this is down to the pure and simple reason that he or she loves Nature. One might believe in the virgin birth, resurrection and walking on water or one might follow the instruction of the Bishop of Durham and disbelieve these miracles. Whatever one sincerely believes, it is clear that Jesus Christ was a righteous and truly holy man. He was undoubtedly a great Magus and healer; also, did his holy circle not count thirteen members? Like the coven leader with his twelve disciples? Think on it. He was crucified for wholly wrong and spurious reasons, and I am certain that had he gone around Essex in 1645, using his magical powers to help and heal – even more to the point, raising the dead - it would not have been long before the infamous Mathew Hopkins would have sought him out and had him hanged. The issue of religious tolerance, it appears, comes down to a question of interpretation, and whether or not the person or persons in power are biased and bigots. Typically, it is usually people that are the problem, not necessarily the system.

Most Pagans respect and revere Jesus Christ as being enlightened and we regard him as a great Magus. Witches and practitioners of the Old Ways have no quarrel with the concepts and doctrine of Xtianity! It is what man has done with it. Man has taken a pure and gentle religion and twisted it into the most hideous genocide machine on earth, and all in the Holy name of Jesus. The Xtians are not alone in this; the Muslims are not too keen on anything that conflicts with their beliefs, either.

Can you imagine the gentle Jesus, the man who threw the moneylenders out of the Temple, standing idly by as an

Inquisitor applied a red-hot iron to the breast of a young girl. All the while reciting, "Repent in the name of the Lord, confess and your torment will end. Forget the burning still to come; it's only the torture that stops." I truly believe that these people were as depraved an example of humanity as you can get, for there are countless records of a victim, usually female, being "put to the question again" in case they had confessed merely to obtain relief from their suffering. No, the gentle Jesus would have had something to say were he to witness such inhumanity. It can only be down to the Xtian concept of man having free will that such terrible acts have been allowed to occur.

One thousand seven hundred and thirty six years were to pass before the horror ended, and one thousand and nine hundred and fifty one before we could breathe easily once more.

Sex and women seemed to worry the clergy the most, so the fair sex bore the brunt of the persecutions. Celibacy was the rule in the abbey and the priesthood, and it was vigorously enforced. The hypocrisy of this dated teaching and the sexual frustration that still builds up is clear from the stream of newspaper reports that we get, worldwide, of sexual assaults on children at the hands of some Catholic clergy. There are currently many cases pending in the USA of people suing the Church for acts of abuse committed by some of their priests.

On a lighter note, I am reminded of the sex-starved and frustrated monks who spent the whole of their lives illuminating beautiful hand crafted manuscripts. A visiting Bishop fondly enquired as to whether they were copied from the original work, only to be informed that each was copied from the previous manuscript because the original was far too precious to use. Thoughtfully, the Bishop ventured that if a spelling mistake should ever be made, then over the space of several hundred years the error would be duplicated, and was it not a good idea after the span of centuries to check the original documents?

The Abbot smiled wanly and in view of the Bishop's position bade the head monk to check. After the Abbot and Bishop had dined, the Bishop asked where the scribe was. He was found weeping copiously in the basement, and when he was brought before the Bishop and Abbot, he was asked why he (now an old man of 93) was so upset. He exclaimed, "The Bishop was right, my Lords, the word should have been "celebrate!" Well, this is only a joke, but stranger things have happened!

Today, in the 21st century, the fear still lingers, and although the Craft is now legal, we are often forced underground by prejudice. We have a case on record going back many years, of one of our people who was an assistant bank manager at one of the big five banks. Secure in his job, he made no secret of his religion and beliefs - but eighteen years on, he is still an assistant bank manager while others now have their own branch. Nothing official is on record, but two of those within the bank who are in the upper echelons confided, "At every board meeting Mr X, who is a lay preacher, mentions it would not be a good image for the bank if it became known that the manager was a Witch". This is always off the record, but the Witch's career is stunted.

Seventeen sixty-eight was regarded as an "age of enlightenment", and at this time, there were strenuous efforts to allay the fear of Witches, particularly in rural areas where old ways died hard. However, Witch-hunting and persecution persisted into the late 1800s. The Witchcraft Act was still on the statute books, despite the death penalty for practising the Craft having been abolished in 1736. Yet, John Wesley, a leading Protestant of the time, was appalled at the growing disbelief in Witchcraft and the growing indifference of the authorities. He wrote at the time:

"It is true likewise, that the English in general, and indeed most of the men of learning in Europe, have given up all accounts of Witches and apparitions as mere old wives' fables. I am sorry for it, and I willingly take this opportunity of

entering my solemn protest against this violent compliment, which so many believe the Bible pays to those who do not believe it. I owe them no such service.

I take knowledge that these are the bottom of the outcry that has been raised, and with such insolence raised through the land, in direct opposition, not only to the Bible, but also to the suffrage of the wisest and best of men in all ages and nations. They well know (whether Christians know it or not) that the giving up of (prosecuting) Witchcraft is in effect giving up the Bible. And again; with my latest breath will I bear testimony against giving up to infidels one great proof of the invisible world; I mean that of Witchcraft and apparitions confirmed by the testimony of all ages."

19

Into the Twentieth Century - The Persecutions Persist

The Witch-hunters are still out there. These zealots are now curbed by common law, but occasionally a clamour inflames authority with calamitous results. We saw this in the infamous Orkneys case, when almost every child on the Island was snatched from its parents and transported to the mainland and to social services. For months they dug, searched, interrogated, intimidated and lied, while searching for occult activity on the Isle and the Satanic "Man in Black" who was said to commune with the children in secret rituals.

How they came to be searching for a "Man in Black" in the 20th century is frankly amazing. Aeons ago, this title referred to a "Summoner", who liaised between covens and who would have been the only point of contact between them. Simple research would have shown that four centuries ago, a craft edict was in place that stated, "No coven shall know where the next abide". The lack of contact between covens was a safeguard, because if a Witch was caught and tortured, he could not give the others away. The only person who could link all the covens in the area was the Man in Black, the War-look, and he was capable of evading capture because he was fit and he had good legs and a fast horse; he would have known every nook and cranny of the terrain.

It was not long before the Orkney authorities uncovered "evidence" that there was such a person, and gleefully they gathered with tipstaff and police, social workers and the press to expose the much-publicised "satanic ring" that they had so skillfully uncovered, thereby to justify their high-handed actions. Once they were certain that they had located this person, they pounced. They went to his door, only to find it opened by a gentle, black-garbed elderly priest who ran the local Sunday school. Did they admit defeat? Did they return the infants? Not a bit of it, they dragged their heels for months, vainly searching for a vestige of Witchcraft and Satanic ritual without success. They even tried to induce the children into making false statements. This performance was so reminiscent of the dark ages when children could send their parents to the gallows tree on a mere word. Eventually justice prevailed and the High Court ordered the return of the children. The children were ultimately reunited with their parents. The poor children were left traumatised and psychologically scarred from the experience of being snatched away from their homes in the middle of the night, delivered into the hands of zealous social workers and left in limbo for months on end.

Much later, the authorities issued a statement to the effect that the practice might not exist. This followed a profound statement from a leading child psychiatrist that, in his opinion there was not even a vestige of truth in the allegations. He did this after studying countless cases, not one of which had been substantiated. In fairness, one must add that the national press reported the facts in full, and the authorities were left with plenty of egg on their faces as a result.

In England, the death penalty for the practice of sorcery was repealed in 1736. In France, this happened in 1745, in Germany in 1775, in Switzerland in 1782, in Italy in 1791, in Poland in 1793 and Spain - reluctant to the last - as late as 1812. America, home of the free, repealed their act in 1781, although it had been mildly relaxed after the notorious Salem Witch trials. Holland had led the way in 1610. By a strange anomaly of fate, Scotland, which had been fanatical in its persecutions, preferring the stake to the rope, followed in 1727. Let me throw a small statistic into the equation and analyse a few facts. It is not feasible to record the Statutes of Repeal for each individual country, so I will record for posterity the following here:

9 GEO. 11, c5 AD 1736. (Ad verbatim)

An Act to repeal the Statute made in the First Year of the Reign of King James the First, intituled, An Act against Conjuration, Witchcraft, and dealing with evil and wicked Spirits, except so much thereof as repeals an Act of the Fifth Year of the Reign of Queen Elizabeth, against Conjurations, Inchantments, and Witchcrafts, and to repeal an Act passed in the Parliament of Scotland in the ninth Parliament of Queen Mary, intituled, Anentis Witchcrafts, and for punishing such Persons as pretend to exercise or use any kind of Witchcraft, Sorcery, Inchantment, or Conjuration.

Be it enacted by the King's most Excellent Majesty, by and with the Advice and Consent of the Lords Spiritual and Temporal, and Commons, in this present Parliament assembled, and by the Authority of the same, That the Statute made in the First year of the Reign of King James the First, intituled, An Act against Conjuration, Witchcraft, and dealing with evil and wicked Spirits, shall, from the Twenty-fourth day of June next, be repealed and utterly void, and of none effect (except so much thereof as repeals the Statute made in the Fifth Year of the Reign of Queen Elizabeth) intituled, An Act against Conjurations Inchantments, and Witchcrafts.

And be it further enacted by the Authority aforesaid, that from and after the said Twenty-fourth Day of June, the Act passed in the Parliament of Scotland, in the Ninth Parliament of Queen Mary, intituled, Anentis Witchcrafts, shall be, and is hereby repealed.

And be it further enacted, That from and after the said Twenty-fourth Day of June, no Prosecution, Suit, or

Proceeding, shall be commenced or carried on against any Persons or Persons for Witchcraft, Sorcery, Inchantment, or Conjuration, of for charging another with any such Offence, in any Court whatsoever in Great Britain.

And for the more effectual preventing and punishing of any Pretences to such Arts or Powers as are before mentioned, whereby ignorant persons are frequently deluded and defrauded; be it further enacted by the Authority aforesaid, That if any Person shall, from and after the said Twenty fourth Day of June, pretend to exercise or use any kind of Witchcraft, Sorcery, Inchantment, or Conjuration, or undertake to tell fortunes, or pretend, from his or her Skill or Knowledge in any occult or crafty Science, to discover where or inn what manner any Goods or Chattles, supposed to have been stolen or lost, may be found, every Person, so offending, being thereof lawfully convicted on Indictment or Information in that Part of Great Britain called England, or on Indictment or Libel, in that Part of Great Britain called Scotland, shall, for every such offence, suffer Imprisonment by the Space of one whole Year without Bail or Mainprize, and once in every Quarter of the said Year, in some Market Town of the proper Country, upon the Market Day, there stand openly on the Pillory by the Space of One hour, and also shall (if the Court by which such Judgement shall be given shall think fit) be obliged to give Sureties for his or her good Behaviour, in such Sum, and for such Time, as the said Court shall judge proper, according to the Circumstances of the Offence, and in such case shall be further imprisoned until such Sureties be given.

[Acts of Parliament, pr. By Watkins, vol xiii, p. 9]

If we take the first recorded Witch trial from old records as being 1209, then Witches suffered the supreme penalty for 527 years in England, 536 years in France and 610 years in Spain, before humanity prevailed and Xtian fervour in their annihilation subsided. Ireland has never (to my knowledge) repealed the Act. It is a matter of national shame that the last execution by burning took place in my mother's lifetime, for she died in her late nineties. The last Irish Witch was Bridget Cleary and the year 1895. This has to be an all time record for the Church, as Ireland tops the league with 686 years of persecution and superstition; almost into the 20th century!

The burning of Bridget was instigated by her husband, who believed that his real wife had been abducted by fairies and that the woman who shared his bed was a substitute. Bridget had recently given birth to a baby, and from contemporary reports, her behaviour was certainly odd. It had all the symptoms of post-natal depression. Her husband and his neighbours set her alight in his kitchen, then waited for his real wife to appear on a white horse at dawn, as they believed would happen. They all went to prison and her husband emigrated to the USA on his release from jail.

To this day, the story is recalled in Ireland by virtue of a children's game called "it" when the victim is taunted by the cry of:

"Be you a Witch or be you a fairy
or be you the wife of Michael McLeary"

In theory, this was the end of overt punishment for a practitioner in Great Britain, for it was written into the statute books shortly afterwards:

"No Prosecution, Suit or Proceeding shall be commenced or carried out against any person or persons for Witchcraft, Sorcery, Inchantment (Enchantment) or Conjouration (Conjuration), or for charging another with any such offence, in any Court whatsoever in Great Britain."

The Witchcraft act still existed though, but two memorable cases were to follow that lead to its eventual complete abolition, and both of these took place in my lifetime. The first to hit the courts was in 1930.

When Princess Margaret was born on the 21st of August in that year, the Daily Mail had the bright idea of asking the astrologer, R. H. Napier, to write up her horoscope. This was the first time that astrology appeared in a newspaper. The overwhelming response from the public led the editor to ask Napier if he could produce an astrology column that could appeal to the public. Napier realised that the only thing that could be done was sun sign astrology. This is because the dates for the sun's entry into each sign are regular (although not completely so) from one year to the next. No reader was likely to know their moon, ascendant or planetary positions, but anyone could look up the sun sign dates in the paper. From that moment onwards, the Mail carried a horoscope column, and in time, almost every newspaper and women's magazine joined in.

Mr Napier went on to make further Royal predictions, the accuracy of which antagonised the establishment. Since then, astrologers have been discouraged from making unpleasant remarks or predictions about the Royals and celebrities, not by the newspapers themselves but by the astrological associations. Some astrology organisations regard it as immoral for an astrologer to write about a person who is in no position to defend himself. Indeed, some years ago, the Faculty of Astrological Studies threw one well-known astrologer out after she made predictions for Princess Diana in The Sun. Some astrologers ignore this edict and still write about Royals and celebrities, but the jury is still out on whether it is right to do so or not.

Napier stated the Princess would be denied marrying the man she loved and that she would ultimately make a loveless marriage. He predicted she would bear two heirs, be divorced and that scandal would follow her. A Mrs. Campbell took up the challenge and charged Napier under the still un-repealed Witchcraft Act! This was despite the fact that Napier was an astrologer rather than a Witch – and all this as late as 1930! Another 21 years would pass before the Old Religion of England would be restored to the people.

Therefore, a simple man who had dared to make a public prophecy was now to face the wrath of the courts, and none would defend him. Barrister after barrister in succession refused the case, as not one of them wished to jeopardise their career by being seen to champion an astrologer. R. H. Napier had been abandoned by the legal system! It seemed that in 20th century England, an astrologer could be called a Witch. Then the so-called Witch would be tried yet again - thus rolling back 300 years of history.

As Napier awaited judicial might, a leading barrister stepped out of the shadows and stated that he would take the case. This knight in shining armour was one Christmas Humphries, a practising Buddhist, who was not influenced by Xtian fervour. The case was sensational, and it culminated in victory for Napier, who was acquitted of all charges. Xmas Humphries went on to become a High Court Judge, his career made overnight by his brilliant defence. During the next 50 years, he acquired a reputation as a humane and merciful man. Humphries died in 1983. Pagans worldwide will always remember him for his heroic stance in their defence.

Before moving on to the second and even more fascinating case, there are a couple of points worth noting. While this book focuses on Witchcraft, it is a fact that Witches are not the only ones who are on the receiving end of bigotry. As you have already seen, astrologers hardly fared any better, but even today, Spiritualists can suffer from the same kind of prejudice and bigotry.

Spiritualism is a recognised religion in this country, and its ministers perform baptisms, marriages, funeral services and so on. Some churches are Xtian Spiritualist while others are simply Spiritualist. If you want to see the same blind and insane bigotry that I talk about here coming from a minister of the Xtian Church, read "Pathway to Spirit" by Ann Caulfield (*Zambezi Publishing*). The story in that book happened within the last decade!

Another point is that, although the Witchcraft Act has been repealed, the Fraudulent Mediums Act and the Vagrancy Act have not. These still groups such people as Spiritualists, astrologers, Tarot readers and the like with beggars!

The Last Bastion

The second case that shamed the nation took place in 1943, and it involved a medium by the name of Helen Duncan. This was carried out under the antiquated Witchcraft Act of 1735 and the Vagrancy Act of 1824. The latter Act came into being after the Napoleonic wars, when poverty was so rife that people did anything, including offering fortune-telling in the streets, to make a few pennies. Some of these fortune-tellers were fakes and they became such a nuisance that the whole business was banned – and still is, in public places. A friend recently told me of a man who gives Tarot readings in a car at a weekly boot sale. Someone will soon have to tell this person that he is breaking the law, before he finds himself "up before the Beak"!

Let us now return to the poor Spiritualist and her story.

Helen Duncan was not a Witch, but a spiritual medium. A Spiritualist's job is "proof of survival", which means proving that the soul lives on when a person dies. The fact that the messages that are channelled comfort the bereaved or even occasionally predict the future is totally beside the point. In addition to being able to produce ectoplasm, (this is not as uncommon as one might think), Helen Duncan gave uncanny insights into what was going on in the Second World War. This was not her intention. Her job was to pass on messages from those who had died. Often these messages describe the moment of death – which anybody who knows even the most basic facts of Spiritual mediumship will understand as a perfectly normal part of a medium's work. In the case of Helen Duncan, someone told the Ministry of Defence that she "knew too much" about things that it wanted kept under wraps.

The event that led to her arrest and subsequent imprisonment was the sinking of HMS Barham in a ferocious naval engagement. The Barham went down with astronomical loss of life at a time when the war was going very badly. It was thought that news of yet another disaster would lower public morale even further, so the official line was that news of the sinking of the Barham must be withheld at all costs. This so-called "Witch" was considered to be undermining the war effort. She knew about the sinking of the Barham because she was being contacted by desperate sailors who had gone down with the doomed ship!

Relatives of those sailors attended her sittings, confident in their belief that their loved ones were safe and well, because they had not yet officially been told that their loved ones were in fact dead. Helen Duncan passed on messages from the recently deceased relatives long before the ship was officially announced as lost. The news got out and the authorities were swift to react. They commissioned an undercover investigation to be conducted into her sittings and séances.

Within days, a police officer stated he had enough evidence to charge her with the Vagrancy Act and for good measure, the Witchcraft Act of 1735. This arrest occurred, despite the decree that came into force in 1736, which clearly stated that "prophesying" was not a crime. More to the point, mediums such as Helen Duncan do not prophesy anything, but this was also ignored. The authorities used the excuse that taking payment for doing "prophesying" was illegal. It was not, as long as the prophesying did not take place in public, so they got that wrong as well. The trial was a national farce, and even the Prime Minister, Winston Churchill, poured scorn on the outcome. This is not particularly surprising, because Winston Churchill himself was an excellent medium, in addition to being a Druid!

Helen Duncan was found guilty in 1944 and sentenced to nine months' imprisonment, this being sufficient time to keep her out of circulation and thus of doing anything else that might hinder the war effort. After she was released, she sank into poverty and obscurity, and she died in 1956.

There have been attempts to charge people since 1951, but these have not been successful. Whenever there have been accusations of Witchcraft, they usually come under legislation on completely separate matters such as intimidation. One case of this occurred when a miscreant was charged at Salisbury

County Court in 1976. He was accused of bewitching a neighbour by posting him a chicken's heart pierced with pins and needles "to work evil and malefice against the victim".

Recent legislation has afforded us greater protection, of which the most notable is "The Universal Declaration of Human Rights". This preceded the repeal of the Witchcraft Act by some three years, coming into force on December 10th 1948. The most notable Statute of this Act was Article 18, which declared:

"Everyone has the right to freedom of thought, conscience and religion; this right includes freedom to change his religion or belief, and freedom, either alone or in community with others and in public or private, to manifest his religion or belief in teaching, practice, worship and observance".

Clearly, this helped to pave the way for the restoration of our liberties, whereby we would have the freedom and right to worship the God and Goddess of Nature as we had before the coming of the Xtians. Theoretically, we can do this without fear of persecution and prosecution. The repeal of the Act in 1951 was welcomed by all pagans, and it reads as follows:

"The following enactments are hereby repealed, that is to say: -

The Witchcraft Act of 1735 in force

Section four of the Vagrancy Act, 1824, as far as it extends to persons purporting to act as spiritualistic mediums or to exercise powers of telepathy, clairvoyance or other similar powers, or to persons who, in purporting so to act or to exercise such powers, use fraudulent devices.

Those who happen to be astrologers, mediums, clairvoyants, palmists, card readers and so forth call this "The Fraudulent Mediums Act". They are very much in its favour, as long as it is used in cases where true fraud has been carried out. They do exist, but the true professionals have no time for frauds because they bring genuine work into disrepute.

The editor of this book is an ex-President of the British Astrological and Psychic Society, and an ex-Chair of the Advisory Panel in Astrological Education. In this capacity, she contacted Brussels to check on any EU laws that might prevent astrologers, Witches, palmists, Pagans and others from pursuing their interests. Brussels wrote back and said that there was no problem. Thank goodness for small mercies!

20

The Inquisition is Alive and Well in the Vatican

When the law sees fit - or perhaps I should amend this profound statement to read, "When the Government sees fit" - then it will ride roughshod over the law in order to force its will. We have seen this in recent years with the unlawful use of the "Parliament Act", which can only be used for "dire emergency", which is usually interpreted as an Act of War. However, we have seen this violated when a democratic defeat has been inflicted on the Government, when in a fit of pique, the obscure "Parliament Act" has been used as a big stick.

Another example is the eroding of our rights. These have been enshrined in the Magna Carta since 1215, although there is but a mere shred left nowadays. Similarly, the further rights afforded to the people from 1688 in a Bill of Rights under Constitutional Law Six; the very existence of this Act was denied when the Government wanted to make sweeping and both illegal and unlawful amendments to Common Law to suit their particular purpose at the time. Is it little wonder, then, after over 600 years of the gallows, the pyre, the inquisition and the legalised Witch-hunters, that we still cannot feel completely safe in our beds at night? Where will we stand if we are taken into the final stage of integration into Europe? Many countries are under the domination of the Catholic Church. Will the theoretical anti-xenophobic laws protect us then?

What is not generally known is that the inquisition has never been abolished. It was abolished in Spain in 1908 during the period of Napoleon's occupation, but not in the Vatican. It is alive and well there, and it is still an integral part of the hierarchy. The office of the Inquisition still resides in a corner of the Vatican; all that has changed is its name. It is now known as "The Department of the Congregation for the Doctrine of the True Faith", but internally, it is referred to by all and sundry as the "Department of the Inquisition", or just "The Inquisition". It even has a "Grand Inquisitor", who is the supreme head of its continued functioning. This is currently Cardinal Joseph Ratzinger. So, can we ever feel safe while the terror merely sleeps?

We have had our champions who avidly upheld all human rights without fear or favour. One such was Lord Hailsham when he was the supreme Law Lord. I had many a conversation with him in days gone by, and I sadly miss his wit and sincerity. We would argue amicably at the Wig and Pen club, which is a Fleet Street rendezvous for lawyers and writers. In 1979 in a historic case, a leading High Court Judge declared in his summing up:

"It is sometimes forgotten that the common law of England for centuries has taken the view that it is an offence for anyone to stir up hostility against any section of the Sovereigns subjects."

So why were Witches throughout the Continent persecuted so perniciously, why should a nature loving Religion whose adherents lived their lives in harmony with the Earth Spirits and who loved the Old Gods, be attacked with the vehemence that they were? The reasons are legion.

The Xtian Church would brook no opposition. They were right and everyone else was wrong. That included other Xtians, if of a different persuasion to their own brand of thinking - of course, depending on who was in the ascendancy at the time. It was by no means a one-sided matter, because if it wasn't Catholics burning Protestants then it was Protestants burning

Catholic heretics. The common denominator to these warring faiths was the unilateral elimination of Witches - and they all but succeeded over the years.

The Church was essentially Patriarchal and the Old Religion was Matriarchal. This does not mean that it was one-sided, for both God and Goddess ruled equally, dividing the year up between them. The Goddess is identified essentially with spring, summer and the more stern aspect of the God with autumn and winter. The Lord Cernunnos (Kernunnos) was the God of Death and of Resurrection, and the Goddess Ceridwen, the harbinger of new life and creation in the cycle of life everlasting. Reincarnation is an essential tenet of the Pagan beliefs.

On a historical note, strangely enough, reincarnation was also once taught by the Xtian faith. The problem that they found was that the peasantry kept to the old ways and converts to the new faith were not increasing, so a new strategy had to be used. It was decided that salvation and life everlasting would henceforth replace the doctrine of life after life. The Church Council of Constantinople met in 553 AD and issued a Bull, proclaiming further belief in reincarnation henceforth would be deemed heresy. So, Church doctrine and ecclesiastical law said one thing on Monday and another by Tuesday. Such was the hypocrisy of the time.

James the First of England, who was also James the Sixth of Scotland, reviled Witches, sorcerers, fortune-tellers and Wise Women. I personally think he just hated women, because most of his edicts seem to be directed against the fair sex. He revised the Bible in 1603 to create what is known to this day as the "King James" version, altering original references to suit his own outlook.

A typical example is the story of King Saul, who sought out a famous woman who lived in the land of Endor. This particular woman was noted for her wisdom and her uncanny ability to solve problems. The mighty King undertook a long journey to seek her wisdom, for such was her knowledge that she was recognised throughout the known world as the "Wise Woman of Endor". "Wise!" James exclaimed, "If she is indeed so clever, then this ability has been delivered to her from Satan himself, so take out the pen and let's revise history once more." The result is that the 1602 Bible reads "Wise Woman of Endor" while the 1603 version reads "Witch of Endor". Women, wisdom and wickedness definitely go hand in hand – he forgot sex!

Joan Usbarne was accused in 1572 of bewitching cattle to death. She was tried and found guilty by Judges J. Southcote and T. Gawdy at the Sussex Lent Assizes. She was fortunate, as she was only was sentenced to one year in prison, during which time she was to be placed in the pillory four times. She would wear a notice proclaiming her a Witch and the crime she had been convicted of, "And there she shall be exposed to the mob for a period of six hours on each of the four appearances".

There are many records of people placed in the pillory being killed through the excesses of the mob. Those placed in the stocks were treated more as figures to be mocked and pelted with filth and refuse. The stocks were often filled with drunks and those convicted of lesser crimes. The locals looked upon them as sport and someone that they could publicly humiliate. Those in the pillory could be stoned, which was a far worse punishment. The sentence often carried the further punishment of having one's ears cut off in public by the executioner, and ones nose slit and a hot iron applied.

There is on record a remarkable case where the culprit, who was a forger, had his ears removed and his nose slit. He then let off such a piteous yell when the red-hot branding iron was applied that the hangman/torturer stepped back in alarm. He beseeched the mob to the effect that he should not continue the punishment, to which end it is recorded that the onlookers were so moved to pity they demanded the man be freed - and he was.

In 1575, the same two Judges presiding at the Sussex Lent Assizes, sent one Margaret Cooper, the wife of a surgeon of "Kerdeforde" to the Gallows. Her crime was "bewitching to death" a man named Henry Stoner, one other man of the parish plus a local woman. In this case, the hanging did take place. She was taken in a cart and hanged on a "three legged gallows" (known as the three-legged mare). She slowly strangled when the cart was led off, leaving her dangling. There is an old woodcut in existence showing the execution, and the event is on record. There are no records existing of the village of Kerdeforde, and one can only presume that it disappeared, along with numerous other little hamlets, when the Black Death devastated Sussex.

1591 saw an unfortunate case when a spinster from the village of Mayfilde (Mayfield) was accused of "bewitching to death an ox valued at four shillings, the property of Magin Fowle, a gentleman of the parish". She appeared before the same Judges and was sentenced to one year (and the statutory pillory). We do not know the details, but the old records say *"mortua est in custodia"* (died in custody).

I found this repeatedly in old records. One entry in Essex alone showed 33 people languishing in gaol on charges of Witchcraft and sorcery. The records state, "Anne Cooper, Rose Halleybread, Elizabeth Gibson and Mary Cooke, these beinge accused for sorcery and Witchcrafte are dead in gaol." The subsequent coroner's inquest records Rose Halleybread, aged 65, died after a "visitation by God". Elizabeth Gibson aged 40, wife of Thomas Gibson; Mary Cooke, 60 and Joan Anne Cooper, 80 all died from the same thing – a visitation by God.

We now go back to 1592, when Agnes Mauser went on trial at the Sussex Summer Assizes. The accusation is not clear, but *"Cul mo incantacone"* is mentioned in the indictment, so we can only presume she was caught making spells or working verbal magic. She got a year (and pillory) from Judges Clarke and Pickering, who found her guilty as charged.

Joan a'Wood was sent before a grand jury at the "Sessions of the Peace" at Seaford in 1577, and the testimony below is recorded as being *"venefica"* (true).

"1578 saw two men charged, answering to the name of Tree, a bailiff of Lewes, Sussex, and his companion one Smith of Chinting. They were sent to the interrogators to be examined for "touching conjuration" and in 1571 a woman suspected of Witchcraft, who it appears was old and feeble to such an extent that she was supported by the parish, was tossed out of the poorhouse and dragged forcibly to the outskirts of the town and banished. Old almshouse records refer to her as "Mother Margery" and state she was a most reprehensible woman, and that one of her alleged victims, while having been bewitched by her, had committed suicide by hanging himself."

One extract details her crimes as, "Such as any Christian harte would abhore to here spoken of, much less used." It is curious to recall that part of the so-called evidence against her was the "discoverie of a goode quantitie of rawe beff that was gon rotten". This, it was decreed, was the reason for the bewitched man to take a rope and hang himself. It was quite clear that as the meat decayed so did the victim; one can imagine them examining the body some days later and confirming that decomposition had set in, thus proving them right.

At least old Mother Margery was lucky to have escaped with her life, albeit she had been banished; just across the border, innocents were being murdered on any pretext. This again shows how much more tolerant Sussex was, for it is a certainty that across the border, she would have ended up at the end of a hempen rope or worse. The last entry on this case a few days later states, "the towne of Rye hath no more trouble now the Witch hath been banished from the poorhouse".

By the 1600s, the persecutions increased in intensity and the local and ecclesiastical authorities now started to administer summary justice. In rural areas mob rule prevailed, often on just the slightest whisper of Witchcraft. Frequently, the local dignitaries would bid the mob to do their work for them or at best, they would turn a blind eye. Such was another case at Rye in 1645. In that year, Bruff and Anne Howsell were suspected of being witches. Upon complaint being laid, the Mayor of Rye, and a number of councillors ordered that they be put to the ordeal of water by being swum.

In public, they were stripped naked and each bound with her right thumb to her left toe and her left thumb to her right toe and then cast into the pond. The result is not recorded in official records but the case is well known locally: a broadsheet that was published some years afterwards refers to them as having failed to survive the ordeal. This is not surprising, as the usual belief was that if she sank, she drowned and if she swam, she was declared guilty without any further evidence being lawfully required. Escaping drowning meant being hanged.

There are records where the swimming was conducted with full ritual being observed when the ecclesiastics were the accusers. Everything was the same as above except that, after the strapping and binding, the accused was sprinkled with holy water and allowed to kiss a crucifix. A rope was then tied around the waist, and at a distance of two "ells" from the body a knot was tied, and the person would be thrown into deep water, the body of the accused had to sink the depth of the knot to stand a chance of being found innocent. Priests conducted the ordeal.

Mass was said to the accompaniment of prayers and psalms. It was mandatory for the accused to confess his or her sins before the ordeal, as there was little chance of surviving. Then, they would call upon God to prove their innocence. Followed by vows upon relics and bones of departed saints, it was all designed to impress the onlookers with the power of the Xtian Church.

1645 saw another case against Witchcraft unfold in Rye, this time the accused were two women by the names of Susanna Swapper and Anne Taylor: their crime was, "That they did councell with spirits" Both the accused received the death sentence. Just before her execution, it is recorded that Susanna "did plead her belly" and was reprieved. Pregnant women were never hanged or burnt in England, as even the authorities here would not allow an unborn and innocent child to die. The Church on the continent unhesitatingly burned them, with one diabolical case of a mother giving birth as she was consumed by fire. Anne Taylor was not pregnant and a date for her execution by hanging was duly set, but she was lucky to be included in a general pardon of felons granted by the reigning monarch in a fit of clemency. At this point, they both disappear from history.

The Last Bastion

Graham King of the Museum of Witchcraft,
in front of an exhibit.

Doreen Valente's altar of High Magic.

Ralph and Audrey Harvey renewing their handfasting vows at an autumn equinox ritual at Stonehenge.

Audrey's initiation into Egyptian Mysteries and ritual anointing by the Honourable Olivia Robertson.

The original temple at the Centre for Pagan Studies at Maresfield. Ralph and Audrey were handfasted there.

Invoking the Gods.

The Last Bastion

Ritual consecration of the wine, using a chalice originally belonging to Sir Francis Dashwood of the Hellfire Club.

Audrey performing sacred Isian rites in the adoration of the Goddess Isis.
Huntingdon Castle in Clonegal, Wexford, Eire.

More Trials and Tribulations

A Witch by the name of Juliana Curtis was tried at Crawley in Sussex in 1577. A spinster of the Parish, she was accused of bewitching Dionisia Snell to death, by causing her to "languish till she did die". Also tried in that year was another woman (name unknown), who did bewitch two pigs valued at ten shillings, the chattels of Richard Roose.

Two Witches by the names of Nanny Smart of Hurstpierpoint and Dame Jackson of West Chiltingdon are recorded as having practised the Art from the late 1800s until the First World War with impunity, because no one ever laid a complaint against them. As we entered the 20th century, the Witchcraft Act had not been invoked for years; it is a pity that this record was despoiled in the 20th century with the 1930 trial of Napier and the travesty of justice with the wartime trial of the medium, Helen Duncan.

In the same year of 1577 in Sussex at the summer sessions, Margaret Barrowe, a spinster of Chayley (Chailey) went on trial for bewitching Isabella Marten, wife of John Martin, who languished until the day of taking this inquisition.

The Sussex Lent Sessions 1580, held at East Grinstead. Ursula Welfare; a spinster of Alfriston, Sussex was accused thus: "That she did bewitch unto death one sow valued at three shillings and four pence, plus eight chickens and two hens valued at three shillings, they being the goods and chattels of

John Blunt." At the same sessions, an unknown Witch who lived at Berwick in Sussex was also tried for "bewitching unto death two Oxen valued at six shillings, the property of William Suzan."

The Sussex Summer Sessions at Horsham in 1579 saw Alice Steadman, wife of John Steadman, a "Wodbrooker", accused of bewitching two cows belonging to William Squirior valued at four shillings and a steer valued at thirteen shillings and four pence. "And that she did also bewitch another cow of William Squirior, valued at 40 shillings, which cattle did calf."

That same year, one of the most dreadful cases of all took place, when Elizabeth Winters went to the stake at Horsham for the crime of "bewitching unto death her husband Mark Winters, who died most horribly as the fire burned slow". It is the only case on record of a Witch burning taking place in Sussex. There is an element of doubt here though, and there is confusion as to whether we owe more to broadsheets of the period embellishing the facts. The records at Horsham museum show quite distinctly that the woman was strangled before the pyre was lit; but yet again, this could be a sanitising of the most barbaric execution of a woman ever to have taken place in Sussex.

Not only is there doubt as to what did happen, but also doubt as to whether another record of a public burning of a woman in that same year by the name of Whalley is that of the same person. My conclusion is that for Elizabeth Winter it should read Elizabeth Whalley, for there was only one burning recorded in 1579 at Horsham, and this was for the crime of poisoning her husband; this event is well recorded. Killing one's husband was considered to be an act of treason, but at the lower end of the scale - hence its name *"petite traison"* or "little treason", a crime always punished by burning. Elizabeth Whalley was definitely strangled at the stake before the flames were ignited. There is no mention at this point in the final records of her being executed or accused of sorcery, strangely enough, only of poisoning.

A further case is recorded in Horsham, years later in 1680. We found records of Alice Nash being charged with the unlawful killing by the use of Witchcraft of Elizabeth and Anne Slater. In 1654, there was another case recorded of one Jane Shoutbridge, also recorded as Jane Shoubridge of Witham. She was accused of using the Art Magical and bewitching one Mary Muddle, a spinster of the said parish, together in an unholy alliance with one Clementine Shoubridge, also of Witham. Therefore, we must presume that the two were related and that the correct name should be Shoubridge. It is a strange case and it was pursued through the courts relentlessly, with them also being charged jointly and severally of bewitching and enchanting one Benjamin Caught. Fortunately, we were now entering the Age of Reason, and both the Witches were eventually acquitted.

All allegations of Witchcraft were meticulously recorded, so there are six cases of "black magic" recorded as "Witchcraft" in the 1579 presentments for the practice of sorcery. One was of Agnes Hyberden, who was recorded as "suspected by her neighbours of being a Witch. "There be common fame that the wife of John Ditches is vehemently suspected of being a Witch also." A Mother Digby of East Harting was accused, but no record exists of the accusation being taken any further. Recorded in the same presentment is an entry to the effect that Agnes Gunnell of Westbourne in Sussex was accused in 1574 of using sorcery for one Elizabeth Knight. The same Elizabeth confessed to this, as the sorcery was intended for the termination of at least one illegitimate pregnancy.

It is recorded in the Horsham archives that the elimination of an unwanted foetus could be attributed to Witchcraft, although a straightforward albeit illegal abortion seems more likely. Found guilty, Agnes was excommunicated from the Church in 1580, but was absolved the self same year! There is yet another record of a Dame Jackson being accused of Witchcraft, but no record of her being sent for trial or ever being tried.

The records also show a case dating from 1603, where Bury churchwardens report, "Old Mother Scutt is reported as being a Witch and assisting the village girls to not be delivered of child". That same year, we find Widow Lickfold being accused of the practice of black magic, sorcery and the use of Witchcraft. It was said, "That she takes upon her the art to find lost things by the use of magic and does deceive the people, and being altogether ignorant, practices physic and surgery in the town of Horsham to the hurt and danger of many".

This is followed by another case in Sompting in 1605. A local butcher by the name of George Sowton was arraigned for practising Witchcraft inasmuch as, "he did use the Arts Magical". Unusually, he appears in further records some nineteen years later in 1624, and 20 years later in 1625 for "supplying a magic bottle of water and a paper with crosses on it to a local Sompting woman to hang about her neck".

There are many strange aspects of this unique Sompting case, which once more reflects the leniency afforded to Witches in Sussex. The outcome of this was as follows:

"What George Sowton did do that one Anthony Nashe and his wife of Yapton, Sussex and a helpful neighbour, one John Walters of Felpham in the same county did do, it be recommended that he be presented before the court for the offence."

It is further reported in the annals of the time that, "The butcher George Sowton as of 1625 had been excommunicated these two or three years, while a George Sowton of Sompting did in 1642 sign an Oath of Protestation – and a convert to the Xtian ways." Was this a case of a son of the renegade George going against the ways of his father? We will never know… and the Sompting case remains a mystery.

Two unusual Sussex Witches were Dame Neave and Witch Killick of Crowborough, who openly practised their Craft and were purported to be expert at lifting the spells of other Witches. By all accounts, they made a fair living, and as was so common to Sussex, they were never prosecuted.

In all the above cases, a strong part of the defence was that the Witches were entitled to practice their craft as they were licensed under the Physicians Act of 1540. This act absolved them from being prosecuted for the practice of Witchcraft. (The same act was also a great help to physicians, herbalists and natural therapists who used astrological knowledge.) The Sussex courts upheld this plea! This once again showed the amazing independence that has characterised this great county as the only place in the entire British Isles to licence Witches – a percentage, of course, going to the church, which obligingly turned a blind eye.

Even so, old laws were occasionally enforced and when one looks back, some of these become farcical. The Morning Post reports the arrest of two suspected Witches in 1780. They were publicly weighed against the church Bible and they were found to be heavier. This was considered a guaranteed sign of their innocence, because true Witches were obviously as light as a feather, so that they could fly! Naturally, an Xtian Bible would also be heavier than they were. They were both freed.

Looking for the moment outside the astonishingly lenient attitude to Sussex Witches, other miscreants fared decidedly worse. Hanging was the usual punishment, but out of the whole of Sussex, Horsham has the most terrible reputation for cruelty. This applied to bull baiting, executions, bear baiting and public mutilations. All miscreants convicted ended up at Hangman's Fair or Hang Town as Horsham was called, for execution, whipping or worse.

Horsham incidentally was one of the few towns where wife-selling continued right up to 1895, and it enjoys the unenviable reputation of being the last town to outlaw wife sales. On one occasion towards the end of this era, a man led his wife to the auction block on a rope halter (as was required by law). When the woman was sold for a gallon of ale and ten shillings, the crowd stoned the erring husband while he hastened off with his money. Changes in public opinion led the authorities in Horsham to outlaw such sales. It is amazing that such an evil law was still in existence up until the turn of the 20th century. It would be 1930 before all women over the age of 21 threw off the stigma of being the chattel of a father or husband and ultimately received the vote!

There are references to an Anne Therston of Holland (Halland) sometimes referred as Great Halland/Holland, who was charged with entertaining two evil spirits, one in the likeness of a bird and the other as a mouse. However, we cannot conclusively prove it was Halland in Sussex. This incident took place in approx 1645. Also indicted were an Anne Cate of Holland/Halland and an Anne Cade. While there is no proof of the exact area, it is worthy of note. Also recorded is one Dame Prettylegs of Albourne in Sussex, described as the "Witch of Albourne", but there is no record of her ever being charged. Both an Anne Cade or Anne Cate (the records conflict on the spelling) and Anne Therston, however, were accused of bewitching to death a butcher and a yeoman.

The evidence in some of these cases seems incredible by today's standards. I have selected two extracts from trials, keeping to the original wording as a blatant example of what the testimony was like and what was believed. I have not been able to locate the full trial records of Cade and Therston, but I did discover that the evidence was preposterous. As an example of the kind of thinking that ruled in those days, I have selected the Mai versus Wods trial as an example. However, if you really want to wade through the vast volumes of the Margaret Mixter versus De Shotley trial, I can recommend it as fascinating, albeit macabre, reading, but it is too long to record here.

16th Century Depositions: British Museum. Add. MS 27402, fos. 104-121

"Elizabeth Mai testatur that the 3rd night she seemed very sick and seed to have very strange fits and desired to ruck downe or lye downe and such fits she had seuerall nights and after they perceived her in those fits immediately this informant

*searched her and cold playnely peceive that her teats wear
newly sucked and that she wiped of the fresh blot fro the ends
of her teats wth her finger, and she confessed that one Japhery
Wods did send her a Toad some 6 years since and it sucked on
her thygh, and after that the Toade came into her woll basket,
and in the time of her watchinge she cryed out & sd that Satan
was wthin and prayed the that watched wth her to hold her
bodie & to worke down Saten wch they - and she thancked the
and sd they had done her grease good and had wrought Satan
out of her and when it Satan was wthin her being asked how he
came into her she sd that on Wod sent it and it came out like a
mowse againe, and that this Wods sent the Toade to her. Jo,
looke testatur vt ante, Sara Wods testatur that she standinge by
the accus, saw a thinge come from under her petticotes in
likenes and shape of a beaur brush and passed vnder neath a
chest but cold not find what became of it and they
chargdgeinge her that was one of her Imps she sd no it was one
of her neybors chickings."*

Those accused of practising Witchcraft were subjected to most
oppressive treatment to induce them to confess. This included
starvation, depriving them of drink, walking them to the point
of exhaustion, plus "swimming" and "pricking". Although the
mob frequently went to excess in obtaining proof, Sussex, in
keeping with the rest of England, never went to the abominable
extremes that were widely practised on the Continent, and in
particular by the Holy Roman Inquisition. I say England, for
regretfully Scotland went to great extremes in obtaining
confessions. The Scots were prone to barbaric public burnings
of those convicted as against the normal and more humane
English custom of hanging.

No one was exempt, and the infamous Mathew Hopkins
once "walked" a Xtian Priest he had accused of being in league
with the Devil. The old clergyman was in his dotage although
mentally bright, but the poor man was "walked continuously
until his legs did swell so he could not stand". It is also written,

"That his feet were broken with raw blisters and he did readily then confess to being a Witch". He retracted his confession once his ordeal was over, but to no avail; he went to the gallows on his forced admission. He was a game old soul and he roundly chastised his accusers afterwards, albeit his protests went unheard. Such was the fear of even being associated with a so-called Witch that his own clergy made no attempt whatsoever to save him.

The aged clergyman demanded full rights to conduct his ending and a Xtian burial, all of which were denied him. It is to his eternal credit, poor old soul, that on the way to his public hanging he recited his own burial service from memory. This act inflamed the surrounding clergy, who at last started to complain at the excesses of Mathew Hopkins. It is interesting that it took the death of one of their own to disturb their consciences.

The seizing and stripping of so-called Witches at one stage became almost a weekend entertainment for the local louts, who singularly seemed to pick on young girls. It was widely believed that imps suckled in the Witches' "most secret parts", so the accused would often be stripped in public and subjected to the most humiliating and disgusting search in front of all those who had gathered to watch the show. If charged by the local authorities, the unfortunate woman often was at least examined in a cell by women, but with a minister coming in to check their findings afterwards.

The idea behind pricking was that a Witch had an insensitive part on her body that was incapable of bleeding. She would have a carefully concealed teat for the Devil to suck. If Old Horny was out of town and sucking from some more delectable creature, then her familiar or imps would be having a ball, so all you had to do was find the insensitive spot and the teat. The process would start with the stripping of the suspect and the shaving of all her body hair so there was no chance of the teat being missed - then the search would start. Any protrusion on the body was confirmation of guilt. A mole, a wart, even a pimple would send a "suspect" to the fire or gallows. The chances of there being no blemish present were remote. If one did not show up, the search progressed to the "most secret parts" and Eureka they always won - female anatomy not being one of their strong points. Then the "pricking" would start.

We all know that a modern injection rarely bleeds, so as the Witch-finders went about their business, it was only a matter of time before they managed to insert a bodkin and proclaim that it had not bled. Looking back, we can well imagine the shock of being naked in those days and the effect of being shaved and pricked instilling such fear that the body would "freeze" and not bleed. However, on the off chance that there might be some blood, the Witch-finder would sometimes use a retractable needle that would not actually enter the body. They wanted to prove their point and collect their fee, so countless numbers went to a hideous death owing to false accusation. This whole period was riddled with hypocrisy. On one hand, if the victim failed to bleed they were condemned. On the other if a person believed that he had been bewitched, he could have a suspected Witch seized and then stab her in the buttocks because if blood flowed from the wound, the spell was negated. All this being the ingenious idea of a man called Zacharias, who was an expert on breaking spells and enchantment. For a suitable fee, he would free you from all aspects of sorcery, to the dire cost of the suspected Witch, of course.

His favourite method was what was known, as the "blooding of the Witch". Custom demanded that the bewitched person must draw blood from the suspected bewitcher by the drawing of the thumbnail of the right hand across the alleged Witches face or forehead. This practise was not exclusive to Sussex, as it existed across the country. In other parts of the country the same tradition prevailed, but it usually only refers to scratching the face.

Justice did occasionally prevail and the following anecdote and result are both chilling and ultimately poetically just. This comes from a "Tryal of Witches" that was published in 1664, and it reads as follows:

"The said reputed Witch-finder acquainted Lieutenant Colonel Hobson that he knew women whether they were Witches or no by their looks, and when the said person searching of a personable and good like woman, the said Colonel replyed and said 'Surely this woman is none, and need not be tried' but the Scotch-man said she was, for the Town said she was. And therefore he would try her; and presently in sight of all the people, laid her body naked to the waste, with her cloaths over her head, by which fright and shame all her blood contracted into one part of her body, and then he ran a pin into her thigh; and then suddenly let her coats fall, and then demanded whether she had nothing of his in her body but did not bleed, but she being amazed replied little, then he put his hand up her coats, and pulled out the pin and set her aside as a guilty person, and a child of the Devil, and fell to try others whom he made guilty.

Lieutenant Colonel Hobson perceiving the alteration of the aforesaid woman, by her blood settling in her right parts, caused the woman to be brought back again, and that her cloathes pulled up to her thigh, and required the Scot to run the pin into the same place. And then it gushed out of blood, and the said Scot cleared her and said she was not a child of the Devil".

By now the Scot had caused a certain amount of suspicion to be drawn to him, so he was forced to retract his guilty verdicts and proclaim some of the accused victims innocent. I do not know whether the gallant Lieutenant Colonel was instrumental in his downfall, but it is on record that the Scot was apprehended and "put to the question" himself. He confessed that he had caused 220 women to be hanged on false evidence and that his motive was gain, for he obtained the sum of twenty shillings for each one that he proclaimed a Witch.

The Last Bastion

Thus end the accounts of the few Sussex Witches whose stories I have uncovered over the years. This compares well in those bad days against the dismal records of neighbouring counties. Essex tops the list for England, with hundreds sent to the scaffold, and Scotland forever being slighted with ignominy for its vehemence in its persecutions and cruelty.

Sussex Ways and Sussex Cures

The very word Witchcraft derives from the old word Wisecraft; or as it should really be, the "Craft of the Wise", which is the terminology from which the word was derived. The old village Wise Woman was healer, midwife, herbalist, vet and friend, thus estranging her from the Church and the local quack, who were ever anxious to eliminate the local competition. The local quack could claim fat fees for treatment, while the old Witch would settle for a bag of plums or half a dozen eggs. The ever-dominant Church could claim a tithe (usually 10 per cent) of a person's legitimate earnings and have a lien on his soul as well! Under this patriarchal regime, the Wise Woman was usually the first to be persecuted and hanged.

The following cures are factual and I record them for posterity. However, no treatise would really be complete without a tongue-in-cheek look at some old country wives' tales set against genuine Witch's cures. Only the village idiot would recommend swallowing a live spider as a cure for whooping cough, but that was actually done. In Sussex, you had to put a large cob (spider) in a slab of fresh butter alive and swallow it. By the rules of sympathetic magic, whereby the rule is "like unto like", one might at least identify with placing a live frog in one's mouth, hoping that the croaky cough would be transferred to the croaking frog itself. Such was the logic of simple country folk at the time.

Criminals believed that the right hand of a hanged man cut off the corpse at midnight, tarred, dried and the fingers soaked in wax, could be lit as a five-fold candle which was known as a "Hand of Glory". If you lighted this and carried it whilst burgling a house, you would never wake the occupants. I wonder how many felons went to the gallows having been caught in the act despite being equipped with a protective hand... Bones of hanged men, who had suffered gibbeting as well, were often prized for a variety of cures. Parts of the skull could be powdered down and used as a general panacea, whilst almost any bone was considered a cure for rheumatism.

In Sussex, a murderer called John Bread was hanged and gibbeted at Rye as late as 1743. Local women stole pieces of his rotting body as a cure for their rheumatism, and records allege that Witches avidly collected up his bones for spell making. Frankly, I cannot think of one good reason that they would want them, and human bones are not, to my knowledge, part of any cure for rheumatism. Witch cures worked: old wives' tales did not. I guess it was a case of "give a dog a bad name" all over again. We Witches got the blame as usual. Apparently, Bread's skull was not pilfered because it was well secured in its iron girdle. It can still be seen in Rye town hall, complete with the original gibbet cage – just ask! Gathering body parts was a favourite pastime in olden times in the somewhat stupid belief that bones of those executed could ward off illness or cure it. Ailments such as the common cold and chicken pox cleared up naturally after a certain period, but the cure would be attributed to the tasty little piece of highwayman that Grandma had procured when she was a girl. John Bread was such an example. Long after his execution, pseudo Witches and pseudo healers continued to glean bits of bodies, and, in many incidents, even parts of the gallows they were hanged on.

Although nothing to do with Witchcraft, I feel that an amazing incident so steeped in blood and gore as that enacted at Ditchling should be recorded. There was a notorious execution in that place and unbelievably, the locals still believe in healing properties associated with the area to this day!

The year was 1734, and the citizens of Ditchling in Sussex were celebrating the weeklong annual fair. On the 26th of May, the fair drew to a close and the many gypsies, beggars and itinerants who had flocked there wended their way home once more. Amongst these was a peddler by the name of Jacob Hirsch. Jacob had not been very successful in selling his wares and thus was somewhat disgruntled when he adjourned to The Royal Oak that evening. It appears that the publican, Richard Harris, was in a buoyant mood, having had a very good week, due to the fair. He unwisely announced that his profit that week had exceeded £20 - a considerable sum of money in the 18th century.

Jacob was well known to Harris; his skulduggery included trading in contraband, particularly tea and brandy, and the publican was one of his customers. Knowing the considerable amount of money that would be on the premises after the fair, the peddler set out to rob him. He chose the simple expedient of booking into The Royal Oak that night and carrying out the deed under the cloak of darkness. Jacob's plan was to lure the landlord into the stable block and murder him there.

He asked Richard Harris for stabling for his horse and requested him to feed and water it for him. Later that evening Harris obediently led the horse into the stable, unaware that Jacob was lying in wait for him. Once the horse was securely tethered, Jacob bludgeoned the landlord to the ground and then, for good measure, cut his throat. Records of what happened next are indistinct, except for the fact that he was disturbed by the serving girl from the Inn. Jacob immediately turned on her and launched a frenzied attack, slashing her wildly with the knife and concluding his dastardly act by cutting her throat.

His perfidy did not even end there. The landlord had been wearing a new riding coat (subsequently valued at 10 shillings) and Jacob swiftly divested the bleeding corpse of this prized article. With two murders under his belt, the peddler now went back to the empty inn. However, it was not empty, because Mrs. Harris, the landlord's wife, was lying sick in bed. Jacob picked up the strongbox, which Richard Harris had left on the counter. The noise that he made when coming back into the pub attracted the attention of Mrs Harris, who mistook Jacob Hirsch for her husband returning. The encounter was fatal, because within minutes her bloodstained corpse lay at the foot of the stairs.

Coolly, Jacob Hirsch returned to the stables to saddle his packhorse. He was confronted by the mutilated remains of the girl, but of the landlord's body, there was no sign! Harris had disappeared! All that could be seen was Jacob's old coat, which he had discarded when he purloined the publican's new one. Both coats were heavily bloodstained.

Panic stricken, Jacob made haste away from the scene and arrived some hours later at a hostelry called the "The Cat". Again, old records differ, as some refer to the Cat Inn at West Hoathly in Sussex, while others state it was The Cat Inn at Turner's Hill in Sussex. Some time later, Richard Harris was found dying in the road outside The Royal Oak, but he lived long enough to be able to identify his attacker as the Jewish peddler, Jacob Hirsh. The dying man was aware that his wife and their serving girl were dead, as he had crawled back into the inn for help only to find them dead. From there, he made his way to the highway, where he had ultimately expired.

A clamour ensued and riders in groups raced in all directions seeking the peddler and his slow-moving packhorse. Jacob saw the first group from his vantage point at the window of the Cat Inn and he made his escape to Salsfield, where a colleague sheltered him overnight. The posse, led by John Oliver, continued the hunt and Jacob returned to The Cat Inn the following day. Now fate took a hand, for the posse was drenched in a ferocious downpour and the men decided to return to The Cat for shelter. This time the peddler had no time to escape, so he climbed up the cold chimney to hide.

Unfortunately for him, the wet and bedraggled pursuers decided to light a fire and dry their clothes. Within minutes, the choking peddler was discovered and taken into custody; the posse also went on to Salsfield House and arrested the man who had sheltered him.

Both men were taken to Horsham Jail and held overnight. Then they were taken to a meeting at Ditchling, which had been hastily summoned by John Mitchell, the Coroner. Jacob was accused of the murders of Richard Harris, his wife Dorothy Harris and a serving maid. Also of stealing a strong box, in excess of £20 in money plus a riding coat valued at 10 shillings. It was a summary trial and both men were found guilty as charged. They were transported to Horsham for sentencing, where they were incarcerated until the 30th of August 1734. The judge sentenced Hirsch to be hanged and gibbeted; his companion received two years hard labour for harbouring a felon.

On the 31st August, Jacob Hirsch was taken out to an area called Hornbrook Hill in Horsham, also known as the "hangman's plait" where the Carfax now stands. He was placed in a horse and cart with the gallows rope around his neck. To the jeers of the mob, he was strangled slowly as the cart moved away. Once he was dead, women surged forward to grasp the dead man's hand in the belief that they would now conceive. Holding the hand of a hanged man was widely believed to be a cure for barrenness. Others would place the dead man's hand on the parts of their body they wanted to heal. The hand of a hanged man was also believed to be a cure for goitre and scrofula.

The final indignity for Jacob was the gibbeting, and it was decided that his body should be displayed outside The Royal Oak as a warning to evildoers on the fruits of crime. The actual gibbet site was a short distance from The Royal Oak, and for many years, Jacob's decomposing and near mummified remains were on public view. Once more, people flocked from all over the country to touch the corpse, thereby seeking a cure;

and if possible, to secure a fragment of the body itself, as in the case of John Bread at Rye. Eventually, the body entirely disappeared as fingers, toes, bones and dried flesh were filched. It is said that Witches and locals even took his teeth as a cure-all.

Long after Hirsch's body had been scavenged, miraculous cures were attributed to the gibbet. Over the years, pieces of the rotting post were purloined as a cure particularly for toothache, rheumatism and arthritis, until eventually, even the last remnants disappeared. Was this the end of the story - and the legend? No, not a bit of it. The authorities decided that such a dastardly crime, combined with local history, should be permanently recorded, and a new post was placed on the exact spot where the gallows stood.

Once again, it was taken, piece-by-piece; the last remnants of this post are now in the care of Horsham Council. According to a brass plaque on the replacement Gibbet, the remains of the old one are currently displayed in Ditching museum. However, when I visited the museum, the people there were completely unaware of the message on the plate. There was virtually nothing of local history there; the majority of the exhibits were centred on the church. They consisted of vicar's vestments, choirboy's gowns and a selection of Xtian carvings, paintings and crucifixes. Nobody at the museum even knew about the plaque directing people to visit it and see the "vanished gibbet", or learn about the locality's most notorious murderer.

On a final note, I must conclude this story with an anecdote from 1881 regarding to Jacob's Post. An old native from Newick informed his doctor, who is recorded as trying to cure a man of epilepsy, as follows:

"Ah Sir, pity sure-a lye he 'adnt a bit of Jacob's Post in his pocket. They do say no one wouldn't never 'ave this yere fallin' sickness if he had a bit o' Jacob's Post loike about 'im. Whoy, Sir, people come from moiles and moiles from round Ashdown Forest way to get a bit o' that poisty so that they shouldn't fall in these yere fits."

Well I guess that this time, we Witches did not get the blame. However, I do have an old bit of Jacob's Post in my pocket. And, do you know... I have never fallen down in a fit. Of such stuff is superstition born.

There are only two traceable incidents of Witchcraft in Ditchling, both of which occurred in the 20th century. The village was rocked by rumour to the effect that a particularly nubile group of young and beautiful Witches were openly practising the Art naked on Ditchling Common. "Shameful!" they cried, "Where have they come from? Who is leading them?" You can imagine the chagrin when the chief practitioner turned out to be a local girl in her teens, whose father sported an extremely high title and who was always in the eye of the media of the time.

Girls locally had readily joined this coven of Witches, and many of them knew every inch of the common. The girl was apparently a weekly boarder at a high school near Burgess Hill, and her classmates were travelling to Ditchling at weekends to dance sky clad in the moonlight. Overtures to Daddy by the enraged Ditchlingites proved successful, and his dear daughter was surreptitiously removed from the school and boarded elsewhere. The coven folded shortly afterwards, although rumour had it that, scarcely three or four years later when the ladies came of age, reunions were held to celebrate the good old days when they danced naked on the heath.

Long before that time, Ditchling Common sported another young Witch. This was a Ditchling resident at a house called the "Jack O' Spades". She spent most of her time rambling on the common, collecting herbs and cast off "sloughs" (snake skins). She became the butt of some quite violent verbiage by passers by on her return to the village each day. She was certainly a woman of power as well as beauty - and she would demonstrate this with impunity to any drover or carter who abused her. She would step in front of the offender, look his horse in the eye and then inform the driver that his animal would go no further until she bade it so. Contemporary reports state that no amount of urging or forcing could make the beast move until the drover apologised to the Witch or placated her with a small gift. Apparently, they soon learned and the abuse ceased.

It seems to be common among accounts of Sussex Witches that they have this ability to command horses and oxen to halt until told to move again. Horse whispering was an old art that all Witches of note mastered, and there are countless accounts on record. Ursley Kemp had a singular rapport with cattle and oxen. Old George Pickingill, the famous Witch of Canewden, whose progeny spread south to Sussex, was notorious for mischievously putting the "evil eye" on the horse of anyone who riled him. There is one report of Old George crossing swords with his milkman and it is said that Old George did not hesitate to let his power be known. This story is a wonderful example of long-distance magic.

The Witch of Canewdon told him that it "B'aint no use bringing yon horse an' cart down this road tomorrer 'cos he won't pass my cottage door". Defiantly, the milkman set out the next day on his usual journey and confidently walked ahead of his horse, which, unaware of old George's curse, dutifully followed its master as usual. Whistling defiantly, the milkman passed Old George's door with a contemptuous glance towards the Witch who stood motionless in the doorway, just watching. Suddenly the milkman stopped and glanced back, aware that the familiar clip clopping of his horse had ceased. Sure enough, right on the boundary of Old George's property, the animal had stopped on an invisible line and refused to move. Even when tempted by his owner, not one single inch further would he go. Old George, still silent, just looked on. So commenced a Mexican standoff. The milkman held his ground and the old Wizard watched. Each waited for the other to give way.

As the sun reached its zenith, it became obvious that the milk would start to sour and be ruined. "Sorry, George," the man muttered. "Horse'll go now", George responded, and off the beast merrily trotted. You did not mess with old George! He passed to the Summerlands in 1909, aged 93, and his obituary stated in a national newspaper that England had produced two of the greatest magicians ever known: Old George Pickingill and Merlin.

Sussex enjoys the reputation of having more than one Wizard, including one who was a mathematical genius. People would flock to him with complex equations, and he would astound them by delivering the correct answers in seconds, all this despite never ever having been given a formal education. He passed into Sussex history in the 1700s as "The Calculating Wizard" and he is reported to have died sometime in the 19th century. He was born with ASP (Aspberger's syndrome), which is a mild form of autism.

Sussex is famous for having another very famous wizard in the 1600s, and this was Earl Henry Percy of Petworth. He was known as "The Wizard Earl of Petworth" and his reputation was such that, combined with his position in society, he was never arrested or charged with sorcery. This was unique for the time. Petworth spawned another famous Witch known as "Butter Ede", and there does not seem any doubt that she was feared.

What is intriguing about Butter Ede is that she would apparently avoid crosses, although one must consider that by playing on this, she would have enhanced her reputation as a Witch. Such was her phobia that the local children would cross twigs or pieces of wood in her path to watch her go around them, and it is said that if they placed two large pieces of wood in the road, she would go home by another route. Again, one would have thought that in the 1600s, when the persecutions were at their height, she would have been seized and tried, but no. In Petworth, we have the only recorded case of Witchcraft being countered by the local people and this occurred by the use of Witchcraft!

The background to this remarkable story is this. A local girl was taken seriously ill, and as was usual in such cases, the local Witch received the blame. Normally a complaint would be made and the suspected culprit "put to the test". We do not know Butter Ede's profession other than that of being a Witch, but she must have worked for someone. It is said that her employer took the heart of a horse, "and did impale it with thorns and pins while reciting the Lord's Prayer (strange mixture)". He then wrote the words "Butter Ede" on a piece of parchment, stuffed the horse heart with it and threw it into a bonfire. The following morning the employer gathered up the ashes and threw them into a stream that ran by Butter Ede's door, whereupon the woman made a full recovery. The casting of ashes from a spell into continuously running water is certainly a typical Sussex practice – although it is also used in London and elsewhere.

Well, old Butter Ede lived out her three score years and ten and was buried in the normal way, with no stake through the heart or impaling at a cross roads, but merely buried nearby because the church at Petworth refused to have her in their back yard. There was some speculation that Butter Ede's body was no longer in its normal form by the time that it lay inside the coffin, because it was so light. Had she turned herself into a cat? Villagers stated that on the day of Butter Ede's funeral, a black cat was seen running hysterically in and out of the Witch's house, but no one opened the coffin to check if Butter Ede was still in it. The situation was not exactly helped by a violent thunderstorm that erupted as the coffin was brought out of the house, and the funeral service was conducted to the accompaniment of thunder and lightning.

This was not Petworth's only Witch, as another is recorded living on the outskirts, in a village called Barlavington. Her name was Sue Redding and she was better known as "Old Sue Reading", so one must assume she was elderly. Despite her years, she was known as a brilliant horse rider and she was said to have mastered the art of horse whispering. If she wanted a mount, none would refuse her and it was said that she borrowed horses to move contraband. She was known to be a smuggler and it was said that she used her Magical Arts to stay free.

One can only assume that the owner of the "borrowed" horse received a portion of the duty-free goods. There are stories of her using the legendary "fith-fath" (shape-shifting) to avoid detection and that she could change shape at will. One story is that on one night, a farmer refused to lend her a horse and thus incurred the Witch's disfavour, to the extent that when he set out one stormy night, he saw Butter Ede standing in the centre of the cross roads, but when he looked again there was only a hare sitting there! It is said the horse refused to pass by the hare and the farmer was forced to return home.

In the biographies at the end of this book, I refer to Rowan, who is a member of Artemis. She has much in common with me, inasmuch as we are both psychic fulcrums for "happenings". I will talk about these in another book, but I must relate an event that took place on the area known as "Jack's Land" at Kingsfold. On this particular occasion, Rowan and a non-Wiccan were walking through this section of woodland when they both became aware of a movement. Puzzled, they looked around, fully aware that something was there yet there was nothing to see. They were in the middle of a small glade in the centre of the woods with only a large bush apart from the trees themselves… yet they knew that there was some kind of presence.

Later, each independently verified that they found the occasion hauntingly beautiful and not in the slightest way frightening, for by now they had realised that it was the bush itself that was the entity, and it was none other than the legendary Green Man himself! To this day, both of them look back upon it as one of the most memorable experiences they have ever encountered. As they both watched, they realised they were watching the ritual mating of the Foliate God with the Goddess, as the bush pirouetted into humanoid shapes as the couple performed coitus. Both of them later remarked on the beauty of the scene and the awareness of their presence by the God and Goddess, the haunting eyes and the privilege that they had been granted to observe such a sacred occasion.

It is probably difficult for non-Witches to comprehend that in this century, such magical manifestations can occur, but practitioners of the Craft Magical will believe it. It is a strange fact that every single Witch, once initiated, receives a "sign" from the Old Ones. This can take many forms and can be anything from haunting Panpipes following them from room to room, to physical manifestations. I have even heard of our people and their offspring telling of near-accidents in their cars and of invisible hands taking the wheel gently but firmly from them and steering them away from danger.

Ancient Sites and Ancient Ways

Chanctonbury and Cissbury Ring have the greatest notoriety in Sussex folklore, having been associated with Witchcraft and magic since time immemorial. Is it true that Chanctonbury is a continuous hive of Wiccan activity? The answer is both yes and no. In the 50s, 60s and 70s, both my own coven of Artemis and many others sometimes met at a secret location on Chanctonbury. There, in a heavily wooded section, we would meet on the occasional Sabbat and conduct our rites. The particular location that we used was extremely difficult to traverse, one side being so steep that only the fittest could access it. When the coven's Summoners sent out the call, we would gather under cover of darkness, often rendezvous with other covens and by torchlight commence our climb. Those were fun days, and we were very merry as we teased the girls who struggled to climb the slippery hillside. Many of us would carry long lengths of rope, and once the ablest had reached the peak, we would knot the ropes and prepare to haul the womenfolk up.

Mark you, the men were not always the first to make the summit. There was one extremely beautiful girl - a keep-fit fanatic - who could surpass some of the fittest of us, and she took great delight in doing so. Her delight was to dance sky clad under the silver moon, and none would ever forget the moonlight glistening on her lithe young body as she leaped and skipped around the circle. One of her favourite roles was to take the part of the pursued in the old ritual of "O I shall go as a hare in spring", and when the coven would try to catch her, she would always elude them and slip niftily from their grasp. They were great days.

Sadly, it is a rarity for us to go there now. The national interest in Witchcraft activities means that curious people and voyeurs tend to go there on such Sabbats that they are aware of, particularly Hallowmass (Halloween), hoping to see the Witches at work and to try and glimpse their sky clad rites.

Once there, we would make our way to our secret clearing and commence to cast the magic circle. Balefires would blaze into the night. At dawn, we would greet the rising sun and perform a dawn ritual, just as we had worshipped the moon the evening and night before. There, under a full moon, we would cast spells and bury secret artefacts beneath the roots of trees where they would never be found, and by moonlight, we buried our Witch bottles. This was a very important part of the coven's training, and the interring of a Witch bottle had to be performed with great care - an absolute essential for this great protection of the Witch, because firstly, the secret must never be dug up in the Witch's lifetime and secondly, while the Witch lives, the bottle or container must not be broken.

Such is the paranoia of the Witch that the secret burying of their Witch bottle is often performed as many as three or four times in the occultist's working life, and each time it will be in a completely different location. It is essential, therefore, that the spot so chosen must never ever be disturbed - so logically - the practitioner looked to nature reserves, National Trust land and Historic landmarks. The sheer vastness of Chanctonbury Ring in the early days made it an ideal setting. It is steeped in history and it has been associated with Pagan worship and the Old Religion almost since the dawn of time itself.

The Witch bottles were buried very deep, because rabbits were the greatest menace; evidence of how deep they could burrow was evident on Chanctonbury from the shards of

Roman pottery that could be seen lying around, as these had emerged from deep underground. Usually we would secrete the bottles under young trees, especially holly, to deter treasure hunters, who could be seen on occasions, scanning the ground with their detectors, ever hopeful of finding buried treasure.

In 1973, a Witch bottle was dug up in Michelham Priory in Sussex. It was a bellarine jar dating back to 1600 and I think it will be added to Sussex Mysteries, for it contained a heart formed from wax, which was pierced with a selection of pins and thorns. Now, old ways of blighting a victim would have used the heart of a goat or a dog, or possibly a sheep or pig - but wax? Why? Could it be someone from the village who had a grudge against the priory or against a specific monk? On the surface, this seems unlikely, as an outsider would have been able to get hold of a real heart, so that leads us to the conclusion that it was done by someone within the monastery, who was presumably barred from the outside world - a not uncommon practice at the time. Certainly, a vindictive Prior would have been able to purloin one of the Bellarine jars used in Michelham. Wax and candle fat would have been to hand to fashion the heart, and as for pins and thorns – well, a walk round the garden would have yielded those a plenty. However, why a man of God had fashioned and buried a Witch bottle in the grounds of Michelham priory 400 years ago will never be known. Alternatively, we must be charitable and consider that perhaps the Prior believed himself to be under psychic attack or perhaps even cursed, so could it have been a counter-spell?

Long before Charles Goring planted Chanctonbury with a wondrous array of trees in 1760, natural growth had already started to cover the summit. Nature added to it from then onwards, to create the intriguing kaleidoscope of twisted trunks that were to give complete cover years later to the Witches' activities. Neolithic man had inhabited the area and excavations have produced much evidence of his occupation. Unbelievably, there is oil in the soil of Sussex, and in some areas, it is still mined even now for small industrial purposes.

This sandy oil is called oil shale, and Neolithic folk were known to use the oily deposits towards the end of the last ice age to keep their fires burning. Flint is also common in the area and this was an extremely useful resource for Neolithic people.

The Romans built a Temple to Diana there, making it sacred to the Goddess. There are the remains of an Old Saxon Pagan Temple just beneath the surface, and generations of locals have slipped away from their villages in the dead of night to worship the Old Gods in secret.

In the burning days, followers felt safe there, for in those superstitious times, the hill had an awesome reputation for being haunted. It was considered the home of fairies, elves, dwarfs and goblins. Spectral manifestations had been reported. It is said that a fearsome Viking who died there still searches for the gold treasure he had buried deep in the hillside years ago. Even the Devil himself paid an occasional visit during his nocturnal excursions, so the locals knew they would not be disturbed. As I said elsewhere, "did not we ourselves create superstition?"

Regretfully, another reason that Witches have all but abandoned the old hill is the fact that every group of pseudo satanists, black magicians and motley weirdoes flock to it. Gangs of Hells Angels practise some occult rite that has virtually no chance of success. These pseudo practitioners of the occult are a danger to themselves; they get hold of some ancient grimoire on ritual magic that was written in the USA circa 2000 by a loony, and with book in hand, they set out to raise the Devil or to implore his help. If only they realised that one of the first laws of the Wicca is a complete and utter denial of this entity!

To a Witch, the concept of the Devil is based on a fallen angel by the name of Lucifer, who fell out with God over a conflict of ideals and ended up being banished. The Church no doubt realised that showing Lucifer simply as an opponent of God (after all, all he did was disagree with the Almighty) and subjecting him to perpetual banishment did seem a bit severe.

The next stage would have been, logically, to demonise Lucifer and associate him with the Horned God of the Witches, then to get moralistic (as the Wiccan God, Cernunnos, was a God of fertility) by condemning sex and pronouncing woman as a source of evil. The final indignity was seen as associating womankind with original sin. Evil is a different matter, and all Pagans and Witches recognise its existence, although we see it as a manifestation of man's unpleasantness. We certainly know what evil is, because we have been on the receiving end of it for centuries, but evil manifested in humanoid form such as the Devil is not acceptable to a Witch. Satan as portrayed in Xtian depictions is always shown with horns and a tail plus a hideous expression, and the image is enough to chill the blood of the most avid Xtian. Certainly, it was enough to frighten poor primitive villagers into obedience and into contributing their tithes. In short, we consider the concept of the Devil as an invention to keep the people in line. Witches have no problem with other religions believing what they will, as long as we can do so ourselves.

Chanctonbury has now been defiled, rendering it unsuitable for religious meetings. The soil is tainted and this has been exacerbated by Aleister Crowley, who stated that he offered sacrifices to his infernal master on its slopes. The followers of the Old Religion have, after countless centuries of usage, forsaken their holy site. In addition, the great gale that devastated the Sussex countryside on October 16th 1987 stripped the ancient ring of most of its trees, exposing the old sites to public view and further depriving us of privacy. After the gale, many of us streamed up the sides of the hill seeking the secrets that the upturned roots might reveal. We were prepared to rebury our sacred Witch bottles. We heard the stricken trees crying and tried to comfort them, then we sadly said goodbye to the land that we once held so dear.

The 1980s were not good for us. The death knell of the sacred hill had been sounded long before the coming of the great storm, so this ferocious gale was merely the final climax.

Additionally, the occult investigator, Leslie Roberts, foolishly declared publicly that Chanctonbury, together with the Long Man of Wilmington, were focal points of Wiccan activity. This was another nail in the coffin of Chanctonbury as a centre for our activities, as on Sabbat days, reporters from the national press, the idle, the curious and the sensation seekers – not to mention the odd voyeur, hoping to catch a glimpse of a nubile sky clad maiden, trudged up the now deserted mound in a vain vigil. No, the witches are long gone.

24

False Accusation is our Lot - Nothing Alters

A man called Leslie Roberts had many friends amongst Sussex Witches, including a particular rapport with the most famous Witch, who was often referred to as the Mother of Modern Witchcraft. This was the brilliant writer and Witch, Doreen Valiente. I am grateful to Doreen and to John Belham-Payne, who inherited her wonderful collection of Witchcraft artefacts, for permission to quote from her poetry. Doreen was not a happy bunny when the trusted Leslie Roberts disclosed what he knew of Wiccan rendezvous points. One group in particular was most aggrieved at his revelation. A Witch family lived in the shadow of Chanctonbury ring, and the family was friendly with Doreen. These people were the descendants of those who had worshipped there for centuries. Doreen did not hesitate to make Leslie Roberts aware of both her and their displeasure. The same scenario was enacted at the Long Man of Wilmington, when the local coven abandoned the hill figure in the 1960s, once again in the wake of Roberts' disclosures. They had worked their rituals undisturbed under cover of darkness for years, so they were also less than amused when overnight they found that their sacred gathering place was attracting voyeurs.

Doreen's artefacts were nearly lost to posterity when Leslie Roberts borrowed them for a lecture on Witchcraft one day in

December 1958 in Brighton. He became carried away with his revelations and started to disclose what he knew of black magic in Sussex. What had started out as a simple lecture on Witchcraft had now become inextricably mixed with the diabolical practices of the left hand path. Roberts was the architect of his own misfortune, because his desire to impress his audience backfired.

When someone lectures, the first rule is to ignore rumours and stick to facts. Once a person earns a reputation as an investigator, he will be approached by every pinhead, eccentric, lunatic and zealot who will recount such and such a story of Witchcraft, assuring him that the story is true. If I were to recall or even attempt to recount the bizarre stories that have been offered to me over the years, I could fill several volumes. People sidle up and try to gain one's attention, or ask questions about sexual activity (favourite topic) sacrifices, nude rituals and raising the Devil. They all know someone who knows someone who has a friend who told a colleague who told them something. These are Chinese whispers to an extreme.

It appears someone told Leslie Roberts that Rottingdean was a hotbed of diabolism and that there was a very large satanic group of black magicians operating in a house owned by the grand master. Such was his reputation that people crossed to the other side of the road if they saw him coming. This means that the man was known! Not only that, but apparently he had openly boasted of performing human sacrifice, including that of newborn babies. This is how such stupid rumours circulate.

Leslie Roberts gave a lecture in the conference room of the Adelphi Hotel in Brighton, and as he addressed the prestigious Forum Society, he blurted out that murder had been committed scarcely three miles from where they sat. As you can imagine, there was a furore and the next thing poor Doreen Valiente knew was that her possessions were in the hands of the police and Leslie Roberts had landed up at the police station – helping the police with their enquiries!

Within days, it had hit the national press and a murder investigation was under way. Leslie Roberts was under pressure to tell what he knew and where his information had come from. The result was sheer farce and a full police operation that yielded absolutely no evidence. When the denizens of Rottingdean were interviewed, it became clear that they had no idea what the story was about. Yes, they had seen the headlines in the Brighton Evening Argus announcing "Police Probe Black Magic Murder at Rottingdean", but that was the extent of it.

The local vicar was most surprised to hear that his sheep were not all white; the village postmistress was as bewildered as anyone was, and said that a black magic group in the village was laughable. The Satanist's house was visited and the somewhat bemused owner was amazed to find that his house had been named. He was a highly respected man and the closest association he could lay claim to with regard to such disturbing matters was having a gnome in his garden!

Part of a police statement read, "The officers concerned made inquiries and found no corroboration of this story and it was quite frankly dismissed as being fantastic". The newspaper headlines now announced, "Police say that there is no substance in black magic story". In addition, all this had happened after it was alleged that Scotland Yard had said, "There is more Witchcraft being practised in this country now than there was in the Dark Ages".

By the 1980s, Chanctonbury was often in the news, and that brought its usefulness to the Witch community to an end. While Traditionalist and Hereditary covens had sought solace in its greenery on specific Sabbats in the past, now many new practitioners headed for the hill to practice their newly founded religion. Soon Alexandrians, Gardnerians, Dianites and goodness knows how many "Hedge Witches" (lone practitioners) went there now. The upsurge of interest in the subject focused on all activity on the hill.

The press had a field day In the 1980s. They completely ignored the hundreds of covens working healing rites and switched their attention to any that appeared dubious. All they wanted was an interview in which questions about sex rites would predominate; hopefully followed up by a photo of a nude female participating in some ritual. The result was that Chanctonbury now attracted such a focus of attention that, sadly, it had to be abandoned by most practitioners. It had become likely that some callous paparazzi with a long distance lens might secretly film sacred and forbidden rites. Forbidden, that is, to outsiders, may I clarify.

Now the hill was becoming a favourite picnic spot and the council had even built a new car park to accommodate visitors. The prevalence of the motorcar meant that Chanctonbury was within the reach of everybody, so hikers and ramblers would park their cars nearby and set out up the hill. Then, horror of horrors, a local spotted a UFO there - and that was it! UFO enthusiasts now descended upon old Witch territory as the stories unfolded of aliens being seen. Personally, the only "aliens" I have ever seen in the vicinity were groups of Hells Angels. Now they really were from another planet! Occasionally a coven will still go there, but it is increasingly rare nowadays.

Witches cannot trust national newspapers, as experience has proved that they are not the least bit interested in the true workings of the Craft, but only seek sensationalism. Having said that, I would like to praise the local press and especially the Evening Argus. Over the years, the Argus has reported on Witchcraft activity in the County with total accuracy - as has Radio Brighton.

Regretfully, there is woman in the area who is prone to hysterical outbursts and who, for some obscure reason, seems to associate any missing cat with Witchcraft. She bombards the press with stupid statements, and I can say that I wish the press would check things out and not publish such rubbish willy-nilly.

To give a typical example, we were once told that some fifteen cats that had gone missing in the space of a week. When the woman concerned was asked to substantiate these facts, she unhesitatingly provided the investigator with the names and addresses of the bereaved owners, together with their telephone numbers. We waited a month and then telephoned every single person on the list. The statistics were a revelation. Of the fifteen missing cats, fourteen had since been found or had returned home, the exception being one that had been discovered run over.

Was our accuser sorry? Not a bit of it. She promptly checked our findings and had the audacity to say that one of the "kidnapped" cats had returned home extremely thin three weeks later. She said that it must have escaped and that we had been starving it during this period. Yet another had returned to its owner with a torn ear. She did not get her letter of protest published to the effect that "Witches torture stray cat", but she would unhesitatingly spout racist trash to the effect that local occultists had mutilated the cat.

The owner was a very kind woman who disagreed with our tormentor. When the woman had taken the cat to the vet, his verdict was that it had been in a typical catfight and that the injury was caused by claws. The woman was good enough to call us and report the vet's findings; she wrote to the press as well, so we were exonerated. Knowing my own and any other coven, any stray cat would be more likely to be loved to death than hurt. I do wish certain local papers would copy the Argus and think before they publish.

You would think that was the end of the matter, but this crazy woman still sometimes rears her head and lets off a tirade against us. Such people are dangerous and they are typical of those who would unhesitatingly have sent us to the gallows years before. In a way, I guess that it is amusing to think that this nutty, cat-loving woman would herself have been given a one-way ticket to the gallows in times gone by...

Patcham Woods frequently features in tales of missing animals, but in one instance, mainly dogs. The area has a somewhat oppressive atmosphere and there is certainly a case to answer here, owing to the occurrence of many mysterious happenings, but in no way can the happenings be attributed to any form of occult activity. Dogs that have disappeared are usually lost minutes after being let off the leash in an area that I have investigated and found to be honeycombed with foxholes and badger setts. Interestingly, usually small dogs suddenly vanished.

Both a police officer and a vicar once entered these woods and never came out again. Despite intensive searches at the time, there was no trace of them and nor were any bodies found. Weeks later, both bodies were found in areas that had already been thoroughly searched. The mystery was never solved, but inquests recorded "no foul play". These incidents immediately added fuel to the haunted reputation of Patcham Woods and resurrected the old chestnut of a secret group called "The Friends of Hecate" that supposedly frequented the woods for a multitude of nefarious purposes.

Charles Walker, a local investigator, is convinced beyond any doubt of the existence of this group, but frankly, I do not believe that there is any such thing. Charles is a respected and ardent investigator of the paranormal, and we have cooperated in the making of the "Hex Files". I have followed his investigations over the years with much interest and I eagerly await his findings. However, I feel that his search for the "The Friends of Hecate" in Patcham is a case of him chasing shadows. Local pranksters try to lead investigators a merry dance by daubing Witch symbols on trees. They even go to the extent of tying branches into strange shapes, leaving those who find them scratching their heads in astonishment. I have conducted many days of investigation in Patcham Woods and I have never found the slightest trace of these so-called "Friends of Hecate". On these expeditions, an RSPCA inspector and a powerful Witch group known as "The Triple Aspect" have often accompanied me. It is the considered opinion of all of us that this group is a figment of local imagination.

There is talk of an underground cavern where devilish practices occur, and this rumour was so strong that we conducted a thorough search of Patcham with an ex-poacher. Within days, we had tracked down this hidden chamber. What we found inside, deep underground, amazed us. It was furnished with every comfort you could imagine, including a radio and CD, etc. - all battery operated. Lighting was from candles and lamps. There were a number of rooms, including sleeping quarters; and there were books on medicine, plant life and fungi. It might have been strange, but there was nothing suspicious.

A watch was kept on the chamber and it was not long before we found the person who had constructed it. He was a member of the medical profession and we were all convinced beyond any doubt that he was just a kindly, middle-aged man who had painstakingly created a little retreat for himself. We had every opportunity to satisfy ourselves that there was nothing sinister there. For example, all the candle wax was white, pink and green – not colours associated with black magic. It was simply a place close to nature where the man could be at one with the trees. He was an eccentric, maybe, but why should people condemn those who are simply different? We Pagans are very aware of how hysteria can grip people when they encounter anybody who is different, because we have all experienced it.

Regretfully, a few weeks later, hysterical groups were combing the woods, hell bent on their own "Witch hunt", and they eventually found the hide and wrecked it. It was destroyed. Had this man lived 300 years earlier, I am sure he would have been left swinging from the nearest tree. This was over two years ago, but vigilante groups still maintain vigil, constantly searching for a group called "The Friends of Hecate". I am sure that this exists only in rumour, a sentiment that is shared by various authorities, which would be extremely interested if there was any real wrongdoing. The police do not lose one of their own without a full investigation - and they say there is no case to answer. Their conclusion is good enough for me.

It is amazing how rumours are started, often maliciously. They then spread like wildfire and they become embellished with each recounting. We have all fallen victim to this over the years, and no book would give us Pagans justice if we did not recount at least two incidents as a comparison.

False Trails

Many years ago, Alex Sanders decided to conduct a ceremony in a remote and unused gravel pit outside Hastings, when he came across a group conducting a full moon ritual of the kind that is usually sky clad. On this particular occasion, a farm worker on his way to work happened to walk by the top of the gravel pit. To his horror, he observed a group of naked men and women dancing around a fire. In seconds, he had observed all the paraphernalia of Witchcraft that was scattered around - broomsticks, cauldrons, goblets etc. Hurrying on, he went about his day's work and recounted later what he had seen to his companions over a drink. They nodded sagely and admitted they had heard stories of such activities in the area and that it was no surprise. The discovery of a coven became the main topic of conversation in the local hostelry that evening, and of course, the question came up. "What were they doing?" Well, our farmhand did not know, so there was a fair degree of speculation. The result being that, undoubtedly, there had been a sacrifice of some sort.

The story reached the ears of the local bobby, who, being a diligent copper, told his sergeant. The sergeant told his inspector, who decided it might be advisable to check that no crime had been committed, so he dispatched a police car to the quarry. After all, it wasn't exactly every day of the week that the police heard of Witches in the area. As was to be expected, the result was completely negative. The site had been left tidy and the only signs of activity were the ashes of the fire and a little candle-wax here and there, around what had been a circle. A perimeter of stones remained and in a neat pile, in some bushes nearby, was a quantity of uneaten food, left for local birds to feast on, as was customary.

His eyes did pick out a maroon stain on the sandy floor of the quarry, and he scooped up a small sample and checked it. The odour of red wine showed that there were no signs of foul play, so he made a few notes in his police book and left. We know that this would have been an offering of a libation of wine onto the earth, to the Old Gods, as is the conclusion of every Wiccan ritual.

Back in the village, speculation was running high, now that the villagers knew that a police car had gone to the quarry. Clearly, there was no smoke without fire, so what had happened? Rumours of the suspected sacrifice swept the village, and the next thing was that a cat had been reported missing. Yes – it's always a cat! How strange? Within an hour or so, women gossiped in the shops, then afterwards they hurried home to check on their feline companions, and by nightfall, there were reports of nineteen missing cats. There were rumours that the police had found blood, that they had brought back pieces of cat fur, and that they had recovered numerous devilish artefacts. As it happens, all we ever leave behind are our footprints and a lingering scent of incense.

By noon the following day, all the cats had returned. The police issued a statement to the effect that there was no truth in the rumours and the whole episode died a natural death. All this happened because of one sighting. I forgot to mention the mass orgy that was also rumoured to have taken place there as well, but no one had reported a daughter missing, so that rumour died a death as well.

The other incident involved me. I have never been fond of sitting about in pubs and drinking, because I much prefer a bottle of wine at home with my family and friends. However, on the odd occasion and particularly on a hot summer's day, I have found nothing more delightful and satisfying than to take a drink at the one pub I regard as my local in Poynings. Here, the publican serves me with an ice-cold glass of sweet cider. I use this country outpost for occasional business meetings, to meet friends and to meet fellow Witches. So our little band all became fairly well known to the regulars as followers of the Old Ways, and were welcomed.

Early one summer evening, I dropped in to keep a rendezvous with a potential initiate who wanted an initial social meeting. To my surprise, I was greeted by a sudden and obvious silence, accompanied by furtive glances from all those present. I found this a complete and utter contrast to the usual repartee. "I hope you parked your broomstick in the bicycle rack, Ralph. You know we've got to keep the parking bays for cars." Or "Hi Ralph, if I buy you a pint can you turn the mother-in-law into a frog?" On this occasion, there was absolute silence and it was obvious that something was wrong.

The barman greeted me cordially, but then he shook his head slightly and surreptitiously lifted his finger to his lips indicating that I should say nothing. Perplexed, I sat down, glancing at my watch and realising that I was early for my appointment. Then it started. A man of some twenty-five to thirty started to speak, and he was immediately egged on by one of the locals in the bar.

Glancing at me, he looked at one of the others in the bar, who said to him, "Go on, tell us some more about what this Harvey fellow gets up to... like the orgies". The man wiped his lips and then started up again, "Always got new girls he has, no one over thirty gets initiated, and then he has sex with them in the centre of the circle - I know, I've seen it."

By now, my temper was starting to rise, but I kept my cool. Hardly able to contain myself I ventured, "Sounds interesting, but where do you know Harvey from?"

"I used to be in his coven" he remarked, "but I left because I didn't like what went on."

"Are you talking about Order of Artemis? I've read about that one."

"The same," he replied, "I've seen awful things happen at coven meetings, so I resigned."

"Describe him to me," I asked. Whereupon he proceeded to give a reasonably accurate description of me - to the amusement of all present. "Are you certain you would know him if you met him again," I pushed home.

"Of course I would!" he reacted, "I worked with him for enough years."

At that point, I exploded, grabbed him by the scruff of the neck and his tie - then as one of the locals sprang to open the door, I literally threw him out of the bar. All the time he was protesting and apologising, saying it was what he had been led to believe. We all had a laugh afterwards, and the proprietor said he nearly died when I walked in. He also assured me that the pub locals had been winding the garrulous idiot up before my unexpected arrival. The stupid man never ever came back. The moral is that, despite the fact that on this occasion I was among friends, in most circumstances, we still have little if any defence against the kind of far-fetched and evil stories that are still perpetuated against us.

In relating the following story, may I emphasise that Witches do not allow children to witness ceremonies. Only the initiated are allowed to attend a Sabbat, and juveniles are most certainly banned. We make it a strict rule that none may join us until they come of age, and that means an absolute minimum of eighteen. In practice, unless the parents are Witches, this is increased to at least twenty. We do have rituals for blessing a newborn baby and this includes a ritual of love and protection for the infant. It is a very moving and beautiful ceremony, and the temple or meeting place is adapted accordingly. For example, no incense is burned, as this would not be good for the child's underdeveloped lungs.

On this particular occasion, one of our people wanted to bring her newly born child up in our faith. As was the normal procedure, she sought the opinions of the Elders who would have to conduct the ritual, and ensure that it was within our ways to bring a child up as a Witch. She was saddened to learn that this was not within our jurisdiction, for there is no dogma in the craft. Our law is that people must choose their own paths, without influence, when they become of age. How many people of other persuasions would choose the religion they had been brought up in, if they had the choice, and if they had not been indoctrinated? My own situation is a case in point. I have five children, and in their early days, if they had been brought up as Witches, they would undoubtedly have been both ostracised at school, and very possibly persecuted by their peers. Children can be very cruel to those who are different.

Looking back, I often wonder if I made the right decision but it was certainly right at that time in the 1950s. I examined all Xtian faiths before embarking them on an Xtian upbringing, and I decided that Methodism was closer to the Xtian God's teachings than the orthodox and rather pompous outlook of the higher churches. Not only that, but the Xtian minister at the Methodist Church in Portland Road, Hove, was a "real" Xtian, who would attend and help a Jew, Gentile or Pagan, regardless of their beliefs.

Therefore, my progeny were committed into his care. The result is that I have five Xtian children and not one of them has become a Witch. The good side is that no one dares to criticise the Craft to them, for they will not hear a bad word said against it. They have spent over forty years living alongside it, and they know its purity with the Worship of Nature, but sadly, it is not for them. This is common where parents are "into" something, but do not insist on their children following the same path. Each person needs to ask his or her own questions and find his or her own answers. As long as there is mutual respect between the generations, that is fine.

Anyway, the new mother understood and accepted the fact that she must allow the child free will, but that she could bring it up in what had now evolved into a freer society that was fast accepting our ways. In other words, she could lead by example. She then asked for a dedication and blessing for the child. This was granted and a date set for the right moon phase. Now a chain of events was set in motion that was to have terrible repercussions. This will give you an idea of what can befall our people and why we still cannot drop our guard.

The woman's husband had no particular faith, but he was quite sympathetic to his wife's religion, so he happened to mention what was happening to a workmate. Within days, this man had related it to another and soon it became a topic of conversation at the local hostelry. From there, it came to the attention of a local freelance reporter, who jumped on the "story".

What happened next is incredible. The new mother received a knock on the door the day that the blessing was to have taken place. She opened it to be confronted by a somewhat ebullient reporter. The following dialogue ensued. (This is as accurately as we can reconstruct it, but with all relevant names, etc. changed.)

"My name is Smith of the Daily Echo - are you Mrs Jones?" asked the reporter.

"Yes," replied Mrs. Jones.

"I believe you are a Witch," commented the reporter.

"Yes I am. Why, does that interest you?" responded Mrs Jones.

The reporter pressed on. "We understand that you are involving a child in a Witchcraft ceremony tonight and I would like a story - and a photo of the ritual taking place as well, please."

"I'm sorry but it is a closed meeting – no one but Wiccans may attend," replied Mrs Jones giving a pleasant smile.

"Okay - sign me up as a Witch - whatever that means."

Mrs Jones laughed and told the reporter, "You would have to study for at least a year before you could even be considered."

The reporter now showed signs of aggression and a nasty tone entered his voice. "What do you do? What is going to happen to that baby? How old is it?"

Mrs Jones replied, "It is a simple blessing, rather like having a baby christened, except it's Pagan."

"In other words you are refusing me entry to see what you do - right?

Mrs Jones started to close the door on the intrusive man, meanwhile telling him, "It is just a ritual of protection for the baby, so that the Old Gods may protect her in the years to come."

Exit angry reporter!

Two days later the headline on an article in the paper blazed "Child dedicated to Devil in satanic ritual in Kensington basement!" The lesson is clear, if they cannot get a story they will invent one. We cannot win against the power of the press in their bid to sell papers, no matter how big the lie.

Retribution!

To give you a further idea of what we have had to endure from the media, I will recount a rather amusing little story that involved our own Artemis coven and the Coven of Tanith. One day, we received a phone call from a villager in nearby Wiston, who reported that a freelance reporter had been asking numerous questions in the local pub regarding Witchcraft activity on Chanctonbury. It turned out he hoped to secure shots of an orgy or two and to sell his story to the News of the World. He had bought many drinks for the regulars in the local pub and he made it transparently clear that he would pay well for information. He offered £100 to anyone who could lead him to the place where the goings-on may be observed. He said that he had inside information to the effect that Witches would be celebrating Hallowmas there. (Xtians now refer to it as Halloween.) The date in his diary was October 31st, so he knew it was true.

After the phone call, the locals hatched a deadly plot. We will never know where this man got his information from, but it certainly was not true... however, the locals decided that if the man wanted evidence of satanic activity - then satanic activity he would get! The medium for the potential hoax was a villager from another area. He dressed in rough, country tweeds and "dropped in" on the night the reporter returned. During the evening, he let drop within earshot of the man that he was the local poacher. He then asked if anybody was in the market for a couple of prime pheasants. The would-be sleuth replied that he was not, but he was in the market for information on Witches and he asked the "poacher" if he knew of any.

"God Bless you Sir," replied the local, "I knows every place they meets and when, Sir," adding, "'tis part of me round on a full moon when I'm out a'poachin'." Then he added "Them's meeting next Saturday, Sir. And oi can tell 'ee that there will be devilish activity there that night: see'd it with my own eyes, I have." He gave a wink, "Skellingtons, grave clothes, you wouldn't believe what they do on Halloween, Sir. Devils, them's are!"

"Jackpot!" The reporter was over the moon! It was everything he had hoped for and more. Fifty pounds changed hands, and our "Judas" was promised the balance on the night. Well, on the great night, the informant kept the rendezvous. On arriving at the car park, he was confronted by a full television crew! The balance was paid over. Our friend was somewhat reluctant to take the money, but he realised that a refusal at that stage would have alarmed the reporter. In the event, our friend gave the reporter's money to charities such as the Woodland Trust and animal welfare.

Off they set on a route the villain of the piece had preset, up Chanctonbury in the dark they traipsed, round and round Chanctonbury they traversed, hauling giant cameras, tripods, sound equipment, recorders and so on. Groaning and sweating, they resolutely followed our betrayer. At one stage, they came down the hill close to where they had started and splashed through a mud pool. Next he took them across the fields to a little hall, hidden right in the middle of the downs, scarcely a stones throw from the ring and only 300 yards from the main road.

Fearfully, he looked at the crewmembers and the reporter, pointing to the little hall from which sounds of great revelry (probably mistaken for devilry) emanated. Screams could be distinctly heard (undoubtedly the ravishing of a virgin) and ethereal music. "In there they be. Devils, ghostees, an' skellingtons like I told 'ee." Then he added, "Oi've earned moi money; an' I won't go no further, Sir, no way. You're on your own now. I wouldn't go further for all the tea in China." They thanked him profusely, and in seconds, he had scampered away. Looking back, I have often wondered why it had not occurred to them that they would need his services to get back - after all, they had walked a good two miles or so around Chanctonbury to catch the coven.

Stealthily, they approached the door, some raising themselves up to film through the windows. Then, with flashlights blazing, they burst in - to find a Halloween party in full progress! Sure enough, as promised, there was a copious array of "Witches", resplendent in pointed hats and broomsticks. Hideous masks covered their faces, complete with long noses and warts. Ghosts and skeletons were performing a danse macabre with an assortment of Wizards and Warlocks. At the centre of the revelry, complete with dog collar, was a vicar with a nun on each arm. I presume that the vicar was a man in fancy dress, of course - although I never ever did find out if he was real!

The crew were not amused. The freelance reporter never showed his face again. The News of the World got no story. And us? Well, we all chuckled. It was the talk of the village for weeks afterwards. The poacher? Oh dear, I am sorry to say that I just cannot remember his name, but if I recall correctly, he did have a rough beard when he first came in the pub… but he shaved it off afterwards – or perhaps simply unglued it!

Pseudo Satanism and Vandals

I was once consulted by the police, who had received a report of a group of satanists who had held some diabolic ritual at Chanctonbury. The rumour started when a rambler had come across signs of black magic and reported them. A police officer was dispatched, but he failed to find the site, until eventually, the rambler led him there. The poor man was completely out of his depth and as a result the came along to consult me. For many years, various police forces had sought my opinion whenever it became necessary. I lecture widely on the subject, and have even lectured to the police at Hove and to the police cadet force.

I am usually consulted in cases of vandalism to graveyards and churches, and I am happy to say that not one incident turned out to be anything other than mindless vandalism. People have often asked me how I can tell that the incidents are the work of these morons. The answer is simple, notwithstanding the fact that the desecrations might be the work of pseudo satanists. One thing that comes over loud and clear is that, if they are playing with the occult, they are playing a very dangerous game. Many of the symbols I have discovered are contradictory. What is referred to as Goblin's Cross or Goblin's Knot predominates in these idiot's minds, as does the pentacle. Give them an aerosol can of spray paint and away they go.

Along comes the investigator and straight away looks for how each pentacle has been painted or constructed; this is a very simple matter to deduce by the trained eye. What the pseudos do not know is the correct way of constructing a pentacle, full details of which I am obviously not going to describe here.

Now let us take the interpretation of differing constructions, which are based on the elements of Air, Earth, Fire, Water and Spirit - each of which has a positive and negative side. So, imagine graffiti in the form of pentacles, etc. everywhere. The trained eye works out what each one is for and finds that, for example, invoking water is followed by banishing water. One cancels the other out. At that point, I can see that this is the work of the uneducated or the amateur.

In the case of the Chanctonbury investigation, I was once called to a situation where, as described above, everything was contradictory. The police reported that they were perturbed. The police officer had seen a crudely made cross which had been hammered into the ground in the middle of the circle. To them, this was a clear sign of black magic or satanic ritual. In one respect, they were correct, and the culprits were quickly identified as an out-of-town group of bikers. They had tanked up at a local public house nearby, before descending en masse to the Ring, where they decided to attempt a somewhat amateurish black mass. Perturbed locals informed the police. Goodness only knows what they got up to, but they certainly did not get anywhere near raising any Power as such. Besides the pentacles that were arrayed against each other, they had cast the circle incorrectly and furthermore, North, East, South, and West were out of alignment, so the invocations would have been in the wrong quarter anyway.

The area showed all the apparent trappings of the Black Mass, complete with pools of black candle grease. Ominously, one area showed obvious signs of blood soaking in, by now covered with a myriad of flies. Discarded beer cans were everywhere, empty whisky bottles galore, but not a single wine bottle. This was indicative of an attempted Mass, so we presume that some poor cockerel or animal had been sacrificed there. This is another indication of deluded Satanism, for, to genuine Witches, the shedding of blood in any form whatsoever, is anathema.

Amongst the debris they had left in the circle was a variety of trash, such as cans, sweet wrappers, used contraceptives and cigarette ends. Now, no coven would ever even allow these into the sacred circle. Let alone leave them there. The Witch's first duty is to cleanse the circle by symbolically sweeping away all evil influences with the besom broom, and when the ritual is over, the circle is banished and left perfectly clean. So, finding a circle such as the police had discovered proved once more to be the work of morons. Many other vital clues concern the construction of the circle - least of which being the correct diameter - and it had been simply scratched out with a stick or some similar instrument. A true occultist would have known exactly how to cast a completely invisible circle. The remains of the fire would have used the old Sussex custom of casting it with soot and ash if it had been done properly, but of course, it had not. On a historical note, again an old custom/ritual has died out with the casting of a circle; soot and ash sealed and protected the circle in the days of yore, and fertilised the soil.

The most damning evidence, though, was the inverted cross in the centre. It was made of two pieces of iron tied together to create a makeshift crucifix. At some point in their amateur ritual, they had driven the cross upside down into the earth at the centre of the circle. Even if they had managed to summon up any power, by driving iron (of all things) into the ground, they would immediately have negated any energy field they might have raised.

In all the 50 years or so in which I have been engaged in investigating haunting, manifestations and all forms of occult phenomena in Sussex, I have only come across two genuine satanic groups, and these are well known to all Sussex Witches. Nowadays, with the invention of the Internet, we make sure they are known. Whenever they are suspected to be active, hundreds of e-mails go out and their every move is noted. One of these groups is particularly dangerous, and the Witches who continuously thwart them are often the targets of their activities. Every now and then (fortunately, rarely), we become aware of what we refer to as muscle flexing and then begins an "occult war". It pleases me to report that these wars are becoming far less frequent now, probably because in every single encounter, the black magicians, satanists and workers of evil have come off second best. Good always overcomes evil - that is an occult fact. There are many Sussex covens working for the good of the community. We have direct links with well over 50, including Hedge Witches. While, by way of contrast, there are only two "black" groups and the number of their followers is diminishing. In fact, one of them is almost extinct, the other however, is evil and run by a mother and her son. To meet them, you would not think that butter would melt in the sweet old lady's mouth.

One thing that annoys me intensely is that people seem to divide Witchcraft into black and white. When there is a benefice reported, they refer to the coven as white Witches, and when a malefice has been committed, it is referred to as black Witches. This really galls us, as there is no such thing as black Witchcraft. All Witchcraft is essentially white! It has to be, owing to the very oaths that a Witch swears at his initiation - for we all swear the oath of "An' Ye Harm None". Those who deviate or digress from that path are not Witches. Something that also makes life difficult for us is the typical dictionary definition of the word Witch; invariably, there are negative connotations included - black magic for one - and, quite frankly, we ourselves would not wish to mix with the kind of person usually labelled by dictionaries as a Witch!

Those who follow what we refer to as the left hand path are evil. That encompasses satanists, black magic practitioners and devil worshippers. We include Voodoo within this category. Voodoo itself is not intrinsically evil, but its macabre rituals make it anathema to us, as they involve animal sacrifice. To Witches, all life is sacred, and the shedding of blood is totally against our beliefs. Books such as The Devil Rides Out are fantasies that are the product of Dennis Wheatley's creative mind. Fantasy is fine as an entertainment, but the damage that he has caused, inadvertently, means that Dennis Wheatley has much to answer for. Inverted iron crosses on Chanctonbury Ring? Fantasy and stupidity, no less…

Bloodsticks, Squares and Circles: Old Lore

This brings me to the use of the *Athame* in modern Witchcraft. Over the years, this has slowly taken prominence over the wand. Metal tools are an innovation within Craft circles, and although metal implements have been used in the past, it was in a completely different format to that which we now practise. The sacred circle has - and will always be - the mainstay of ritual, no matter whether this is in Witchcraft or Ritual Magic. The essential element in these conjurations is to work in a circle. With Ritual Magic, however, it is often also necessary to create a triangle outside the circle.

The circle is a sign of Power from the Old Gods, and it has been recognised as such by humankind since time immemorial. The sun and the moon are round, the planets are round and the cycles of the year show a revolving, circular pattern. The signs are everywhere. Notwithstanding this, we should not overlook the old country practice of working in a square, particularly when the persecutions were at their height, as described earlier in this book.

One thing, however, that always remained unchanged was that there was no Athame as such. All the rituals - the casting of the circle, the consecrations and so on would be done with a wand of wood. The wand is still an essential ingredient to a modern day Witch, but it is not used to the occult extent that it should be. Sussex Witches always used the wand as a major implement to conduct their ceremonies; the Athame was called simplistically the knife and its use was essentially to cut herbs and flowers for use in rituals. I used several sources when researching the background of the Sussex wand and its importance in ancient Witchcraft. One of these was the Jarrett coven from Kingston, which is now no longer in existence. The sole survivor and last of the line is Doreen Jarrett. Her roots span the centuries, and fortunately for us, she is alive, healthy and still practising.

The Jarrett Witches were truly hereditary. They belong to an ancient bigradal tradition, where women taught daughters and sons. While writing this book, I am also carefully recording the old practices for posterity. Doreen's knowledge is vast and it must not be lost, so I am extremely honoured for her to have asked me to elevate her to the Third Degree by our trigradal system. This high-powered ritual is planned for Beltane this year.

Doreen's mother was descended from Wise Women and Witches, and she trained Doreen Jarrett in her early days. This coven never used metal in the casting of a circle, and their own unique wand was used for all its conjurations. Most of the Witches had two wands – one that was the healing or invoking wand, and another, referred to as the bloodstick. This would be carved with twenty-eight notches upon it, followed by a further two notches, followed by a further one.

I think the bloodstick is a unique example of ancient times that remains in existence. By tying a small thread around a certain notch, a girl could calculate her exact moon time and monthly cycle. The other side of the wand had nine deeper notches. This would be used, roughly like an abacus, to calculate fertility and conception periods, and once a conception had been achieved, to calculate the birth of the child 278 days later with great accuracy.

The old covens around the Lewes area of Sussex did not have High Priests and Priestesses. Their elected male leader was always referred to as The Lord or The Magister and the High Priestess was always The Lady. People came from everywhere to consult them for their knowledge. If a Witch did not wish to be disturbed, he would keep his broomstick inside his house, but if he was happy to receive visitors, the broomstick would be placed outside, on the right hand side of the door, as a clear signal that Mr and Mrs Witch are "at home". Children were brought up to be fully aware of their mothers and fathers religion, but they would be packed off to bed once the ritual started.

Doreen tells lovely tales of how, as a little girl, she used to creep out of bed onto the landing and listen to the Witch chants down below, so that by the time she reached eighteen and could join the coven, she had spent many years learning the words by heart. Her blood stick was given to her when the first signs of puberty appeared, and before her initiation. The arrival of the first menses was the signal that the potential Witch was now blossoming into womanhood, and that she had paid her first tribute to the moon.

Doreen's mother and father were great animal lovers, as are all Witches. They were particularly perturbed by the behaviour of a certain drover who regularly crossed the old drover's way through Kingston. The man would take his load to market and then, together with the villagers, he would spend the evening following the sales in drunken revelry. In the early hours of the morning, the cottagers whose houses lined the old drover's way (passing the tree upon which Nan Kemp was hanged) would be disturbed by the thunder of horses and carts galloping to wild whoops as the drovers raced each other home.

The drovers always urged their horses on with a minimum of encouragement, but one particular brute would thrash his horses unmercifully in order to win the race. In the event, the Jarrett Witches decided to "put the mockers on him" to quote an ancient phrase. The following month as he passed by on his way to the sales, the Witches stood at the crossroads and warned him not to thrash his horses, but they were treated to ribaldry and blasphemy. In the early hours of the morning, the drover's race came through, but as it reached the Witches' house, the drover's horses pulled up violently and would not move any further.

The Jarretts dared the drover to strike the horses again and vainly he tried - but nothing he could do would induce the horses to move a single inch. It appears that in his drunken stupor, he then fell asleep and tumbled into a ditch. He spent the night there, awaking wet and cold the following morning to find his horses had taken themselves off to a nearby field. None of his efforts to round them up succeeded, and a very humble drover apologised to the Jarretts and promised to treat his horses well in future. When he returned to the field, his carthorses came to him in a docile manner, submitted to being placed in the shafts and continued on their way. This story was told and retold by the drovers for months afterwards.

A Sussex Mystery

Sompting Church is the setting for this most curious episode in local history and folklore, and it is the scene of one of the most bizarre of all the Sussex mysteries. Sompting Church is somewhat of a mystery in itself. It was built almost 1,000 years ago and its construction contains Roman bricks from a nearby site that contains the remains of an old Roman dwelling. There is talk of a Temple dedicated to Diana being close by. These remains in themselves show that this little acre was inhabited by Roman settlers, with a distinct possibility that a Celtic settlement had preceded it. It was the wont of the Roman invaders to settle their own people on Celtic lands. Apparently, some time in the past, the funerary remains of two Roman soldiers had been discovered in the churchyard, and strangely enough, the ecclesiastical authorities interred these in the church wall.

The floor of the crypt was solid, but a slab was discovered many moons ago and it appeared to be a grave. When the huge slab was lifted, a large, extensive cavity was revealed. Then as a torch plunged into stygian darkness, the explorers recoiled in horror...for there was not one skeleton, but thirteen! Twelve bodies were laid in a circle. They were ramrod straight but with their heads inclined towards the centre, while in the centre were a thirteenth skeleton and the remains of a chair or throne, which could be identified only by its rivets and metal attachments.

This was not the first time that a discovery of this kind had been made, for there is a previous one on record as well, identical in every way. Twelve bodies were in a circle and a thirteenth in the centre. Like the first, the central body was also a female, although there is no record of the remains of a seat in the second case. Once again, it was beneath a church floor in a building that had been constructed on an old Pagan site on the Continent. It was the custom in early years when newly arrived Xtians erected their houses of worship upon our sacred sites to prevent us from gaining access to them.

Subsequent investigation showed the central figure to be that of a woman of about thirty to thirty-five years of age. Around her neck were amulets that, outwardly, were Wiccan or Pagan, but an exact description of them was withheld. The remaining skeletons turned out to be alternately male and female. Six of each sex and of variable ages. Other artefacts were also found within the circle, but no further information is available to date. We know that, days later, the skeletons were removed for examination and the vault either filled in or sealed. The discovery was hushed up, and it would have remained a secret, had it not been for the fact that some considerable time later, the bodies were unceremoniously returned, each in a plastic bag.

The sexton was summoned. He had been present when the bodies had been found and when they were removed. He was instructed to bury them at a designated site within the existing graveyard. At this point, the mystery deepens. Apparently, he had been instructed to dig in virgin ground that was not consecrated, but his spade reached no more than a foot or two into the ground when a virtual charnel house of bones appeared. It seemed that he had disturbed a large site of old burials.

It was decided that this jumble of bones could only have come from an old plague pit, because the bodies were heaped one on top of the other. Another possibility was that the unfortunate people had been victims of a massacre, or that they had fallen in battle and had been hastily interred there. Whatever the reason, he could not continue. At this point, he was told to place the thirteen skeletons on top of the remains that he had uncovered, and cover the whole site up afterwards with the newcomers on top of the old burials.

When I interviewed him, it was clear that he had been uneasy at the way that the thirteen bodies had been re-buried. Six sacks held thirteen skulls and a jumble of small bones - vertebrae and metatarsals and so on. Others held hipbones, leg bones and an assortment of arm bones and so forth. He commented that this was not a very reverent means of disposal. He recounted that any old burials that needed to be re-interred were always meticulously kept together, as was the Xtian custom. With that in mind, the conclusion must essentially be that these thirteen bodies were most certainly not Xtians. The people had been Pagan and this may even have been a complete Witch coven! If so, what were the circumstances of their burial? Why were the bodies laid out as they were? Could they have been walled up alive? This seems an unlikely theory, as the precise layout of the skeletons tended to disprove this. If they had died naturally, they would have been found curled up in a variety of positions.

Was their presence known or unknown at the time the church was built? Had local Pagans secretly interred their deceased people in the dead of night? How was it that all thirteen had come to die at once? What were the findings of those who had removed them earlier from their sacred resting place? Why had the discovery never been publicised?

The story does not end there. At this point, the gravedigger felt that he could not carry out his original instructions to toss them on top of this old charnel pit, but orders are orders; so, he tried to lay the skulls out in a line and attempted to place the jawbones beside them.

He made a start and he had actually buried a few skeletons and spaded the earth over, when to his surprise he realised that two of the skulls were back out of the grave and sitting on top again. One skull that had been sitting on the earth, suddenly leaped off and landed at his feet - his own words. The message to him was clear. Hastily he gathered up the Pagan skulls and replaced them in the plastic bags, covered up the area as quickly as he could, and unhesitatingly filled in the ground. He was completely unnerved at this experience.

He said he did not consult anyone as to what he did next, but on his own initiative, he selected a spot near a tree and secretly buried them there, along with a sprig of oak as a gesture. He then covered up the new interment, placing some old masonry on it to give the impression of an older grave. He placed old gravel on it to disguise the newly dug earth, and there the group lies, sleeping peacefully to this day. The years have passed, sextons have come and gone, as have gravediggers and parsons, so I can write this secure in the knowledge that our benefactor, who gave our fellow Pagans a decorous burial will not be identified.

Ḥerbs, Cures, Recipes and Old Witch Lore

Herbal remedies were once the order of the day and they worked. Many plants were called locally by the names of their healing attributes. Such names as bright eye, feverfew, heartsease and ridflea passed into the English language. Each identifies the particular attribute of its herb. Some have passed into the realm of myth and legend that endures to modern times. These amusing cases, rather than describing the specific property of the herb or weed in question, have given rise to superstition about it instead. A typical example, so beloved of schoolchildren in my day, were such superstitions as not to pick dandelions, as it was believed that if you did, you would wet the bed. There was always someone who knew somebody who had picked a dandelion and wet their bed! Thus is superstition born.

Let us go back to the old properties of this beautiful yellow flower (*Taraxacum Officinale*) that was widely distilled and used as a diuretic. The old village Witch offered it as a cure for dropsy, so the memory remained that it drew water out of the body and made a person pee - to coin a phrase! Three centuries years later, all that remains is the fact that the old name for a dandelion had been forgotten, but its properties were remembered. The name had been bastardised to mean to wee or to wet in the bed. The dandelion's magical qualities were known throughout Europe and in mediaeval France; it was called *piss en lit*. (Actually, it is still known by that name in France.) The plant's roots were dried, powdered and used to aid digestion, and it is now known to be a detoxifier.

So much for history, but let us look at some old Sussex cures that have survived and that are known to work; I do not doubt that these may well have survived in other areas as well. I could devote so much space to this one subject that it could easily warrant a book of its own, but I will keep it short. Please remember that, with all the medicines and the like mentioned in this book, it is important not to try things casually, and without full understanding of all possible effects, such as not using sterile ingredients, or perhaps overdosing in some cases. The information in this book is not offered for direct medical purposes, but as data for the sake of interest or for further investigation in conjunction with professional medical advice. It is unwise to experiment with medical matters - the old Wise Woman would have known exactly what she was doing!

The common cold and the influenza virus, which have plagued humankind for centuries: the old village Witch knew a trick or two. She could sell her cold cures and earn money to put food on the table. The main target of her foraging along the country lanes was the good old-fashioned ladies' tree or sacred elder (*Sambucus Niger*).

At the end of her day, she would return with a sack of wild parsnip to roast and with which to make wine, apples to ferment for cider and a big bag of elderberries to make her cold cure. This one fruit alone would see she did not starve through the winter. Come the season of colds and coughs, the old village Witch could call upon her stock of boiled and distilled elderberry to ease the symptoms of colds and flu when an outbreak swept the village. The elder tree contributed not only its berries, but its leaves and flowers as well. Elderflowers were made into wine, but they were also a favourite ingredient in pancakes, and they were considered a cure for hay fever - to name but a few remarkable properties. Once home, the Wise

Woman would boil the berries in a proportion of five to one. Five times the weight of elderberries to one measure of pure honey, comb and all. Then she would strain it though a cloth and bottle the mixture to sell later. Then, off with her basket and back to the woods once more for St John's wort, wolf bane and wild garlic.

I have experimented with the elderberry cure, substituting sugar for honey; it most definitely works, but honey is better. It was known as Robin's Juice after the God. Later, this was abbreviated to Rob-juice. This is now the subject of research by scientists, but we always knew it... What is not generally known is that a devastating flu epidemic swept Israel in 1992 and this was countered by using elderberries. Why, when this simplistic Witch cure was so widely known, has it taken so long for modern science to recognise it? Adding a little modern touch to it, I add a teaspoon of Venos Expectorant (the old-fashioned, dark, treacly one) to three tablespoonfuls of the Witch cure, plus a dash of lemon juice, a pinch of nutmeg and a touch of cinnamon. Therefore, I turn the old Witch's cold cure into an even more effective cure for the flu in the modern age. Taking two aspirins with it helps to keep a temperature down. The ancient Wise One would have used willow leaves and boiled willow bark, with the injunction to take this three times a day in hot water for the cold or flu to abate.

The Wise Woman would gather spider's webs in a grass circle first thing in the morning for the treatment of wounds. The webs had to be newly spun. She would fold a long blade of grass into a circle and remove the web from behind to keep it intact. She would repeat this process until she had a thick layer that she could lay on the wound. Sometimes she would scrape the green mould off old cheese and bind this on as well. We now know that the latter is the basis of penicillin.

Honey was known for its curative properties, both internally and externally. It was used to boost energy levels. Some of these old ways have survived and others are being rediscovered. Aintree hospital in Liverpool has just announced that a series of experiments has begun to investigate the healing properties of honey. This follows the discovery that, when it is applied to wounds that have become resistant to modern antibiotics, they healed within days. Honey has been found to be particularly useful in the case of leg ulcers, which are notoriously hard to heal. However, before you plonk on some honey from your jar, bear in mind that the honey used in hospitals is kept in sterile conditions.

Another old remedy was to take a freshly laid hen's egg, remove the yolk, then whip the white into froth. When this was applied to a wound, healing followed swiftly. When looking back at the inheritance of old-time Wise Women, Cunning Men and Witches, we ask ourselves just how much knowledge has been lost over the centuries by the attempted genocide of these old practitioners. By a strange anomaly, the egg white cure is also being revived. It is being brought up to date by aerating the egg white with pure oxygen. This is exactly the same process the old Witches used by the simple expedient of vigorous whipping. We may still live to see a Witch, complete with broomstick and cauldron, on a hospital board... (black cats and toads being forbidden on the grounds of hygiene).

Foxglove (*Digitalis*) was used to alleviate heart conditions. Beware, as this is a very potent poison. Belladonna was also known and used. Even the humble stinging nettle had its uses, as it is rich in iron. It cured anaemia and it is a jolly good substitute for cabbage when used as a boiled vegetable. Before eating nettles, one must ensure that they have been grown in clean conditions, wash them thoroughly and only use the tender top shoots. It goes without saying that it would be wise to wear rubber gloves while gathering the nettles.

More recently, antiseptics were made by the simple method of crushing wild or cultivated pears to extract the juice, marinating cloves and cinnamon in it, together with lemon juice. This is a most powerful antiseptic. Cloves have antibacterial properties, as has cinnamon. In the east, these have been used for centuries past. Cloves are also helpful in the case of toothache, so if it is not convenient to get to a dentist, try using a pestle and mortar or some other tool to crush a clove, soak the dust in a little whisky and apply the mixture to the tooth. Then drink more whisky to cheer yourself up. This cure carries the following warning: "Do not drive or operate machinery after using!" This recipe came from a now long dead pharmacist in Wimbledon!

Weeds often served dual purposes, depending on whether you were a Witch or a peasant. For instance, if you were a follower of the Old Religion, *cinquefoil* would be an essential ingredient in the making of a love spell and in divinations, so a sprig of dried cinquefoil would be part of every good Witch's inventory. Strange, is it not, that many village houses also kept cinquefoil as a deterrent against evil spirits?

Heartsease and henbane likewise were an essential addition to any love spell, a great favourite of Witches and sorcerers. (Be careful with henbane though, as it is highly toxic – better to put it on an altar than to ingest it.) Oberon commanded Puck to bring him heartsease and lay the concoction on the eyelids of the sleeping queen Titania, so that upon waking, she would fall in love with the first person she sees. The idea being that the young suitor avidly waits in the hope that her eyes alight upon him first. Don't try it, though – remember what happened to Titania! She fell in love with an ass-headed person by mistake...

In the days of the persecutions, people were advised to also keep bunches of vervain, St. John's wort, dill and trefoil as a protection against the powers of Witchcraft. An old adage runs:

"Trefoil, Johnswort, Vervain and Dill.
Hinders Witches at their Will."

One could go on for ever with this fascinating subject, so let me close this chapter by answering a little question that by now, must surely have entered your minds when I referred to the Wise old Witch gathering Elderflowers for wine and to make pancakes. Pancakes? Yes pancakes. It is very simple, so let me put you out of your misery and give you the old Witches' recipe.

"First make your batter in your usual way by mixing flour, eggs, a pinch of salt, a good pinch of baking powder and milk (I do not know if baking powder or bi-carbonate of soda was around in 1600). Mix well, then simply add whole elderflower flower heads to the mixture. Deep fry each pancake for one minute, remove, put onto a warmed plate, sprinkle with sugar and eat. Delicious! Pagans and peasants put honey on their pancakes, as there was no sugar available to the common people in those days, although sugar was imported for those who were wealthy."

Banishing rituals are many and varied, and they can take many forms. I have seen a number performed over the years, mainly centred on diseases and growths. A typical one would be for cancer, for example. The Witch would make an image of the cancer from a substance such as clay and treat this magically in such a way that it reduced in size over a period of time. I have known rituals where the effigy has been placed in holy water (ours, that is - not the Xtian variety) and over a number of weeks, it would be left to dissolve, accompanied by a magical evocation to kill the growth. Another method is to allow the elements to destroy it over time by placing it outdoors until it is washed away by rain or broken down by ice. This is considered one of the most effective methods of all, because it understood that the God and Goddess send the forces of nature that ultimately destroy the disease.

Another ancient way was to take a word and destroy a letter a day or a letter a week, depending on how ill the person that the Witch is working on happened to be. The great secret was that that each time the Witch did this, the remaining letters must still have been able to make a word until the illness was cured.

A typical example would be to take a word with a magical number of letters, such as seven or nine, and reduce these over say seven or nine days or weeks. One magical seven-letter word used for healing, for example, is arataly. So, over a period of time it would be reduced a letter at a time to rataly, then ataly, taly, aly and ly: each time making a word. The Witch would write the word and ceremonially burn it, one letter at a time, followed by the chant, "Arataly, Rataly, Ataly, etc."

When such invocations are performed in a circle, the results are outstanding; the success rate is so high that even the most ardent doubters have to dismiss coincidence. The greatest pity is that only three rituals can be engendered at any one time, with the third invocation being the most powerful and delivered to the sickest person. It breaks our hearts to select three out of the many sad cases that are submitted to us on a regular basis. The criterion that we use is to work on those who are very young and whose lives are before them, and then take each case from there on its merit.

The Days of the Ĥempen Rope

How lucky Sussex was, to have escaped the extremes of the persecutions. Sussex was the last county to be Xtianised, eventually falling to the influence of a monk named Dicul who established a following in or near Bosham in Sussex, long before St. Wilfred, who is generally attributed as being the harbinger of Xtianity here. From this humble beginning, the rot set in and eventually, the county outwardly went Xtian; however, its Pagan heritage was never far from the surface, and the Pagans held out for nearly 1,000 years before succumbing.

Although we regard the burning days from 1500 to 1700 as the worst period of our suffering, oppression both by religious and civil authorities has been with us since the first edict was issued. This was issued by the Roman conquerors, who were here for some 400 years, and they imposed the Twelve Tables on the British populace. Of these, besides the Bible oratory, were statutes that included death amongst their punishments.

Further punishments were recorded by what was known as the *Sententio* of Julius Paulus, who wrote the offences it contained into law. These initially were comparatively mild for first offences such as prophecy. The offending soothsayer would be given a sound beating and promptly (if he could still walk) be escorted outside the city limits with a warning not to return. Woe betides he who ignored the warning and decided that the citizens of that particular town just had to listen to what he had to say. (Come to think of it, this was rather stupid, for if they were really good at the art of prophecy, they should have been able to forecast their own fate!) They would be recognised, seized, given another beating even more severe than the last one and thrown into the local gaol somewhat unceremoniously. There, they would be ill-treated, almost starved for an indeterminate period and eventually expelled yet again with a warning. This was only the beginning; if you made charms, plotted, cast spells, worked any form of magic, conjured spirits or brewed love potions, then the penalty was to be nailed up on a stake.

On a historical note here, and contrary to what is generally surmised, crosses were not used for crucifixions. It was quicker and easier to find a tree so that two people could be crucified at the same time - one each side. This saves the price of a carpenter, the cost of wood and the cost of an extremely expensive commodity – that of iron nails.

Practising magicians fared even worse. They also automatically received the stake and a pile of brushwood for their funeral pyre. Another edict known as the *Lex Cornelia de Sicariis* went as far as decreeing that if you made an offering or sacrifice that was somewhat dubious in its intent, you could be punished even if you had done no wrong or harmed nobody.

We all know the Roman Catholic Church went to near hysterical extremes in both punishment and persecution in their desire to exterminate the opposition, the penalties growing in severity as the years passed. Here in England, it started with Theodore, who was Archbishop of Canterbury between 668 and 690 AD. This extremely fervent Xtian was not too bad a fellow, but he really did believe that he was right and all others were wrong. He set out, albeit quite gently, to suppress Paganism. His successors built on his *Liber Poenitentialis* until it was supplanted by the infamous *Malleus Maleficarum* - the Hammer of the Witches.

The *Theodores Liber Poenitentialis* comprised some 50 chapters of ecclesiastical law, of which the 27th dwells on offences such as idolatry and sacrilege. The following is a small sample. As you will see, this man was a fervent believer in what he did, but he is one Xtian whose hands are not stained with blood.

From *The Theodores Liber Poenitentialis:*

Section 1   Sacrificing to Demons: one to ten years' penance.

Section 6   Consulting or divining by birds: three years' penance, one of which spent fasting on bread and water.

Section 8   A layman or cleric practising as a magician or enchanter to be unfrocked and expelled from the Church. (It looks as though some must have tried to have it both ways here!)

Section 9   To destroy someone by evil spells: seven years' penance, three of which shall be on bread and water.

Section 10 Frequenting soothsayers or they who make divinations: five years' penance, one of which shall be on bread and water.

Section 13 Any woman who uses divinations or practices devilish Witchcrafts: one year's penance.

Section 20 To be an Astrologer and who by the invocation of demons has turned a man's reason: five years' penance, including one on bread and water.

Section 21 Raising storms: five years' penance, two of them on bread and water.

This was the situation up to 690 AD. Then King Wihtraed decided to increase the penalties and fill his purse at the same time by the time-honoured custom of governments and monarchs imposing fines. Oddly enough, it was the husband who was punished if his wife was caught practising Witchcraft. Should it be the man who was discovered offering up to devils without his wife's knowledge, then his *heals-fang* (fine) was "all his substance".

That year, a penitential was issued that was clearly a rebuke to the followers of Pan, Herne or Cernunnos. At that time, the enemy was the old God of the Forest. The persecution of the Goddess was still around the corner, and in its wake, the ultimate persecution of all of womanhood. The locals would dress up in animal forms and joyously enter the forest to sing, dance, and make merry. All the local villagers energetically joined in the celebrations alongside the local Witch coven, which performed publicly for all to witness them in the old coven circle dance. As they cavorted with their assortment of weird and wonderful costumes, they would imitate animals and birds and chant *" Oh I will go as a wren in spring, with sorrow and sighing on silent wing"*. This role would invariably be played by a woman. The men would usually take on animal parts and the womenfolk the more gentle creatures such as birds and fish.

This verse would be followed by the participant singing a tribute to the Goddess, *"And I shall go in our Lady's name - aye till we go home again."* This verse has now become *"Aye till I come home again"*. The men would respond by one of them jumping into the circle and singing of the animal he represented. For example, *"Then I shall go as an Autumn Hare, with sorrow and sighing and mickle care"* and would identify with the God. In modern Witchcraft, the High Priestess now seems to play all the roles, be they animal, bird or fish, leaping around the circle as the covenors try to catch her. Each gesture would be symbolic, for if the Priestess became a mouse, then the coven would all become cats and try to ensnare her. However, the origins go back to the mummery of the days when everybody dressed as an animal.

A song that was sung around the balefires really aroused great emotion from the participants as they joined in the chorus. Villagers dressed as animals would leap and dance into the circle. Once more, they would imitate animals and birds as they sang, but would also hold their arms out to represent trees. The song is The Lord of the Dance. It was also known as The

Dance of Life. It has probably been copied into countless Books of Shadows over the years, and is regularly sung and enacted at full moon gatherings and Sabbats. Witches have a beautiful ceremony called Cakes and Wine, and it is traditional for the Lord of the Dance to be sung to the accompaniment of laughing, singing and handclapping.

The Lord of the Dance: The Wiccan Dance of Life

The opening verse below becomes the chorus after each verse is sung and enacted.

"Come now and join us in our song,
Come now and mingle with the Pagan throng,
Cast off your cares and dance quite free,
Dance with the Lord of the Dance merrily.
I dressed in horns and an animal skin,
Love I teach is never a sin,
I'll dance with you, if you'll dance with me,
For I am the Lord of the Dance you see.
I danced in a cave when the world was new,
I danced in a circle, and the early morning dew,
I danced the round that will always be trod,
And I danced as a Priest of the Horned God.
I dance in the morning when the stars are bright,
I dance in the wind and the dark of the night,
I dance in the light of the noonday sun,
And I dance for all, for with me all are one.
I dance in the rocks, and I dance in the trees,
I dance in the flowers, as they dance in the breeze,
I dance in the water, and the air and the flame,
I dance in the Earth and I'll always be the same.
And now we dance as we did of old,
So mote it be till the sun grows cold,
And Moon Goddess no longer sheds her light,
We always will dance on the Sabbat night.
We dance as we raise up the cone of Power,

We dance as of old, at the Witching hour,
We dance for health, and for joy and good,
We dance in a grove in the depths of a wood.
We dance between the worlds, and we talk with our dead,
We look into the future, and we know what lies ahead,
We can see into your soul wherever you may be,
For we dance with the Lord of the Dance do we.
In the worlds beyond the worlds, they dance, as do we,
They form the Circle round and they work the Mystery,
They gather at their Sabbats when their festivals are near,
And they reach towards the stars as we do down here.
We teach that all is life, and that death is not the end,
For the Horned God is everybody's friend,
So we circle around, and we learn the mystery,
For rebirth is part of the dance, you see.

In his ritual role, the coven's High Priest represents the male aspect of the creative source of life, while the High Priestess represents the female aspect. Such celebrations often ended in coupling in the woods, to earth the Power that they had raised. It was under the rule of King Wihtread that such activities could be punished. The edict running:

"If any go at the New Year as a young stag or a cow, that is, if he shares or dresses in the habit of wild beasts and is clad in the skins of cattle and puts on the heads of beasts, then any such who thus transforms themselves into the likeness of beasts are to do three years' penance".

Once more, the years have rolled on, for the edict specifically refers to the New Year, which was, of course, a time of celebrations for new beginnings, but this particular ritual was traditionally performed at Lammas. There is an anecdote that throws an interesting slant on the ritual of dressing up in animal skins, and the trail leads us to Frant in Sussex, an old town with an unusual history.

Near Frant, an abbey once stood that was noted for its decadence in the eyes of the Church authorities. This was Bayham Abbey, and it was the home of a sect of White Canons. Apparently, they were highly popular and loved by the simple villagers. There is an interesting history of continuous rebukes from the ecclesiastical authorities against the denizens of the abbey. For over a hundred years, this was like water off a duck's back, as the edicts were ignored. The climax came in 1525, when Cardinal Wolsey became completely exasperated by their antics (which appeared to include poaching). He closed the abbey down and evicted the brethren. This gesture turned out to be a highly unpopular one, for, apparently, the citizens of nearby Frant rose up and broke in to the now deserted abbey and set the White Canons back on their thrones.

What is so interesting is that the men of Frant (subsequently arrested and punished) marched on the abbey dressed as wild animals. They were described as being "clad in animal skins". Some dressed as donkeys and more significantly, goats! A clear symbolism of their Pagan heritage and the Old God - but strangely, they seemed sympathetic to these Canons. The mere fact that the Canons were out of line with Church doctrine meant that they were probably in accord with the Pagan traditions of the immediate area, hence the abbey's forced closure.

So, go to the Sabbat at thy peril and you will enrich the King's coffers. At that stage of the early persecutions, the authorities realised the Craft was a wonderful cash-cow, but only in the burning days did they kill the goose that laid the golden egg. In the tenth century, the death penalty could be imposed, but fines were preferred. An old record quotes a "*theow*", who made an offering to devils, had to make a "*bot*" of six shillings or his "*hide*". A hide was a measurement of land that could be seized and sold.

By the eighth century, Ecgberht, the Archbishop of York (735-766) increased the fasting punishment to seven years for some offences, such as "slaying with spells". Sacrificing to demons by a strange logic, was upped to ten years' fasting. The penalties increased under both Guthram and Edward, and it is during this period that I found the very first reference to Witches as Wiccans, and from then onwards the reference becomes commonplace. I quote from a record of the time:

"If Wiccan or Wigleras (diviners) perjures or morth (kills by secret, such as spells and curses) workers, or foul, defiled, notorious adulteresses be found anywhere within the land: then let them be driven from the country and the people cleansed, or let them totally perish within the country, unless they desist, and the more deeply make bot."

King Aethlstan ruled between 925 and 940 and the death penalty became far more frequent. However, there is a strange quirk of law here that I feel should be vice versa, but one can only quote from the evidence available, therefore:

"If the Witch confessed to lyblacs (acts of witchcraft) and morthgaeds (secret killings by conjuration), he or she should be killed, but if he or she should deny it, then they faced three ordeals, that commenced with an assumption of guilt. First the suspect was imprisoned for fifteen days, and then was bailed by relatives who had to give the King fifteen shillings, and pay the wer (compensation) to the deceased relatives and enter into borh (surety) for the Witch to desist from spell making and the like."

Xtianity was now about to be vigorously enforced upon the people, whether they liked it or not. The worship of the Earth Mother and the Woodland God prevailed and the churches were split into two, as we have seen earlier in this book, thus allowing the New Religion and the Old Religion to live in harmony side by side.

In 958, King Edgar came to the throne, and now the heat was about to be turned up. He instructed every Xtian priest to promote the Church doctrine zealously and to extinguish heathenism for good. Pagans were driven out of the churches that had been built on Pagan sites during this period. Old customs and practices were barred, sacred sites were destroyed, sacred wells were filled in and the villagers barred from worshipping at those sites. Where it was not possible to eradicate them, such as at holy lakes and waterways, then the order was to stay away. All forms of necromancy, divination and enchantments, which usually took place at *frith splots* (sacred spots) were outlawed. Tree and well worship was forbidden, stone circles were smashed or fired by burning in gigantic bonfires and when they grew hot, the priests threw cold water on them so that they contracted and splintered. Those that were too large to destroy were toppled into pits and buried; much of Avebury was destroyed in this period, so we can only wonder at the original majesty of it.

A giant circle once stood at Hove in Sussex, but this was destroyed. One particular monolith contained a type of fool's gold that glittered, giving rise to the area becoming known as the Goldstone ground. In recent years, a gigantic monolith was uncovered that had escaped destruction, and today, one of the surviving stones can be seen opposite what was the Goldstone Football Ground in Goldstone Park. This went on until Edgar passed away in 979 AD.

And so the years passed. The Witan of Ethelred had expired and Cnut now reigned as monarch, assuming Kingship in 1014. Penalties for *morth*, *blot* and *fytht* (bewitchment to death, idolatry and pertaining to illusions) were now enforced in a new secular digest. Now the King could impose a fine and increase his coffers, if you so much as even loved the Craft (to quote an old edict of the time). This edict seems to have been exclusive to Northumbria. 1038 saw the passing of old King Cnut (Canute), and in 1066, England fell to the Norman invaders, heralding a new wave of oppression under William the Conqueror.

For some reason, Witchcraft and poisoning had become inextricably interlaced. By strange coincidence, this leads us back to where it all started with Exodus XX:II, with the original meaning, "Thou shalt not suffer a Poisoner to live". Over various mistranslations, this became "Thou shalt not suffer a Witch to live". Nevertheless, there it was, killing by *venomo* (venom or poison) was now categorised as Witchcraft, even though the guilty had not the slightest connection with us. Poisoning even came to be known as a Magic Art, despite the fact that absolutely all those who lived in the country knew the lethal qualities of the aptly named death-cap fungi and deadly nightshade, to name but a few of the lethal concoctions that could be made with little effort.

I am still searching old records to discover whether an adder or viper was said to be bewitched when it bit someone. If this happened, I am willing to bet that the accident would have been laid at some local Wise Woman's door. By this time, the penalties that could be imposed were extended to cover perpetual banishment as well as the statutory fines. A case in 1567 shows how the evil art of the poisoner had become associated with the Old Ways. It is likely that this was because the local healer was known to be continually brewing potions and thus became an obvious target.

The indictment read *incantatione et veneficia*, showing there was no difference as the authorities saw it between *veneficium* or *incantation*. Oh, how the odds were stacked against us. Even *incantamentum* came to mean enchantment or to charm. Back to William the Conqueror, whose hand lay heavily upon every one of the now broken, though not subdued, English. Life was probably harsher than it had been for many years and justice for the indigenous people was a travesty. This was the case right up to 1087, when this bloodstained man, on his deathbed, craved forgiveness for all the sins he had perpetrated on the people he had ruled.

Henry the First (1100 to 1135) introduced *sortilegum* (sorcery) and *maleficiis* (Witchcraft) to a new category of "those practising certain arts". This covered an extremely broad range of what these "arts" were, placing these citizens into a section henceforth referred to as *vultivoli*. Records of this period are sparse, mainly due the fact that England was practically destroyed by a civil war at that time between Queen Maud and King Steven, who both contested the crown.

We jump to 1209, when the first case of that century recorded in a Norfolk plea was put before the *Curia Regis* by Agnes, wife of Ordo, a merchant who accused a person named Galiena of *sorceria* (sorcery). The records show that Galiena was delivered unto the "ordeal of iron" (*judicium ferri*). Interestingly, it appears that King Henry was relatively lenient, as there is a remarkable drop in cases being brought before the civil courts. However, the Church and ecclesiastical authorities were still active outside the common law of *Lex Non Scripta*, which dealt with heathens, Pagans and heretics. *Note:* no mention of Witches.

I will not bore the reader further with more of these early statistics, but I will mention that Edward made a great play on seizing land and chattels as a source of wealth. He introduced the fate of burning at the stake to the law books: hanging offences increased, as did mutilation. Witches were now joined by sodomites, corn burners, renegades and disbelievers. It became a bounden duty to deliver such as these up to the public executioner as an example of a *"come born mareschal de la Chrestiente"* (a good marshal of Christendom). So, as we entered the thirteenth century, Witchcraft mainly dropped out of the civil courts jurisdiction and passed into the truly biased hands of the Church, which had a free hand to do whatever it liked.

The fourteenth century saw ecclesiastical powers further increased, as the Church decided to add moral offences such as promiscuity and affairs of the heart to the list of crimes. Witches were considered to be highly promiscuous and Sabbats were thought to be one long round of orgies and merrymaking.

By the fifteenth century, a certifying by way of a conviction for heresy was enough for the unfortunate person to be handed over to the secular powers for the appropriate punishment, and of course, this included Witches. Henry the Fifth sent letters of patent in 1406 to the Bishop of Lincoln, decrying scandalous conduct. However, scrying, prophecy, charming, fortune telling and the like were no longer regarded as great crimes, though they were punished. It is enlightening to see how offences such as these, which had at one time brought crucifixion, were given comparatively light retribution. I think it would be appropriate here to record the results of a case that took place at York in 1467.

The register of Archbishop George Neville that year records a William Byg, known as Lech of Wombwell, who was convicted of professing to trace thieves by magical use of a crystal stone. He was ordered to do penance with a paper scroll on his head inscribed *"ecce sortilegus"*. On his breast and back, a notice proclaimed *"Invocator spirituum"* and *"Sortilegus"*. This was not bad compared to being nailed to a stake. It would have been hoped that a more humane attitude was entering the equation by now: however, this was not to be, for the burning days were just around the corner.

NB: Interestingly, the word *sortilege* still exists, and my dictionary defines this as "divination by drawing lots". A second point is that the notices would have been a wonderful advert for the man's talents – as long as ordinary people could read them, that is.

Magical practice was referred to under the evil serial killer, Henry VIII. He distrusted doctors and physicians - probably with good reason. He lumped these together as practitioners of probable diabolical arts, with their bloodletting and leeching. He demanded that they be examined and approved, long before they dare lay hands on the Royal personage. He wrote:

"The science and conning of physyke and surgerie being exercised by a grete multitude of ignorant persons and that artificers as smyths wevers and women boldley and custumably take upon them grete cures and thyngys of grete difficultie in the which they pertly use socery etc."

An Act of Parliament was passed to stamp out this evil in this reign, but it was later repealed - probably at the instigation of prominent physicians.

Henry V111 even allowed his second wife, Anne Boleyn, to be accused of sorcerie. She was a good Kentish girl, whose hometown was steeped in Witchcraft. He called in his physicians to examine her – informing them, *"She hath a third teat upon her bodie and there is to be found six fingers upon one hand."* A third teat means a third nipple. Rumour has it that Henry had a habit of taking his potential wives to bed well in advance of his weddings. If Anne Boleyn had had an extra nipple, surely Henry would have been aware of it. An extra finger was not exactly easy to hide, so if this was the case, it could hardly have come as a surprise to either Henry or the Court.

Anne had lived most of her life in the French court, later residing at Hever castle in Kent. The accusation of being a Witch had no foundation at all. Another of his wives, Anne of Cleves, lived in Sussex at Lewes - and that was a town steeped in Witchcraft.

Under the rule of his daughter, "Bloody Mary", it was dissenters of the Xtian faith that were far more likely to go to the stake than so-called Witches - although she condemned her fair share of those as well. It was at Lewes in Sussex that an *Auto da Fé* of Protestants was held on the direct orders of Queen Mary. Naturally, many people in those days would happily burn anybody if they were not Catholic, just to give them a foretaste of hell.

Such was the impact of the mass burning of dissident Xtians that to this day, Lewes traditionally burns the Pope in effigy alongside Bloody Mary on November the fifth every year. In earlier years on bonfire night, many old Pagan rites were re-enacted, such as the rolling down the hill of burning tar barrels. Another old Sussex custom that has since died out was known as egg pacing. Sussex Witches would boil eggs with the skins of onions to turn them bright yellow. Village maidens would also hard boil the pacing eggs and paint them in a kaleidoscope of colours. Participants rolled the eggs down the Sussex hills. This was an old Pagano/Witch rite in honour of the Goddess, Ostara, and to Eostre, the Goddess of Fertility. (Two names for the same "Easter" Goddess.) This rite was re-enacted on the Devils Dyke near Hove each Easter as well. After the celebrations, the eggs would be dipped in a holy well or spring, so that they would be blessed with curative powers. Once this ritual was over (and the eggs eaten), it would be combined with an old ritual that is highly popular with Sussex Witches today. This is known as the Dawn Ritual. When the sun came up at the climax of the ritual, all the Witches would chorus in unison, *"The sun shouts!"*

I have never ever seen the burning of a Witch in effigy at Lewes, and few women, most recently Cherie Blair, a year or so ago. Rumour has it that at least three more are being made of her for the next celebration. Strangely enough, only one effigy of Tony Blair is under construction to date.

Dozens of effigies are made, usually depicting unpopular local dignitaries and councillors in addition to politicians - but as I have said - never a Witch. Perhaps it is some subliminal relic from the old days that make Sussex people unwilling to burn what they regard as "one of their own".

As we witnessed in the case of Anne Boleyn, Royalty was not exempt from being accused of Witchcraft, although in England it was comparatively rare. The greater power or influence the accused had, the better the chance of it being quashed before reaching a tribunal or preliminary hearing. Church policy stated that once someone was accused, it was better for an innocent person to die than for the prospect of a Witch being erroneously acquitted! There were certain exceptions where the death penalty was not applied, and once again, probably the most famous of these took place in Sussex.

The scene this time was Pevensey Castle on the south coast. It was in this forbidding and grim setting that Joan of Navarre, the Dowager Queen of England (1370 to 1437) was incarcerated in 1403, accused of Witchcraft. The wording on the indictment reading, *"That the Queen did by sorcerie and neocromancie for to have destroyed the King"*. Joan was the second daughter of the monarch, inaptly named Charles the Bad, who was King of Navarre in France.

Joan had a somewhat chequered background, having been married previously to John IV of Brittany when he was Regent. In 1401, she was married to the King of England, Henry IV, by proxy. She sailed to England to be married with full ceremony in 1403, leaving her Breton children under the guardianship of Burgundy. She was clearly a wealthy woman, for after being accused of bewitching the King, the revenues that derived from her estates in Burgundy became forfeit to Henry, allowing him to further his expansionist wars into the remainder of France! She was imprisoned at Pevensey Castle for the remainder of her life and she died there in 1422 and was buried at Canterbury.

Edward VI became King in 1549. Archbishop Cranmer sent out a questionnaire to the bishoprics throughout the country asking, *"Whether you know any that use charms, sorcery, enchantments or Witchcraft, southsaying (soothsaying) or any like craft invented by the Devil"*.

Elizabeth I ruled in 1558 when the Queen's Attorney demanded the Bishop of London to *"procede by suche severe punischment"* against those who were out of step with the Church. The following year, 1559, saw the additional line, *"specially in the time of women's travel"* being added. The persecutions were now really upon us, as a new bill making enchantments a felony was preferred to the Upper House. Scarcely a year later in 1560, our people were being arraigned before the Assizes as of old.

This was not enacted in every place, and there is not a single record of it being enforced in Sussex, other than the cases mentioned earlier. It is estimated that close on 2,000 people were arraigned within a year throughout England. Sussex escaped most of it, although with some notable exceptions. At

Cuckfield, there is a record of a suspected Witch being hunted down by a pack of hounds. She was caught and savaged to death, after which the huntsman is reputed to have carved out her heart and impaled it on a stake. Apart from such grisly incidents as this, Sussex was indeed a charmed Pagan county. At this stage we were not alone, for parts of the north of England were also declining to respond with the degree of savagery demanded of them by the authorities. For example, while most Witches were being hanged elsewhere, at Hart in Durham in 1582 a Witch who was convicted was sentenced as follows: "Allison Lawe, a notorious sorceror, Witch and enchanter is sentenced to do penance once in the market-place at Durham with a papir on her head, to be repeated at Hart, and once in Norton Church."

On this note I will finish, as the volume of cases from this time onwards would fill a book with a saga of terror, bestiality and torture.

Where do you Bury a Witch?

Where do Witches get themselves buried? After all, they are banned from all Xtian ground. A great furore occurred in Sussex in the early 1980s when Artemis lost one of its highly regarded brethren. He was a practising devotee of Witchcraft, but he came from an eminent local Xtian family. The family had long despaired of enticing their relative back into the Church, but they felt that they should inter him in the family vault or one of the privately owned burial plots where large numbers of the family had been buried over the years. The vault was reserved for specific relatives; and in any case, it was full. The problem started within the family itself, before the vicar added his personal pennyworth.

The general consensus of opinion was that, although the old chap had been much loved by all the family, it did not somehow seem right and proper that a practising Witch should be laid to rest amongst the his God-fearing ancestors. One elderly lady who seemed to be the next candidate for the vault, stated that in her opinion great-uncle Arthur, who was a deacon in eighteen hundred and something, would turn in his grave if the man was laid to rest anywhere near him! It transpired that Auntie was herself chary of being buried close to a Witch when she too passed the great divide! After much discussion, it was decided the most favourable outlet was to cremate the poor old Witch and cast his ashes to the winds, as that way everybody would be satisfied. The chap's widow, although also a Bible-thumper, said that her late departed husband had made her promise that his mortal remains would become earth nutrient, and that he would become worm food. She went on to state that cremation was too reminiscent in his opinion of the burning days. In those days, the clergy wanted to ensure that that all trace of a condemned Witch was erased completely and utterly. On principle, our Witch was not to be eradicated. He wanted his six feet long and six feet deep - and come hell or high water, he would have it!

The family met again, and after lengthy discussion, they came to a decision. The decided to bury him on top of an obscure relative who had departed this life in 1790, and whose grave was only discovered after detailed research into parochial records. The vicar confirmed that there was plenty of room there for another interment and he would instruct the sexton to dig it the following day. The bombshell came when the vicar enquired as to what were our friend's favourite hymns, because for a small consideration, he would instruct the organist accordingly.

We only heard the remainder of the story second hand. Apparently, the silence was eventually broken when a bolder member of the illustrious family announced that the deceased was not a "churchy" sort of a person. This did not deter the vicar one iota, for he smiled sweetly (knowing that the family was wealthy) and announced that it would be rather nice to give the dear departed a good send off. Indeed, the vicar offered to say a very special prayer directed to the Almighty himself. This would crave indulgence for one, who according to his records, had been baptised there some 80 years ago, and therefore, was still Xtian, whether or nay he had been particularly zealous in attendance.

Apparently, they shifted somewhat uncomfortably from foot to foot, and then announced that he had not just lapsed but had become just a teensy bit Pagan over the years. In fact, very Pagan.

"Pagan!" the Vicar exploded! "You mean he was not even a nominal Xtian?"

Sadly, they nodded their heads and muttered something to the effect that their relative had renounced the Church and gone his own somewhat Pagan way for nigh on twenty years. A nice simplistic send-off and a swift interment were all that they required.

We gather that vicar's curiosity got the better of him, so he pressed his questions home more directly, eventually dragging out the word that no one would utter! The deceased was a Witch! Bingo! All the largesse in the world: bribes, blandishments, pecuniary rewards and handsome fees so offered would not get him to bury a Witch in his Churchyard! Oh no, on that point he was adamant. The mere fact that the family physically owned that particular plot of land meant nothing. He was the vicar of all he surveyed and was the final arbiter in this matter. Our friend was not going to lie amongst good Xtian folks. Besides, what would the Bishop think? Not to mention all those nearby Xtian souls from other families if they knew a confirmed Witch was lying close to their relatives. Just think what would happen on resurrection day!

In fact, in a fit of pique, the vicar implied that the family would have more chance imploring him to inter the family cat there than a Witch! The wrangle went on for quite a few days to no avail. Then the local undertaker stepped in. Our friend was getting a little bit ripe by now, so he asked the family if they could they please come to a decision. As it happened, there was an epidemic of flu at that time and his establishment was full up, so the space was needed.

The next stage was now pure farce, for the only compromise that could possibly be reached was to deposit the mortal shell into un-consecrated ground – if there was any to be found. The vicar pulled his hair out and burned the midnight oil to find the boundaries of all the consecrated land. This turned out to be almost all of it - except for a small piece by the rubbish dump and church incinerator where all the dead and faded wreaths and flowers ended up.

You would have thought that would be the end of the matter and that the dear old Witch had found his eternal resting place at last. Apparently, the plans of the graveyard were very small and the vicar had to measure out the area in minute detail just in case a little bit of our friend's body should protrude onto consecrated ground. Can you imagine the situation that must have gone through the mind of God's emissary on earth? What if 90 per cent of the poor old man's body ended up sitting on a pile of hot coals in Hades, while his right arm was in Heaven?

Having meticulously measured out the area, the vicar went through the full panoply of de-consecrating it, just to make sure. Honour was satisfied. A small length of string was stretched by the side of the plot so that the line of demarcation between consecrated and un-consecrated land was now clearly defined. Local Witches had the last laugh, though. A few days after the funeral, they erected a small wooden marker over the grave and paid their last respects to a most venerable man whom they all loved. The little plaque's last lines read:

"Alas, alas, we both did die
But she lies just as snug as I"

A magnificent headstone to a lady happened to be a mere few inches away from our friend, but in holy and consecrated ground. The irate vicar had the marker removed within hours, stating it was not an "approved" marker. Such is the lot of the practising pagan.

There is divided opinion amongst the Craft as to whether they should be buried or cremated when they pass on to their beloved Summerlands. For some, like our friend, the memory of the burning days still lingers. Others love the idea of becoming part of Nature and returning to mother earth as in days of yore, yet they are mindful that land is becoming scarce.

Beauty, Death and Resurrection

Many years ago, the Order of Artemis tackled this problem and I consulted numerous Witches from many covens. It seemed that not only Pagans, but many Xtians as well, felt that cremation and the usual scattering of the ashes left no lasting memory of a loved one. On the other hand, as the years went on and partners themselves grew inevitably older, it became less and less possible to visit a cemetery, whether it be a grave or an urn containing the deceased one's ashes in a Garden of Remembrance. So, what is the solution?

I wrote up a ritual and devised a completely new approach to the issue. The custom is now predominant amongst Sussex covens, and strangely enough, has been taken up by many Xtians as well, but devoid of the ritualistic side. The entire concept is beautiful and it keeps the loved one with the family for as long as they wish. At the end, it reverts to the earth. Therefore, here is the Pagano/Witch way. Amend it as you wish.

"Find ye a large pot or vase that is both beautiful in appearance and unbreakable; and that will mellow and weather with the passing of the years. Many concrete and stone containers can be found in high-class florists and garden centres, often in the Graeco-Roman style, ornamented with depictions of ancient Gods and Goddesses, nymphs and pards, Pan and satyrs. There are also beautiful "Wedgwood" style depictions in green and white or blue and white of vines and grapes that are reminiscent of Bacchus. These represent the ancient Deities who we worship.

Having obtained such a container of considerable size, bear in mind the amount of earth and peat that you will require. Collect the ashes of the deceased from the crematorium and mix them with seven times the volume of earth and peat mixture - seven being a mystical number. Next, line the bottom of the urn or container that you have chosen liberally with sweet smelling potpourri. Ideally, this should be homemade, but there are many ones readily available on the market. Cover the bottom liberally so that no part of it can be seen, and moisten the potpourri mixture with scented oils and perfumes as you wish. Musk, jasmine and honeysuckle are favourites. (I know of one woman who requested that her mortal remains be fragranced with a bottle of her favourite perfume, so even at the closing ceremony of her life, the earth from the vase would exude the special fragrance for which she was known.)

Add a handful or so of the special potpourri to the earth, peat and ash mixture and remix it all again. Then pour the mixture into the vessel you have chosen, covering the scented potpourri at the bottom. Add earth, but do not fill the jar completely; leave at least four inches or more free from the top. All of those present (and you can make a little event of this) will be invited to add three heads or stalks of lavender to the pot, and then to sprinkle these with rose petals or any flower heads that they think are appropriate to the deceased.

Now we come to the climax. This will endure for a long time, or if cuttings are taken, then forever. Mutually decide on a plant that has been chosen for longevity, such as a rose bush or a tree, especially if it was a favourite of the departed or their next of kin. (All Pagans and Witches revere trees.) Wiccans tend to go for very large Greek style pots and plant a Rowan tree in it, this tree being especially relevant to them. Now plant it in the container, saying whatever words you feel are appropriate to the occasion. Top the pot up with pure earth or loam as you wish, ensuring that the ash and peat mixture is completely covered with pure earth.

Drink a libation to the departed and to the Old Gods, then pour a libation of the wine (not spirits) into the pot. All of those present can do this as a gesture, but do ensure that the libation is only a token. Then water the pot well.

Over the years, the last mortal remains of the loved-one will be slowly converted into a living, breathing and beautiful plant. What you will see growing will be a living symbol of the person, forever displaying beauty and perhaps fragrance. The departed is now part of the plant as it draws nutrient from the remains. The ashes will nourish the plant for many years. What we have achieved is a beautiful transmutation from the dead to the living in the circle of life. The loved one is now the plant.

Each passing year it will display its fondness for you, identify with you and reward you with its green beauty and flowers, blooms or fruit. It is something you can talk to, something or someone you can unburden yourself to, for the plant is now your mentor. It will grow larger and more beautiful as you yourself grow older. It will respond to the love and attention you bestow upon it. It is, in fact, a living depiction of your loved-one. If you move house, the loved-one can come with you. It is a living monument.

Sadly and eventually, when your own day comes to enter the Summerlands and when the Goddess calls you, you and your partner or loved-one can be joined together with the same ritual. Over the years your own ashes, with the roots of the plants now entwined and enjoined are forever in a loving embrace with he or she ye loved.

"So mote it be."

On a final note, I am minded to quote an old inscription that I found in a book of classical quotations, and which gave me the inspiration to create the ritual above. Archaeologists found it on a smashed Etruscan vase, and it is poignant in its sadness and simplicity. It is as written below:

"You may break; you may shatter the vase as you will.

But the scent of the roses will linger there still."
May the above be of comfort to those who have been bereaved
and who read this book and adopt this Wiccan rite.

Finale

I will end on a final note of statistics and humour. Readers will undoubtedly find it interesting to note the ratio of planetary sun sign rulers that belong to the 100 initial members of both sexes (67 women and 33 men) who entered Artemis. The dominating planets of those who are particularly attracted to the craft are as follows:

Planet	Number
Venus	25
Mercury	19
Saturn	15
Mars	15
Jupiter	13
Sun	7
Moon	6

Of the first 100 women whom I have initiated, including the 67 from our own coven, along with those I initiated at the invitation of other covens, the figures alter. However, once again, Venus dominates.

Planet	Number
Venus	39
Jupiter	18
Mercury	13
Saturn	10
Sun	7
Moon	7
Mars	6

It comes as no surprise to me that Venus dominates, as this planet combines love and power. Venusians are not especially academic, so they are not usually drawn to astrology. The planets that can cope with the maths and memory required for astrology are Mercury, the Sun and Saturn. Neither are they particularly drawn to Spiritualism, because one has to be mediumistic for this to become a main interest. Spiritualism attracts Lunar, Jovian and Neptunian types. Venusians are tactile, practical and close to the earth, so they would appreciate both the practicality and the nature-loving aspects of Witchcraft. Nor does it surprise me that the fair sex shows the more aggressive Mars at the bottom of the list. What has always surprised me is that Moon and Sun signs are less prevalent statistically than Mercury and Saturn.

I would be very interested to receive figures from other covens to see if this trend is a constant figure. It would be interesting to see whether it alters with different persuasions of the Craft - i.e. Hereditary, Traditionalist, Gardnerian and Alexandrian in the early days, and in different countries.

Well we have dwelt long and hard on the Old Ways. Many people reading this book will recognise those to whom we have referred obliquely. Those of Artemis will remember the call of the wild as we worshipped in the ancient Woodlands bequeathed to us years ago. The years have passed and it is time to move on. After over half a century of running Artemis, the grooming of my successors is now underway. Tanith, the High Priestess to whom I owe so much, has moved back into the area and she has relieved me of the great workload that running a healing coven involves.

She trains the new initiates in the ways of magic, and she has already produced fine graduates. Others are coming along who have the potential to be High Priests and Priestesses in the future. The foundations of Artemis are well laid, and it continues to expand and spread the belief in the Goddess and God of Nature to all. And me? I think it is time to sit back and be an Elder of the Craft now, and to watch the movement that I created all those years ago as it prospers. It is time for me to write new books and to formulate further lecture tours.

I understand that America now has in excess of 1,500,000 Pagans. Most importantly, the Wiccan and associated Pagan religions are recognised by law. Their marriage services are valid and binding. The time is coming when we too in the UK must press for recognition of Wicca as a true religion that is accepted by the State, alongside our Hindu, Buddhist, Spiritualist and Muslim brethren who have established their own Temples and places of worship within the British Isles. This should now happen, or the original religion of these isles will still be unrecognised.

Constant overtures to the Census Office are met with platitudes. They tell us that accurate figures have still not been formulated, so we cannot yet press for legal recognition of the Old Religion. This, notwithstanding the fact that if at least 30,000 people declare that they belong to a specific faith, the law entitles that religion to be formally recognised. There are far more than 30,000 Wiccans in this country.

Protestors who objected to declaring their faith have recently started a movement to encourage malcontents to declare themselves as Jedi Knights. The subsequent figures revealed that vast numbers did so. In theory and in law, enough did to establish the Jedi Knights as a religion, but the authorities in their infinite wisdom rejected the statistics as "frivolous".

How strange it is that in this computer age, the statistics for Jedi Knights were immediately available, and that they could tell us instantly many other statistics. But Pagans? Sorry... the figures were not available!

I completed my USA Wiccan tour in 2003 as a guest of Levanah Shell Bdolak, who is the head of Clearsight in America and Japan. She generously sponsored the tour and paid all our expenses. This culminated in a week in the Wild West in Arizona and a shootout at the legendary OK Corral in Tombstone. This was very un-Wiccan but great fun. A second tour is currently being discussed for Florida later this year and a tour of Portugal next year.

The lecture tour of California in itself would fill a new book, for the disparity between American Wicca with its sects and schisms could envelop volumes. Their ways are many and varied. However, they are set upon a determinable course, in the adulation of Pagan ways in which the Earth Mother and God of Fertility predominate. The important issue is their complete and utter dedication to the Goddess. Those who I met who followed the Old Ways closest were Isians who combined Wiccan practices with the rituals of The Fellowship of Isis.

When friends and Witches realised that finally, I had decided to write a book on Witchcraft, I was asked repeatedly, "Will you show love spells?" and, "Will you tell about aphrodisiacs?" Well ladies, now it is in print, you can see that the answer is no! We cannot have wicked witches running around enchanting every desirable male who they behold, nor vice versa. As for aphrodisiacs...well, perhaps not that either. However, as it is the fair sex within my coven that press me to tell all - I will break my rule (just for the women's sake) and talk for a moment about aphrodisiacs.

One ancient recipe for love from the sixteenth century (and I use the word love lightly here) is a combination to help you conceive and to revive interest physically in a flagging lover or husband. So here we go:

"Take ye a living fish and place it head first and wriggling inside thy most private parts and leave it there until such time as you are sure it is dead, then remove it intact! Next, you cook it in butter and serve the fish to thy lover. This dish will by now have been transformed, magically with your love juices into a most powerful aphrodisiac, and it will drive him mad with desire for you. It adds "and thou wilt conceive".

Do let me know if it works as I will include it in my next book, but all invitations to a fish supper will be declined!

In conclusion: Sussex - indomitable Sussex - has always been at the forefront in the expounding and preservation of England's proud Pagan heritage. Now in the Age of Aquarius, let us press for the legal restoration and recognition of the religion that was so violently wrested from us.

So mote it be.

Appendix

The following are extracts from tours and books. They give the background to a number of eminent Wiccans or supporters of Wicca who are prominent in the world of Witchdom and the media. Below is part of the publicity campaign that preceded the American tour of California and Arizona in 2003.

If you wish to contact the author or if you have any enquiries about The Last Bastion, please feel free to send an email to bastion@zampub.com, or write to Ralph Harvey, c/o Zambezi Publishing Ltd, at the address in the front of this book.

*NB: **Editor's note:** You will notice Ralph being referred to as Sir Ralph Harvey. This is correct; Ralph is a member of the European peerage, although he doesn't often use his title.*

The Notice

This coming spring (2003), Sir Ralph Harvey, founder and High Priest of the Order of Artemis in England will be coming to the West Coast to visit and Lecture. This is an experience you cannot afford to miss...

Sir Ralph Harvey is one of the last of the Elder English Traditional High Priests of an era that is quickly becoming history. A contemporary of Doreen Valiente, Ralph Harvey has the genuine personal history of the "pre-history" of the modern Craft, as he was active in the 1950s, attending many coven gatherings. He knew all the greats who have sadly passed on and he gave the eulogy at Doreen Valiente's funeral.

Sir Ralph Harvey joined the early Traditionalist covens, and he worked closely with the well-known Gardnerian English covens. He has a reputation for researching the old ways to preserve and bring to light the true Wiccan ways that have been hidden through the centuries and that only survived through a few families that kept the old ways.

With the experience Ralph has acquired through the years, he has documented and preserved many of the old hereditary ways, which were fast disappearing. The Order of Artemis was originally founded in the 1950s after the repeal of the Witchcraft Act. His major coven was strictly hereditary in its practices. After the rise of Gardnerianism, the ancient and strict rules of the Craft that they had practiced so avidly were relaxed, and it was decided to adhere to as many of the old ways as possible, but to bring them into the twentieth century.

The Order of Artemis became the very first coven to throw off the hereditary trappings and update the old tradition so that it would be in keeping with the times. It retained the vast majority of the old hereditary principles, but brought them into the twentieth century, creating a new principle in Witchcraft, which has come to be known as Traditionalist. They maintained all the old traditions but updated certain aspects that had become archaic. The Order was reconstituted in 1978, and it has continued to expand ever since. Ralph Harvey has well in excess of one hundred covens worldwide. They are now found in France, Ireland, Scotland, Wales, Australia, New Zealand, Isle of Man, Canada and Spain. As these groups hive, the number of covens that have sprung from the loins of the Order of Artemis increases.

Ralph is perhaps the last of the old line of the Elder Priests and Priestesses in England. He is also one of the most famous and respected exorcists in England, often being called upon by the police for aid. Ralph's ghostly experiences have been documented and featured on numerous television programs, and in August of this year, he was featured in a program about Wicca for Japanese Television.

Ralph often lectures throughout England about the search for, and the finding of, the famous original, alleged, nine covens founded by old George Pickingill. George was the last descendant of Julia the Wicce, the Witch of Brandon who was killed in 1071. He formed the basis of much of the modern Craft that Ralph holds so dear. One interesting aspect is the fact that the New Forest coven into which Gerald Gardner was initiated was one of the famous nine covens of Old George Pickingill that had survived the persecutions. He speaks about how these ancient traditions and ways have been preserved. He tells of the concepts that survived, albeit in an altered form to become the modern Craft that we now know.

It is a rare treat to hear Ralph speak. He is warm, fun-loving and an extremely knowledgeable and powerful Wiccan, who shares his knowledge of history and Craft practices in a gentle, witty, loving manner that endears all who hear him.

This coming March 2003, Sir Ralph Harvey will be speaking about the ancient roots of Wicca, and how these relate to our modern practices. You will not want to miss this! Sir Ralph Harvey is a genuine living page of history.

Levanah Shell Bdolak
Wiccan High Priestess and director of Clearsight, Malibu. California USA
Encyclopedia of Witchcraft and Neo Paganism (2003)

The International Encyclopaedia of Witchcraft and Neo Paganism that is published in the USA and Canada is the Who's Who of the Wicca, and is the biggest tome on the Craft ever known.

The following entry was submitted after an increasing number of Witches in the USA refused to accept as a genuine Crafter anyone whose roots did not go directly back to Gardner. Erroneously, the tendency ignored the old Crafters who pre-dated 1951. To these people the Craft as such, commenced with the publication of Gardner's Witchcraft Today. The fact that the Craft had survived countless years before Gardner emerged on the scene was conveniently overlooked by our American cousins. To them, Witchcraft only began in 1951.

Repeatedly, visiting American and Canadian Witches would visit us and tell us that they were all Crafters, and that they had been initiated by people whose roots were faultless. However, because they were not Gardnerian, they were not accepted by the Wiccan community. Worse still, people now required what were humorously called "Puppy Papers", documents that substantiated their Gardnerian roots. Professor Shelley Rabinovitch PhD, a cultural anthropologist and sessional lecturer in Religious Studies at the University of Ottawa in Canada, has studied Witchcraft worldwide. She wrote the following article in the 2003 edition of The Encyclopaedia of Modern Witchcraft and Neo-Paganism (Kensington Press). She currently teaches Witchcraft, magic and occult phenomena there.

Shelley Rabinovitch's Entry

The large section on Ralph and Audrey Harvey covers the same ground that is in this book. I do not wish to run the risk of boring you or to sound as though I am blowing my own trumpet, so I will not repeat it in full here.

It starts as follows:

"The Order of Artemis was founded in 1959, eight years after the repeal of the infamous Witchcraft Act, but its roots commenced in the early fifties. Count Ralph de Straet von Kollman, who writes and lectures under the name Ralph Harvey, desperately tried to hold to the old hereditary ways..."

It ends as follows:

"In March 2002, Ralph initiated his hundredth Priestess, thus furthering the expansion of the Craft and Artemis. The covens emanating from his work in a span of over 50 years are many. At the age of 75, he is one of the last of the old school of Witchcraft."

Professor Shelley Rabinovitch PH.D
University of Ottawa

The following acknowledgments, tributes and thanks go to prominent Wiccans and Promoters of the Old Ways. These people have been my colleagues for over 50 years - and they have featured prominently on the Wiccan scene. My book would not be complete without mentioning them.

The Museum of Witchcraft, Boscastle, Cornwall
(www.museumofwitchcraft.com)

Set in a rural harbour village on the north Cornish coast, the Museum of Witchcraft offers its visitors a factual insight into Witchcraft throughout the ages, including information on prominent figures from recent history to today. Graham King, the current owner and a Wicca practitioner, hails from Hampshire. He purchased the museum seven years ago at Samhain from Cecil Williamson, who had built his collection over many years – opening the first Witchcraft research centre on the Isle of Man in 1951, and arriving in Boscastle in 1961, where the museum now resides.

N.B: Please remember that the recent devastating flood in August 2004 caused damage that may only be repaired some time hence, and some exhibits are very likely beyond repair. The following information is therefore subject to change by the time the museum reopens, hopefully by Easter 2005.

The *"mages"* or *"magi"* section of the museum displays a gallery of prominent characters, including Cassandra Latham, village Wise Woman of St Buryan, Vivianne Crowley, Patricia Crowther, Sybil Leek, Gerald Gardner, Robert Cochrane and George Pickingill. As you enter, one of the first exhibits you see is the fragmented robe that was donated by Ralph Harvey of the Order of Artemis. The sleeves show fading and ancient symbols, one of which is the lost Sigil of Power. How many modern day Witches would recognise it as they enter the twenty-first century? It is there to find - for those who seek.

A new addition in 2002 is a collection of Alex Sanders' regalia, including a sword and mask with photographs to confirm authenticity. There is also a huge amethyst and an altar slab used by Alex and decorated with symbols more commonly associated with ritual magic.

A scrying crystal belongs to Austin Osman Spare, who was an artist, witch and writer. There is also an early wax cylinder recording of Aleister Crowley quoting excerpts from the "Gnostic Mass". In the gallery are an Enochian altar and tablets that probably originated with Doctor John Dee, who was the court astrologer, apothecary and magician to Elizabeth the First. Edward Kelly is also displayed.

Other ritual tools are an enchanting moon crown made by the late Hereward Wake, Magister of the West Country coven of the Silver Wheel for female initiates. An athame of "Athene" has been donated by Audrey Kemp, Ralph's wife, who is a High Priestess of the Order of Artemis. Simple and hand-carved, it depicts the early workings of the Craft as it was, when tools were simplistic.

Beside a mystical four-foot ceramic hare-lady, the sacred beast of Eostre and a classic shape-shifting creature, is documentation on the burial of Joan Wytte, "fairy woman of Bodmin", circa 1813. Cecil acquired her skeleton and displayed it for many years. Graham and others felt she needed a more respectful remembrance, so they have buried her near Minster Church, with a stone plaque nearby.

A recent donation of dolls made with horsehair and hay, and magical animal oils from a witch in West Penwith shows that poppetry is still alive and well. The collection of Mandrakes, on loan from the family of Bob Richel from Amsterdam, shows an example of plant and herb lore used for magical purposes. With emphasis on male fertility, these are aphrodisiacs. In addition, they are used as bringers of good fortune, narcotics and anaesthetics.

This text summarises a taste of the varying paths of the Craft that have existed and that still exist today. There is much depth that just cannot be exhibited, but with the library available upstairs for serious students with an ever-expanding catalogue of subjects, may the Museum continue to educate and entertain.

Thank you, Graham, for help with this book and for your continuing support.

John Belham-Payne Biography;
The Centre for Pagan Studies
(www.centre-for-pagan-studies.org)

At an early age, John Belham-Payne discovered a spiritual calling and attended his local church. He soon became disillusioned, and it was not long before he left to seek other faiths. Like many others who discover Paganism as their chosen path, John studied several other religions first. However, in those days it was difficult to find anyone who could teach Witchcraft.

Patricia initiated John into the Craft alongside John Edwards, who was a traditional Welsh Witch, on Samhain 1973 when John was twenty-one. Moving to London to pursue his musical career, he worked as a solo Witch for a number of years, until he met Ralph and Audrey Harvey, who ran the Order of Artemis in Hove, England. John was then initiated into that coven by Isis the High Priestess.

In 1995, he and his wife, Julie, set up the Centre for Pagan Studies (CFPS) in an eighteenth century barn at their Sussex home. Doreen Valiente became a firm friend and supporter of the work of the CFPS. John and Julie nursed her round the clock during her last short illness, and John held her hand when she passed into the Summerlands on September 1st, 1999.

Doreen bequeathed to John Belham-Payne her famous collection of Witchcraft artefacts, her extensive library and the copyright on all her poetry, as well as all her research material and the magical inheritance passed on to her from Gerald

Gardner. The collection includes many items that Gerald Gardner made for her, in addition to some of his ritual items, together with Gardner's original Book of Shadows and Doreen Valiente's Book of Shadows. These are thought by many to be Witchcraft's most important existing documents.

Doreen had asked John to perform her funeral service, and this was done in full accordance with her wishes, at Bear Road Cemetery in Brighton. The crematorium chapel was ornamented in true Pagan style, and four leading members of Paganism delivered eulogies and tributes to the great mistress of magic herself. These included Emrys, a leading Witch and Druid, his wife Sarah and me, representing Artemis.

The Rev John Belham-Payne of the Centre for Pagan Studies conducted the service and oversaw the funeral arrangements. John personally took Doreen's ashes to a secluded woodland glade that was dear to her heart and where she had earlier spent time with the man who was destined to be her husband. Here, on the next full moon, her ashes were reverently scattered by John. Doreen was seen by many people as the head of the Gardnerian Tradition of Witchcraft. John promised Doreen he would continue the work that she had started, and help to move the Craft of the Wise back to its roots.

In 2000, John and Julie moved to Spain. This freed them to restore and archive Doreen Valiente's famous collection of Witchcraft artefacts and to publish her book of poetry, entitled "Charge of The Goddess". In 2001, John was admitted to the Aquarian Tabernacle Church, thereby being given the honorary title of Reverend. John is a longstanding committee member of the Pagan Federation, and is a long-standing member of the National Conference team.

Together with a travelling exhibition of the artefacts of Doreen Valiente, John Belham-Payne runs a series of lectures to raise funds for a suitable, permanent venue for a Study Centre and Museum, so that the Doreen Valiente collection and library can become available to those who seek knowledge. John has never run his own coven. He travels extensively throughout the world, giving talks, and he is always honoured to be asked to act as a guest at many meetings. Despite the fact that he was Doreen Valiente's last High Priest and ritual working partner, he remains loyal to Ralph and Audrey Harvey, considering them his High Priest and Priestess to this day.

NB: More information can be obtained from the web site wwwdoreenvaliente.com

Justin Hankinson and Jonathan Tapsell - Hexagon Productions and Organisers of the Occulture Festival

Justin and Jonathan are two of Britain's leading experts on Witchcraft, Magic and Voodoo and the police, public and media frequently consult them. Their famous cases include the death of Nicholas Gargani, the Clapham Woods mystery, the British remote viewing programme and the exposé of the Order of Nine Angles.

Television and radio credits include The Scream Team for Living TV, The Hex Files - made in conjunction with Ralph Harvey and the Order of Artemis, and a documentary of modern Satanism. In addition, a BBC Radio programme on Occulture and a film about Chaos Magick. In the publishing field, the pair is responsible for producing the last book of the famous English Witch, Doreen Valiente, with her "Charge of the Goddess". This was commissioned by the Centre for Pagan Studies.

Perhaps the most famous and influential of their projects within the esoteric domain was the formation of the Hexagon Archive, an independent resource that collects and preserves rare artefacts and documents pertaining to the occult. These include the Crotona Fellowship Papers that are linked to the New Forest coven of Gerald Gardner.

In the year 2000, to mark a new era in human rights, the pair founded the Occulture Festival. This annual event champions religious rights and spiritual freedom. Occulture is held in Brighton annually now. It has featured some of the world's leading occultists as well as famous actors, filmmakers, intellectuals and writers. International organisations, such as the Tibetan Government and Amnesty International, have attended the festival in support of the many good causes highlighted during the weeklong event. Occulture may not have made the Guinness Book of records, but it is the proud owner of the world's largest Enochian chess set, peopled by 36 human chess pieces!

Peter Hill, Personal Witchcraft History

Peter Hill is also a Witch of the old school. He is now in his 75th year. He is one of the stalwarts of the Craft, having been re-initiated into the Artemis coven in 1981. An old Harrow School boy, he has been interested in Witches and ghosts since he was a small child. He remembers riding around the garden on a broomstick and trying without success to take off. Of such material are future Witches made... His days at Harrow were not happy ones, with beatings and compulsory Christianity continuously being rammed into him. This swiftly disillusioned him with Xtianity. The late Miles Charlesworth, another member of Artemis, was also an old Harrovian. He told similar tales and he drifted away from the faith he had been born into, completely rejecting the Xtianity that had been so violently forced upon him. He joined the coven of Artemis in 1981; the same year that Peter left the coven of Arachne to pledge his loyalty to The Order of Artemis. Myles was 72 when he made the decision to become a Witch!

Peter's mother was a Spiritualist who used to take him to séances at the London Spiritualist Alliance in the West End of London. He found the meetings most interesting and based his early religious views on Spiritualism rather than school Xtianity. One day he found a copy of the Key of Solomon, and as had others before him, practised Ritual Magic - albeit somewhat unsuccessfully. as Peter now humorously recounts.

During the 1950s and 1960s, the Sunday papers ran sensational articles about Gerald Gardner and other Witches, which intrigued him further. Looking south from the farm that he owned, he could see Chanctonbury Ring. Peter's wife, Pam, was a schoolteacher who taught nearby. One day, she told him that one of the daygirls who lived in Ditchling village was a member of a Heredity coven in the village. This girl was in hot water for instructing some of the boarders in Witchcraft, one of whom was the daughter of a press baron. It was a nine-day wonder and it was swiftly swept under the table. He does not remember if the Witch was expelled or merely told to stop her activities.

Peter Hill found that the income from farming was falling and he decided to sell up. He then moved to Littlehampton, where he was engaged in road haulage. He also owned a fishing boat. It was through fishing that he met Brian Parkin, who was also a fisherman at that time. Brian was equally intrigued by the occult, and the two became firm friends. On the death of his mother in 1981, Peter inherited her house. He sold his own home and bought a holiday cottage in Boscastle, a place he had always been drawn to, and the home of the Museum of Witchcraft.

It was not long before he decided that he would like to join a coven, but he did not know how to find one. One day, he answered an advert for a vacancy in a Brighton coven. The people concerned lived in Kemp Town, but he was not accepted by them as they were only looking for couples.

Later, he heard of another coven run by a Paul and Andrea Foreman. Peter was accepted by them, and eventually initiated into the coven of Annisweb. They had been in Alex Sanders' coven at Selmeston years beforehand, but left after a short time and decided to take their own path, forming a coven and then seeking tuition where they could. They also knew an old Hereditary Witch from Abingdon who used to instruct Andrea in magic. They also had knowledge of Plant Bran Craft, which was a very well known coven. The maiden was called Angela and she lived at North Holmwood near Dorking.

The coven of Annisweb, according to tradition, always worked sky clad. At the winter solstice, they elected a Lord of Misrule and played naughty sexy games sky clad. A Witch called Annie, who had previously been in a coven in Lake Lane, Barnham, was also a member, and she formed a close friendship with Peter. Both of these Witches were also destined to join Artemis before long, and to become valued members.

Peter found the coven of Annisweb too restrictive, so he left them. Peter was now covenless, but fate was to lead him into a new path. A chance meeting occurred. He was sent to hire a fancy dress from Harveys of Hove, the Film and Television costumiers in Trafalgar Road, Portslade for a party. Here he met Ralph and Audrey, who knew he was an ordained Witch. They invited him to a Sabbat at Warnham, Kingsfold. The Witch, Annie, came along too. Although Annie had her own coven as well as belonging to the Annisweb group, they both decided that they would be happier with Ralph's Traditional Artemis coven. They were duly admitted and have remained, happily, ever since.

With the passing of time, Peter was elevated to the second and Third Degrees by The Lady Tanith, High Priestess of Ralph's coven. Ralph calls her, "the finest Priestess I ever had".

While living full time in Boscastle, Peter met many local Witches, including Cassandra Latham, the village Witch of St. Buryan. She stayed with him at Claremont when she came to Boscastle on business. Peter went to some trouble to cook a nice meal, but when he offered her Glenfiddich whisky, she refused - informing him that she did not drink spirits, she only invoked them and commanded them to do her will! While Peter was in hospital at Hayle for a hip replacement, Cassandra visited him. Others in the ward noticed that his recovery was accelerated by her visits. The results of her visits were so obvious to other patients that he told them that she was a practising Witch. She is now the official Pagan Chaplain to the hospital. Who says Witchcraft does not work!

In 1984, Peter Hill's fellow fisherman, Brian Parkin, joined Artemis and he became a very powerful Witch in his own right. Brian was a jolly "hail-fellow-well-met" character. He could so easily have been identified with the God Bacchus. Brian was trained by Tanith, the High Priestess of Artemis. His wife soon followed him into Artemis, and she was trained by Ralph.

Sadly, Brian and his wife Jill ultimately divorced, and some time afterwards, Brian remarried a girl by the name of Sandy. True to form, she completed her year-and-a-day and is now ensconced within Artemis, having been initiated in 2002 - eighteen years after Brian's first wife was admitted.

Witch Rowan

No biography would be complete on the Wiccan scene, without reference to the one person within Artemis upon whom the mantle of power will ultimately fall. Rowan, as he shall be known as in this book, came into Artemis when Annie's Arachne coven decided to amalgamate with us. Rowan has to remain anonymous, as have others in this book, because of their professions, but he is well known among us.

A most able Witch of the Third Degree, Son of a Belfast Protestant father and a Jehovah's Witness mother, he was soon to eschew Xtianity and embrace Witchdom. He had grown up in a Xtian atmosphere, having lived with his father and mother until the age of seventeen, in addition to a zealous Protestant grandfather who was head of one of the largest Orange Order Lodges in East Belfast. Rowan's ancestry goes back to the Normans, and he can claim a family link to Romany Gypsies. It was not long after he set out on the Pagan path that his mother, who until then had been a devout Jehovah's Witness, became completely and utterly disillusioned with the entire Witness movement and left it, never to return.

Rowan was an immediate candidate to be a Witch, having spent his youth working with the Royal Society for the Protection of Birds, the British Trust for Ornithology, the Sussex Trust for Nature Conservation Woodsville near

Henfield and other animal conservation groups. By the age of fifteen, he carried quartz stones everywhere, was an avid reader of Witchcraft, astrology and magic. At sixteen, his Xtian mother caught him reading books on the Craft. It was a great disappointment to her to find that the son she had reared as a Xtian had turned out this way. After all, she had chosen this path for him in his formative years. This did not deter him, and in 1986, the turning point in his life came via a trip to Glastonbury, where he experienced a unique spiritual event from which he never looked back.

Rowan had decided to camp at the base of the hill and he was returning to his tent after watching the sunrise, when he became aware of a voice subliminally calling him from the woods. The wood was on the opposite side of a fence, and he found himself being drawn irresistibly towards it. Climbing the fence, he was confronted by a strong breeze, which ceased the moment he alighted on the other side. As he recalls to this day, all was peace and tranquillity there. Suddenly he was aware of a movement and he saw a dark-skinned fawn-like creature that seemed to be beckoning him to enter the woodland. As he now recalls and states, "Normally I would have been afraid, but there was a gentleness in this creature that I found reassuring". Rowan decided to follow, and the creature kept stopping to make sure he was still behind as he was led deeper and deeper into the woods. Eventually it stopped at a badger's sett. It beckoned him yet again, and a few paces further on he found himself in a clearing and alone!

Everywhere there were foxgloves, which were his favourite flower. For some unknown reason Rowan instinctively picked one, and instantly found himself back in the real world again. Suddenly he felt afraid. Around him, the wind was howling, and he knew instinctively in that moment he had committed a cardinal sin by destroying a thing of beauty. At that moment, he understood he had received an occult lesson. Rowan apologised to the woodland spirits around him and instantly all was calm again. So, who was the wondrous creature that had manifested itself before him? Puck? Pan? The Horned God? He did not know. However, he knew he had been called to follow the Old Ways and that this creature was his friend.

Rowan was by now hopelessly lost in the woodland and called upon the "fawn" for help. The response was no more than a shadow, but he followed it and it led him back to the precise spot where he had entered the wood. He thanked the entity and continued back to the camp. From that point onward, his path was to lead him to a coven and initiation. This was almost three years to the day after he met the fawn-like creature at Glastonbury. Fate had set him on the path to Witchdom.

He joined the coven of Arachne, but soon Arachne joined Artemis. Rowan took the first steps along the long, tortuous path that will ultimately lead him to being a High Priest of Magic in his own right, and with his own coven one day.

The Triple Aspect!

The Triple Aspect is a formidable group of Witches who have worked together for the past nine years. Between them, these three, who have hearts of gold, have over 65 years of experience in all aspects of Witchdom at their fingertips. Their powers are formidable. Within the top echelon of Craft circles, they are humorously referred to as "the three whose fame lies enshrined in what we call that unmentionable Scottish play". These three draw on many traditions, having a wealth of experience and knowledge gathered over countless years of practice. Over time, their different skills and strengths have been finely honed and pooled to create their own unique method of working and healing.

Their individual spiritual searches have taken them onto many and varied paths and initiations, including the mysteries of Traditional (Hereditary) magic, Welsh Celtic magic, Qabalah, Esoteric Women's mysteries, Northern traditions, Earth Magic, Chaos magic and even Obeah. These skills were further reinforced by the study of esoteric philosophy and psychology. One can also add a wide range of healing and therapeutic techniques to the list of their accomplishments.

They have worked their magical techniques worldwide, but with particular emphasis laid upon groups in Glastonbury and Cornwall. The positions they hold in normal life mean that their colleagues would probably be shocked if their Witchcraft practices were to become known, so they have to remain anonymous. I believe that in a certain government office, one of them is regarded with awe and great respect.

Working together as a triad and mirroring the process of stripping down towards eventual Cronehood, they have gradually discarded many of the ritual embellishments that were deemed necessary in the past. Now, they work directly and intuitively with the elements and energies, observing the festivals of the year and healing, cleansing, banishing and when necessary, even binding an evildoer. In addition to this work, they pursue the art of herbalism in the study of healing techniques. Working on many planes of the esoteric, they combine spirituality with divination. This group, known as the Triple Aspect, also works under the Title of The Midnight Temple of Kehtti Hotep.

Ray and Lynda Lindfield

Two Witches whom I must include are Ray and Lynda Lindfield. They are Wiccan enthusiasts who entered the Craft at the height of the Witchcraft upsurge that gained momentum in the early 1980s. They were drawn together by a common fascination with the occult whilst living at St. Leonard's in Sussex.

The nearest known coven was that of Alex Sanders at nearby Selmeston, and it was at Sanders' hands that Lynda was ultimately initiated in 1985. Ray was initiated by Sally Taylor, who ran the Folkestone coven. Folkestone was unique, as Sally's husband, Dave, was a serving police officer who made no secret of his Wiccan activities. Kent probably had a large number of serving police officers of all ranks who were

Witches, which meant that David Taylor was never ever questioned by any of his superiors about his active participation in Witchcraft rituals. When working with Sally, I discovered some of the illustrious police officers who were Wiccan.

Ray and Lynda alternated between Sanders' coven and Sally's. They gained much occult knowledge and experience during this period. Sanders health was fading rapidly by 1986, and they left him by agreement to continue their training with Sally and Dave. Such was their ability, that within months of their arrival they had been elevated to the Second Degree of the Craft. They progressed rapidly to their Third Degree from then onwards. Their Third Degree was a great occasion, and we of Artemis were invited to witness their elevation.

This was a great occasion, and the first of many rituals that we celebrated with the Folkestone coven. They were a humorous group that delighted in playing tricks on visiting covens. Sally had one favourite prank, which was to open the valve of a sluice gate below ground and flood the Temple with water from the nearby sea. Sally would carefully check the tides, her Temple being underground. Once the rituals were finished, the coven members were up to their necks in seawater, swimming around the raised Altar. They were fun days.

It was at Sally's that we were introduced to them, and there was an immediate rapport. So much so, that when Sally moved further south and Ray and Lynda moved further west to Eastbourne, they decided to become Traditionalists and join the Order of Artemis, whilst still keeping to their own inimitable roots. They were welcomed into Artemis and they brought a wealth of knowledge with them. This mutually rewarding friendship has stood the test of time. They have worked with many of the greats of the occult and Witchcraft world, being friends of Doreen Valiente, Janet and Stewart Farrar and so forth. They also had, and still have, strong links with the Berkshire coven of the White Hart, run by the High

Priest and Priestess, Ian and Sheila Atkinson. These two are leading Berkshire Witches who introduced them to the more formal magical practices, based on the teachings of the Servants of Light. This organisation was run by Dolores Ashcroft Nowicki and it was inspired by Dion Fortune and Butler's own brand of magic. Interesting, the editor of this book once gave an astrological lecture on the moon to 500 members of the Servants of the Light at one of their annual conferences.

The death of Doreen Valiente on September 1st, 1999 cut short further opportunities for Ray and Lynda to study with her. They were originally introduced to Doreen by John Belham-Payne, who founded The Centre for Pagan Studies at Maresfield. All three ministered to Doreen as she lay dying.

More recently, the Lindfields have devoted their energies to the local Eastbourne Pagan Circle, arranging seasonal rituals on the beach, plus occasional workshops. They both see their work in the local Pagan community as the focus of their energies, enabling others to share in the rich experiences and knowledge. This has brought Ray and Lynda a great deal of fulfilment over the years.

Bibliography

Modern Works

The Encyclopaedia of Modern Witchcraft and Neo Paganism, by Shelley Rabinovitch and James Lewis.
Witchcraft for Tomorrow, by Doreen Valiente.
An ABC of Witchcraft, by Doreen Valiente.
The Rebirth of Witchcraft, by Doreen Valiente.
Eight Sabbats for Witches, by Janet and Stewart Farrar.
The Witches Speak, by Patricia and Arnold Crowther.

Ancient Works

Witch Hunting and Witch Trials, by C. Ewan L'Estrange.
Compendium Maleficarum, 1608 Guazzo.
The Lawes against Witches and Conjuration, 1645.
Malleus Malleficarum, by Sprenger James and Kramer Heinrich. Revisions 1494, 1496, 1595 and 1620.
Sumtibus Claudii Bovrgeat 1669, by Nider Formicarius de Maleficius.
Discoverie of Witchcraft, 1584, by Reginald Scott.
Demonologie and Witchcraft, 1585, by Sir Walter Scott.
Witches Apprehended, Examined and Executed, 1613.

Epilogue

Here is one total non-acknowledgement, followed by a real thank you...

No thanks whatsoever to the mindless, prejudiced religious bigots, who broke my windows, broke into my museum at Newhaven, smashed my exhibits and forced its ultimate closure. The ancient exhibits you mindlessly destroyed can never be replaced and are lost to history. The Xtian tracts, papers and foul letters that you constantly left behind, together with your cryptic, vile and obscene notes, were sent for recycling in the interest of ecology, which is so dear to Pagan hearts.

Until then, I had no idea that the human mind could devise such hellish torments and tortures as those that you stated awaited me in hell. The reason for the eternal torment you say awaits me was the crime of loving all things in nature, for worshipping trees and animals and for respecting all womankind as being reminiscent of the eternal Goddess.

Finally,

On a kinder note, may I say how nice it was to meet the really godly and goddessly folk who replaced you when the Messianic Jews took over your old hall in Portland Road. They were as kind as the evangelists were wicked. They bestowed love and understanding on all of us, in contrast to your vitriolic spewing of hatred. They welcomed all our people and coven members to their Synagogue events: and in a spirit of tolerance, they deigned to attend some of our open discussion evenings, where Jews and Pagans mingled in peace and harmony.

It was refreshing to discover people who practised what they preached. We remember that Jewish prophets, who lived long before Jesus, said that the core of their religion is "Do unto others as you would be done by". We also know that the trials and tribulations that Jews have endured over the centuries were (and still are) an exact replica of those that we ourselves have suffered. May the Old Gods bless them!

Index

Index

Tarot Mysteries

"The Origin, Symbolism and Meaning of the Tarot Cards"
by Jonathan Dee

People often ask Tarot readers how the cards came into being, only to receive a garbled or incorrect answer. Historian, experienced Tarot reader and direct descendent of the remarkable Dr. John Dee of old, Jonathan has extensively researched the cards to reveal such startling facts as that the two Arcanas derive from entirely separate origins.

Jonathan also shows how scholars over the ages have linked the cards to various spiritual ideas, including the Qabalah.

Each card is thoroughly interpreted - as closely as possible to its original meaning - but adapted slightly to make sense to a modern reader.

Jonathan reveals the spiritual links between each card and its astrological, Qabalistic or mythological connections.

All the cards are illustrated, using Jonathan's own beautiful, medieval-style drawings.

ISBN 1-9030650-24-0   *£10.99*   *336 pages*

Modern Palmistry

"A Unique Guide to Hand Analysis"
by Sasha Fenton

This is a comprehensive manual, useful for beginners and experienced palmists alike. It covers every aspect of handreading, for the purposes of prediction, character reading, love, money and health.

In-depth coverage includes the way that past traumas are reflected on our hands, as they are in our psyches and even on our spiritual pathway.

Sasha's well-known writing style makes easy work of complicated theories, while Malcolm is an artist as well as a palmist, so this book is packed with over 200 beautifully explicit and accurate illustrations and actual palm prints.

"... an eminently practical work which deserves a place on the reference shelf of any potential palmist"
Prediction Magazine

ISBN 1-9030650-23-2-   *£10.99*   *208 pages*

Practical Spellcraft

"A First Course in Magic"
by Leanna Greenaway

Rarely do we have the opportunity to benefit from years of experience, as Leanna demonstrates spellcasting in a gentle and safe manner.

These spells work, for the simple reason that Leanna has been using them all her adult life, perfecting them to her high standards. This book also links to her successful postal courses on magic and spellcasting.

In addition to traditional methods, Leanna brings us bang up-to-date with her innovative approach to using such modern gizmos as text messaging and the email for making and transmitting spells.

The many spells in this book are designed to cover most of the daily situations that beset us, but Leanna also suggests adapting spells for more specific purposes.

ISBN 1-9030650-22-4   *£10.99*   *192 pages*

How to be Psychic

"A Practical Guide to Psychic Development"
by Sasha Fenton

An authoritative guide, with information on everything relating to psychic events and experiences, even including how to work in the psychic field.

The book draws on Sasha's own long and successful career and those of many of her colleagues. Sasha covers everything from simple techniques to the truly strange and mysterious, using fully her gift for explaining complex and esoteric subjects clearly and logically.

Every chapter offers hands-on exercises for readers to try for themselves.

Knowing how important, yet easily overlooked they are, Sasha points out danger signals and offers workable techniques for psychic self-defense.

ISBN 1-9030650-25-9   *£8.99*   *176 pages*

Zambezi Publishing Ltd
"Much more than just books..."

All our books are available from good bookshops throughout the UK; many are available in the USA - sometimes under different titles and ISBNs used by our USA co-publisher.

Please note:-

Nowadays, no bookshop can hope to carry in stock more than a fraction of the books produced each year (over 130,000 new titles were released in the UK last year!). However, most UK bookshops can order and supply our titles within a matter of days. Alternatively, you can find all our books on www.amazon.co.uk.

~~~~~

If you still have any difficulty in sourcing one of our titles, then contact us at:-

Zambezi Publishing Ltd
P.O. Box 221, Plymouth
Devon PL2 2EQ
UK
Fax: +44 (0)1752 350 453

web: www.zampub.com   email: info@zampub.com

(Want to join our mail list?
It is infrequent and NOT shared with anyone else - just email us
your details, specifying snailmail or email preference).